Tweens

What to expect from – and how to survive – your child's pre-teen years

Andrea Clifford-Poston, M.Ed. is a UKCP registered Educational Therapist and has over 30 years' experience of working with children and parents in schools, clinics, hospitals and the home. Andrea trained initially as a primary school teacher and taught in various London schools. For sixteen years she was the Teacher in Charge at the Child Development Centre, Charing Cross Hospital, and for many years a visiting lecturer to the Music Therapy Training Course at the Roehampton Institute. Andrea is a regular guest expert on *The Times* Parent Forum and has contributed articles to a number of leading childcare magazines, including *Nursery World*. For the past thirteen years she has been in private practice as a Child & Family Mental Health Specialist. Her previous publications include *The Secrets of Successful Parenting*, now in its second edition.

Tweens

What to expect from – and how to survive – your child's pre-teen years

Andrea Clifford-Poston

ONEWORLD

OXFORD

TWEENS
WHAT TO EXPECT FROM – AND HOW TO SURVIVE –
YOUR CHILD'S PRE-TEEN YEARS

Oneworld Publications
(Sales and Editorial)
185 Banbury Road
Oxford OX2 7AR
England
http://www.oneworld-publications.com

ISBN-13: 978–1–85168–380–2
ISBN-10: 1–85168–380–1

Cover design by Mungo Designs
Typeset by Saxon Graphics Ltd, Derby, UK
Printed and bound by WS Bookwell, Finland

Cover photographs © Digital Vision Ltd

For Morris, Tina, Rachael and Anna Clifford
Who make all the difference

I am grateful to Harriet Matthams for permission to reproduce her poem "*Volcanic Anger*" and to Michael Parkinson for his poem "*Angry I Ams*".

Disclaimer

Wherever actual quotations and family stories have been used permission has been sought and kindly granted. However, names, dates and any other factors affording recognition of individuals has been changed to protect confidentiality. Any similarity to any child, parent or family, alive or dead, is therefore purely coincidental.

Some of the views in this book may have appeared earlier in a slightly different form in *The Secrets of Successful Parenting – Understand What Your Child's Behaviour is Really Telling You*, Andrea Clifford-Poston: How To Books, 2001.

Contents

four
Cool or mateless ...?   72
Too many feelings in search of an identity

five
"That's so not fair ..."   97
Boundaries and discipline

six
Keeping a head in school   125

Acknowledgements

I have written this book and I take full responsibility for the views expressed in it. However, I cannot take full credit for them or for all the creative thinking behind them. They have arisen out of my conversations and relationships with so many people; family, friends and colleagues from several different disciplines and many persuasions have facilitated my thinking. My first thanks must go to the tweens and their parents with whom I have worked who have taught me so much more than I could ever teach them.

The idea for the book arose out of conversations with Adam Phillips and I thank him for the generous spirit he has brought to our meetings. His wisdom and clarity of thought have been inspirational and his compassion and humour have brought out the best in me for this book; that he has also provided its most original, creative and best thoughts is grossly unfair!

The late Dr. Hugh Jolly and the original team at the Child Development Centre, Charing Cross Hospital, London did much to help me to extend my knowledge and thinking about the middle years of childhood; special thanks to Rosemary Richards who first encouraged me to write about my work.

Kay Alderdice, Veronica Austin, Cheryl Batt, Morris and Tina Clifford, Nick Hollis, Jenny Marlow, Sally Richardson, Liz Roach, Barbara Ross, Theresa Satterthwaite and Tessa Smith have all made invaluable contributions to the text. I am grateful to Sarah Adams for her enlightening conversations on Chapter 6.

To Fay Bartram, Daniel Clifford and Scott Peters ... Respect!

Penny Carter has not only typed the manuscript, managing to translate my incoherent ramblings, hesitations and deviations into a coherent text, she has also provided me with an invaluable parent's view from the very first word.

My editor at Oneworld, Christina Wipf-Perry, has provided helpful insights as well as firmly ensuring that I met my deadline (well nearly!).

My gratitude to the late Murray Cox FRCP is at the very edge of language.

Finally, I could not have written this book without the patient and loving presence of my husband who has done so much more than manage to provide exactly the right balance of comfort and confrontation to ensure its completion.

Introduction

So why would you want to read yet another book on parenting? And why would I as a professional feel the need to add to the vast quantity of books available to parents? Hopefully, the answer for both of us is that this book will fill a current gap in the market for parenting books. I have worked with children and their parents for nearly thirty years in all the major child settings, schools, hospitals, clinics and in private practice. Over the last few years I have realized, and this may be your main reason for reading the book, that childhood is changing. Not only are children maturing physically earlier but they are much more exposed to and influenced by the media than previous generations. A teacher recently asked a class of ten year olds, *"How do we learn what is right and wrong, where do we learn how to treat other people?"* Quick as a flash a child replied, *"I watch The Simpsons,"* and then went on to elaborate how Bart had shared a much loved toy with his sister. Here was a youngster getting his identity and values from the media. In the same vein another teacher became concerned about six-year-old girls in her class wearing fake tan, crop-tops and mini-skirts to school; the boundaries between adults and children are blurring.

We have grown used to the accepted stages of child development: infancy, childhood and adolescence. What I hope to address in this book is a new stage of childhood, separate and distinct in its own right, the tween. They are no longer children preoccupied with play but nor are they, as so often described, "teenagers at ten". They have a different preoccupation to children and yet can swiftly slot back into childhood; the latest Barbie doll or Game Boy may be equally as important as the latest hit single! They share some of the same preoccupations as teenagers, especially around self-image and independence, but I hope to show how they have a very different slant on these preoccupations.

We are not the only ones to recognize this new phenomenon. Advertisers are beginning to regard tweens as the new economic market, carefully researching their preferences and interests. Increasingly, tweens have their own music, fashions and growing culture.

Maybe you are reading this book because you have recognized childhood is in transition. Tweens are both newly recognized and not yet fully understood which means this book can only provide you with a map of their world, it cannot provide a detailed guide or a definitive blueprint for parenting! Nor indeed would I want to, for if every child is a bit of an experiment, then the tween years are going to be the most experimental for parents. All experiments involve risk: the risk that the experiment will not work, or may go wrong, or provide a completely different result to the one hoped for by the experimenter.

How we think about parenting affects the way we think about children. Is parenting a skill that can be learnt like playing the piano or golf? In this sense the more lessons you have, the more you practise what you have been taught, the better you are likely to become at it. Or is it an art, a gift, a talent with which you can explore and experiment? Or is it a combination of them both? If parenting is a taught skill then there is a right way of doing it, which implies there is a right way of parenting this new stage of tweens. What I hope you will find in this book is the reassurance that parenting tweens successfully is much less about getting it right and more about not being afraid to get it wrong. There are as many ways of parenting as there are children. The risk of thinking of parenting solely as a skill to be taught and learned is that, as every parent knows, all children are different. What works for one child, or even two children in the family, suddenly doesn't work for another. This is almost inevitable because, in a sense, every child in the family has a different parent because you are different, even if only in subtle ways, with each of your children. And what would parenting be like if we could get it right? Imagine how the relationships between parents and children would be affected or different! You would certainly not have needed to buy this book (and I would not have needed to write it) because there would be no new understandings of behaviour, no shades of grey, no ambiguity, no uncertainty and maybe even no mystery in parenting.

I have written this book around the most frequently asked questions from parents about their tweens, their relationships with family and friends, their issues at school and, most of all, their relationship with themselves as emerging teenagers. I have also tried to address worries such as, "*What can I do about my tween keeping bad company?*" by trying to understand the difference between ordinary tween risk-taking behaviour as a means of gaining independence and delinquency. Whilst helping parents to know when they should be worried about their tween's behaviour, I have also tried to use real-life examples to illustrate how differently any tween and their parents may perceive a given situation and the impact those different perceptions may have not only on the parent/tween relationship but also upon the whole family.

I firmly believe that parents are the best experts on their own children. Sometimes they need some help to dig deep to find their own resources; sometimes they need to know other parents are struggling with the same issues; and sometimes they need some insights to help them decide what is best for their individual tween and family. I hope you will find all three in this book. Most of all I hope the book will remind you that when you decided to have your children you probably did so because you thought it would be fun!

Andrea Clifford-Poston

What kind of teenager will I be?
The task of being a tween

"They change during these years, they move from being a child, to being a boy-man and then a man-boy ..."

(mother of a thirteen-year-old boy)

Nine-year-old Amy sauntered into a family gathering sporting pink jeans, a lavender crop-top, pink baseball cap and a pair of heart-shaped lavender sunglasses. She made a beeline for ten-year-old Max who was propping up a wall on the fringe of the group trying to effect an equally cool look. They stood chatting for a couple of minutes until Max's mother called them to eat. They ignored her. She called them again, Max shrugged his shoulders irritably and snapped, "*Whatever, whatever.*" Max's mother sighed, raised her eyes heavenward as she commented to Amy's mother, "*Six months ago they would have been playing happily on the swings together ... now they're teenagers at ten.*"

Later in the afternoon Amy and Max's parents were amused to see Amy had shed her baseball cap and sunglasses. She and Max were racing around, roaring with laughter as they played an improvised game of cricket with the younger children. "*Look at that,*" said Amy's mother, "*they're just kids really, she's still my little girl.*"

It is a mistake to think of tweens as either teenagers or small children. They are children in the sense they are not adolescents; they differ from small children in that they are not primarily preoccupied with play. As they develop the capacity for abstract thought, they become preoccupied with a whole range of seemingly adolescent issues – boy/girl friendships, appearance and image, and moral issues such as animal rights and drug taking. But tweens are not teenagers either. Although at times they may seem to share the same preoccupations, tweens have a very different slant on worries from teenagers, illustrated by one mother's story of her three sons, aged six, eleven and fourteen years old. All three boys had wanted a tube of hair gel (the youngest possibly because the older two wanted one!) She described how the six year old bounced into the room, plastered in hair gel, asking for admiration of what a cool guy he was! The fourteen year old would amble into the room, preening himself with a nonchalant air, desperately trying to convince everyone he was cool; the eleven year old tried to slide into the room without being noticed. When a comment was made about his hair gel, he immediately went upstairs and removed it. He was having a private rehearsal of what it would feel like to be a teenager and when he realized the rehearsal had become a public performance, he quickly withdrew from the show!

There is a huge difference between an eight year old and a twelve year old. The tween years are a time of the most rapid and dramatic change in development since conception. Many eight year olds are still very much children preoccupied with school, play and their place in the family; others may have begun to "put away childish things" and become more preoccupied with the world outside home. They may seem very sophisticated, sneakily watching over-age films and talking about love, sex and being gay. However, they are equally as likely still to believe in Father Christmas and the tooth fairy. Some eleven and twelve year olds are clearly adolescent and becoming sophisticated in their interests and preoccupations outside the home. However, even at twelve years old, given the choice of being with the adults or children at a family party, they are likely to choose to be with the children whereas, of course, a teenager would want to be with the adults. So the main difference between an eight year old and a twelve year old is a matter of preoccupation. There are two ends of a continuum: eight year olds are likely to be more preoccupied with childish things and twelve year olds are more likely to be preoccupied with teenage things.

We can also think of differences in an eight year old and a twelve year old in terms of bodily strength. Tweens are not as strong as adults but they are much stronger than children. An aggressive eight year old may feel like killing someone but is unlikely to be physically capable of doing so. By twelve years old tweens may be having real struggles with their aggression and their fantasies about their aggression. Late tweens have to struggle to integrate their feminine and masculine feelings and desires. And this is a complex matter today because the boundaries between boys and girls in children are much less clearly divided than they were in the past. The old order of "pink for girls, blue for boys" has gone; boys may very well be dressed in pink just as girls may very well play rugby. Indeed, boys have lost many of their rites of passage. Historically, they were dressed in girls' dresses until they were four or five when they moved into trousers, giving a clear sense of identity. Then there was the tradition of boys wearing short trousers in their primary years, moving into long trousers as a clear indication of their masculinity around seven or eight years old. Similarly, girls at one time wore typically Alice in Wonderland hairstyles and were dressed solely in pretty dresses and hair ribbons until school age, when they might move into thick tights and pinafore dresses with their hair tied back or plaited until they were old enough to put it up and mimic their mother's clothing. Ribbons today have been replaced with hair slides and fastenings worn by females (and sometimes males) across the age range. From babyhood, little girls may wear unisex tracksuits, sweatshirts and jeans. They may have short hair or long hair may be worn tied back or up at any age. There is no distinct clothing ritual defining the move from toddler to schoolgirl to adult woman.

In this book we are thinking of the tween and teenage years as a continuum but also as two very distinct stages of childhood. Like all stages of childhood, the tween years are a transition, not only a transition from child to teenager but also from dependence to independence and for the developing tween independence means much more than the ability to cope alone.

"I'm really scared about puberty because I used to hear my mum screaming she hated my sister ..."

Tweens are in a state of transition as their sense of self, of who they are, is becoming fluid. They are coping with the idea of becoming a teenager. They are also coping with the idea of not being children any more. Of course, I don't mean that either of these thoughts are conscious in the tween's mind. What I mean is that tweens are likely to be feeling confused; they are confused because they know things are changing for them and they are discovering new bits of independence, which can be both exciting and traumatic. They are confused because they are sure they are loved and lovable in their "childhood identities", but they may be beginning to have secret worries about how loved and lovable they will be as teenagers. Teenagers have a bad press and this may be particularly true in families where the older siblings have had difficult and turbulent teenage years. There is an interesting difference here between teenagers and tweens. The "bad press" of teenagers means that families are surrounded by stories about teenagers. Most of these are mythological and many are blatantly untrue. But this does not affect these myths and stories having a profound affect on families in terms of how they may anticipate the teenage years. Until recently, however, tweens had no press at all. As parents, you will not even have had myths on which to base your expectations of life in the family with a tween.

How is it for you?

Every transition for a child is a transition for a parent. When your child started school there was a sense in which you went back to school. When a ten year old asks for a mobile phone, you begin to realize that implicit in that request is the fact that they are developing a life independent of you. You sense that they are beginning to move out of your orbit, to want to be beyond your control. Many parents find themselves surprised and bewildered at how early such requests may be made which is interesting because you are likely to have been filled with an enormous sense of pride if your child achieved any other developmental milestone early – walking, talking, learning to read – so what is it about the onset of the tween years that is different?

> "We're bewildered ... we expected it at thirteen but not at ten ..."
>
> *father of ten-year-old girl*

There seems so much to look forward to when children achieve other milestones – learning to walk or talk often means you and your child will have so much more to share. The onset of the tween years makes you realize what you have always known: that some day your child will grow up, leave home and lead their own life independent of you. Of course, that is not to say this independent life won't include you, but childhood has begun to pass for you both. You may feel shocked, sad and bewildered. Transitions can be difficult for many reasons but not in the least for the way they may highlight worries and anxieties that have always been present but ignored.

Your tween may be sharing your feelings of shock, sadness and bewilderment. Tweens and parents have to get to know each other again. Children tend to regard their parents as an extension of themselves, if you like as parts of their own bodies. After all, particularly in the early years, you are likely to have been as available to them as their own bodies. So we can say that growing up means distancing ourselves from our parents' bodies. You can judge how independent your child is at any stage by thinking about how separate your bodies are, i.e., how much you are still feeding, bathing, dressing, etc. And this is a two-way process because for tweens, independence brings a dawning sense of a world outside their bodies and their needs, a world which is beyond their control. Tweens are beginning to realize what, in some sense, they have always known: that their parents have lives which exclude them. They may be worried or anxious that you have a life beyond their control, for just as you are having to get to know them as an emerging independent personality, they are having to get to know you as a person other than a parent. They may be unsure of how to handle this new experience. They maybe just don't know what to do. This would lead us to believe that perhaps you are most in touch with your tween when you simply don't know what to do with them! Indeed, we could say that you will know that your child has reached the tween stage, regardless of whether they are nine or twelve, when you find yourself not knowing what to do with them in a new and different way.

The difference between a tween and a teenager

Teenagers are primarily struggling with the questions:

- What will life be like for me as a grown-up?
- What kind of a grown-up do I want to be?

and tweens are wrestling with:

- What kind of teenager will I be?
- What kind of teenager do my parents want me to be?
- What kind of life can I have outside the security of home?

In Chapter 2, we will explore at length how the family colours these questions for a tween and also how the tween colours and so changes the family. For now we are going to think about the qualities that go to make up a tween and how these qualities help them to explore and negotiate their task of growing up. Understanding the nature and tasks of tweens may help you, if not to feel more skilled as a parent, then certainly to tolerate feeling deskilled as a parent.

The life tasks of a tween

- Learning that loving and hating are two sides of the same coin.
- Beginning to have a sense of privacy which excludes parents.
- Tweens begin to realize the limits of their parents' understanding of them. This is both very freeing and very shocking.
- Coping with life outside the home.

Learning that loving and hating are two sides of the same coin

Tweens are beginning to practise their ambivalence! One minute happy to be a child, one minute almost teenage, the next minute unsure whether to be child or teenager. One minute deep thinking and resourceful, the next, irresponsible and impulsive. The swing from charming and co-operative to stubborn and bloody-minded may occur in a second. Today she is intent on being a nun, working for a religious charity abroad. He is going to be a writer, a poet. The next, the bright lights of show-business beckon them both. Parents may feel trapped in an atmosphere of impending crisis, bewildered by the inexplicable sudden changes of mood and mind.

"The best thing about being twelve is that you are treated more grown-up."
"And the worst thing?"
"You can be left at the house by yourself."
twelve-year-old Max

An eleven-year-old girl had refused to join a family party, spending the time in her bedroom, laboriously and meticulously painting her nails. At tea-time she emerged making dramatic, eye-catching hand movements as she spoke. She was the picture of cool sophistication until her mother handed her a plate. "*Oh, mum,*" she cried, "*you know I like my sandwiches cut in triangles not squares,*" adding peevishly, "*Oh, they're not the same, I can't eat those.*"

Tweens will show how they are struggling with strong feelings of love and hate in many ways:

- They seem to hate you
- They practise teenage identities
- They are confused about what they want

Loving and hating are an ordinary part of everyday life. Indeed, we can argue we are only as good lovers as we are haters; these feelings are two sides of the same coin. So as adults we struggle with our ambivalence about people. We like them, even love them, but they annoy us or let us down. For the tween these passions may feel a matter of life and death. People regarded one week as close friends, their only confidants, are next week experienced as a threat or a liar and betrayer. They will never speak to them again, and yet their deep distress belies the cry of "I hate her". Sure enough, within a few days the tweens are inseparable again. For the tween in question the feeling is "only I have ever felt like this, how do I know I will survive it?" Nowhere is this more true than in tweens' relationships with their parents.

"No age is so apt as youth to think its emotions, partings and resolves are the last of their kind, each crisis seems final, simply because it is new."

George Eliot,
Middlemarch

It is a sad fact that your tweens are more often likely to hate you than love you. Why should this be?

Try looking at it from the tween's point of view: "*I woke up one morning when I was ten, and knew I hated my mother,*" exploded Sarah, "*I hate everything ... everything about her ... I mean it's so stupid, you've got to do this and you've got to do that, and you've got to do it this way because it's the proper way. It just makes me want to do it the other way ... then they say it's because they care ... I don't bloody want them to care ... I just want them to realize I'm growing up.*"

"Why is my eleven year old so hostile? She seems to have only two moods – bad or indifferent ... what can I do about it without losing my cool?"

Sarah knew her parents loved her. How did she know? Because as a child they were able to anticipate and meet her needs. As a child, her developmental need was that her parents would provide an environment in which she was safe to grow and develop. One of the ways her parents kept her safe was by supervising her closely, they "kept an eye on her". Sarah had been glad of this, she felt safe and secure, happy to be dependent on their protection. As a tween, however, she has different developmental needs. Now she is thinking about practising keeping herself safe, being independent of her parents' care and protection. As far as she is concerned, their concern for her, on which she has so relied in childhood, has now become an obstacle to her own independent life. She is rather reminiscent of another twelve-year-old tween confined to a wheelchair which dominated the family living room. She had always enjoyed her special place, literally in the centre of the family, but as she approached her teens she found this place emotionally confining and restricting. Even if your tween is not yet showing signs of wanting to go out from home independently, they will definitely be wanting to practice independence inside the home.

We can understand Sarah's treatment of her mother as her way of telling her she loved her mother so much, she could only bear leaving her if she turned her into some bad witch she would be only too glad to leave and never miss. And like all tweens, she was trying to have it both ways, because she also had the fantasy that if she was independent of her parents, it wouldn't matter if she hated them because, as an independent person, she wouldn't be dependent on their love to survive as she had been as a child.

Sarah felt if she could stop her parents caring for her, then she could be independent. For her, the only way to "cut the cord" was to be horrid to her parents in an attempt to cure them of their love for her. Many tweens share this fantasy meaning of independence. Sarah was quite confident that if she was allowed more independence, then she wouldn't hate her parents quite so much. So in this sense, tweens believe that independence is both a cure for their parents' love and also of their own hate.

"There's all these things I want to do ... just things ... I've got lots of ideas ... and they [parents] are just a brake on everything."

Sarah

Sarah needed her mother to show an unbreakable goodwill, to tolerate a degree of her hostility whilst at the same time setting firm limits on what was and was not acceptable. But that is so hard for parents to do! Sarah's mother felt rejected, disappointed, a failure and unloved. She was spiralling into a pit of depression and inadequacy but saved herself one day by humorously pre-empting one of Sarah's onslaughts. "*And, yes,*" she said, "*you've had rotten luck, of all the parents you could have had, you've got us – the lousiest, most unreasonable in the world. But you're stuck with us. How on earth are you going to cope?*"

> "After a morning of constant barraging, I just feel furious, I just feel like hitting her. And then I say something I can't believe I've said! I think, how on earth could I have said that? It's not only that I'm losing her, I'm losing myself at times."
>
> *Sarah's mother*

Needless to say, Sarah did not respond with anything other than a flounce from the room. But her mother had regained her equilibrium, she had got in touch with the extremeness of Sarah's behaviour and instead of justifying or defending herself against it, was able to see it for what it was, extreme, and in this way she recovered her sense of being "a good enough mother". As a result, Sarah began to feel more contained, less able to triumph over her mother by grinding her down – an experience which pleased, but also terrified her.

Sarah's story raises the question, "Is growing up something we actively do, or is it something that happens to us?" Tweens can be very frightened by the intensity of their hatred for their parents – because, of course, another part of them doesn't hate you or wish you harm at all. They learn to tolerate and manage their capacity to hate, and also the experience of being hated, by the way you tolerate them hating you.

The British Paediatrician and child analyst, the late Dr Donald Winnicott, describes how the more secure and loving a childhood you have managed to provide for your child, the more you can expect a turbulent adolescence. Your child will have learned to trust the world and so feel free to love and hate the

> "You mean it's a good thing if she hates me ...?"

world, and free to express that ambivalence knowing that they will be accepted whatever version of themselves they are being. Tweens have a predicament – they love and hate their parents. It is not uncommon for children to wish their parents dead, or at least exiled for a while. Of course this doesn't mean they literally want to murder their parents! What it means is that when children become enraged with their parents they may, consciously or unconsciously, wish they were dead or that they could kill them. But it is also imperative for them that the parent survives, that the parent doesn't go away physically or emotionally. Tweens may wish or pretend their parents are dead as a way of seeing what life would be like without them. "Life is not a rehearsal," goes the graffiti, but youngsters rehearse a life independent of their parents all the time.

Loss and change dominate the tween years for you as a parent. They may also dominate the tween's life. As I said earlier, sometimes just feeling "at a loss" means you are deeply in touch with your tween. I realize it may not feel like that! But think back to when they were babies. Anyone who has held a crying baby knows that babies communicate by projecting feelings, i.e., they make you feel what they are feeling. And so it is with tweens. They frequently feel "at a loss and don't know what to do". They may communicate this to you, and ask for your understanding, by making you feel the same way.

How do you become a teenager?

When I met David he was on the point of being expelled from school because of deliberately flaunting school rules, and his generally "outrageous behaviour and appearance" – the last straw had been his dying his hair in a beaver style pattern. He sat sullen and belligerent as his parents recounted an impressive list of his crimes and misdemeanours. As the list progressed, David's look changed, almost imperceptibly, to embarrassment and distress. I decided to rescue him.

"My twelve year old just doesn't seem to care ... about his appearance, his behaviour or his school work ... how can we get him to pull himself together?"
parents of twelve-year-old David

"*David,*" I said, "*it sounds as though you're working very hard to convince people you really don't care about them or what they think of you.*"

"*Well, no,*" he shrugged, "*I don't, it's up to them, it's up to them whether they like me or not, I can't do anything to make them, can I?*"

"*What would be different if you did care, if you were really trying hard to get people to like you?*"

"*Dunno,*" he shrugged, "*I mean, they might not ... they might not like me.*"

Here is the tween's predicament. David wanted the adults to care, on the other hand he did not. In the struggle to establish for himself who he was, he was practising being who he was not. However, he also wanted the adults to understand this "loutish youngster" was not him, but he also needed to feel free to be loutish! He also understood he could not *make* people like him. In his ambivalence he was not taking the risk of asking to be liked for fear of rejection. His extreme appearance of "not caring" was a paradoxical way of his showing how deeply he did care. Tweens' behaviour is also influenced by their thinking about how to be a teenager. They will see teenagers "acting out", i.e., behaving in reckless and rebellious ways and then model their behaviour on them, without understanding this is an act on the teenager's part. I will talk more about this in Chapter 4.

Tweens don't know what they want

Impatience, urgency, the demands for needs to be met *now* may be difficult to manage but they are a symptom of the tween years. And it's all about bodily needs! Some tweens try to cope with their emerging sexuality by being intense and confusing about other matters. Here we see again the continuum. A nine year old knows what they want, a twelve year old doesn't know what they want and may be as shocked as the adults around them at the strength of their own turbulent feelings. One of the tasks of the tween is to find words and people to talk to about how they feel.

> "My tween is always in a hurry ... or have I suddenly got slow ...? How can I make him more patient?"
>
> *mother of twelve-year-old*

Impatience is an interesting symbol of the huge transition that takes place in the tween years. Your nine year old may get impatient or irritated with you whereas a twelve year old is likely to have a real sense of urgency about their desires and needs, more typical of the teenage years. Many young-sters see growing up as something magical that can be done overnight like learning spellings for a test. (If Romeo and Juliet had been less impatient, their story may have had a happier ending!)

Being grown-up is partly about being able to veer from one emotion to another without always experiencing the extremes of passion or being completely devastated. Tweens need adults to help them to develop an internal "gyroscope" so that, whilst still able to experience the highs and lows of life, their basic stability and equilibrium is maintained.

Managing ambivalence

There is no cure for the tween years! This is not a problem to be solved, it is a time to be lived with and negotiated. In many ways your role as a parent is to tolerate these feelings, to bear them and contain them. Remember, when *you* don't know what to do that is likely to be how your tween is also feeling.

- Give them words for what they are feeling, for example, "I can see it's *confusing* for you ..."
- Accept how they are feeling, e.g., "You feel you need this right now ..." If your tween thinks you know how they feel they may stop trying to persuade you of how they feel!
- Reassure them that what they are feeling is normal, e.g., "Everyone feels *confused* at times ..."

Beginning to have a sense of privacy which excludes parents

It was towards the end of her last summer term in primary school that Marie's parents sought my help with her management. She had become increasingly "headstrong and difficult", but the last straw had been when she had lied to her parents over her whereabouts on a Saturday afternoon. She said she was "round at a friend's house" but instead had gone to the local town with friends, missed the bus home and, to the anxiety of her parents, was out after dark.

"My eleven year old is lying to me ... does this mean she's going off the rails ...?"

Marie's parents

Lying is always a worrying behaviour for parents, but Marie's parents were panicking. "*She's going to the senior school in September,*" said her mother, "*there are all sorts of influences. We're afraid of her going off the rails ...*"

Tom's parents ran a tight ship. Although supportive in many ways, they found it difficult to adjust to his burgeoning independence and, in an attempt to protect him, insisted on an early curfew, much earlier than that of his friends. Tom was embarrassed at always "having to leave first", and one evening decided to stay alongside everyone else. His worried father went to look for him, and was horrified to find him sitting on a wall with his friends, sharing a bottle of cider.

The importance of secrets and lies

Secrets and lies are an important way of your youngster establishing their independence. Freud said that the child's first successful lie to its parents is its first moment of independence; it proves to the child that the parents can't read their minds. This is why the sharing of secrets is often seen as a barometer of the warmth of tween friendships.

"We recently found our eleven year old drinking … we were so worried. Is this the thin end of the wedge? How can we stop him going BAD?"
Tom's father

Tom and Marie were beginning to have secrets from their parents, and a different kind of secret to those that they had had in childhood. In early childhood, simply having a secret is exciting, the nature of the secret is almost irrelevant. For the tween, secrets are about developing their own independent world.

Of course, part of Tom and Marie's parents' anxiety is that so many of the tween's secrets are beginning to be around feelings and thoughts about sexual relations. They are beginning to feel invaded with curiosity about the pleasures and fears of sex. They may try to find out about sex by noting your response to their behaviour, be it flirting with sexual relations or

"I just wonder what they're up to …"

telling dirty jokes. They may let you know, consciously or unconsciously, about a risky situation they have been in as a way of gauging your reaction. It may be a rather perverse way of asking, "Was this a safe thing to do?" without being seen to be asking your advice. For parents this can be painful, because you are beginning to realize that not only can you not protect your youngster all the time, but that your youngster is toying with the idea of not looking to you for protection.

Many adults feel lying is never acceptable, such behaviour is seen as being detrimental to an overall search in life for truth and goodness. At the same time, many people will admit to "white lying", not so much trying to deceive someone else as to protect them from pain. The feeling is that there is no real harm done by their giving, for example, a ficticious excuse not to accept an invitation. Other people may tell the truth but a slightly askewed truth.

Lying seems to be part of life. D. H. Lawrence said that we need to lie like we need to wear trousers. For some reason we all need to conceal ourselves from, as well as explain ourselves to, others. Most people would admit, even if only at times, of trying to create a false impression in many parts of their lives. It may be living in a particular house or driving a car beyond their income, or it may be exaggerating the size and importance of a job. So there is a sense in which adults make things up all the time, whether it be to impress, to dress down, or to emphasize a point or detract from a point. In this sense, lying is shifting the focus, "putting a gloss on" one aspect and hiding another. It is a way of living. And indeed, sometimes we have to lie in order to tell the truth. What looks like lying may in fact be a way of making the truth palatable. But many people will despise others found to have been "living a lie". Is this because part of being human is living with the fear of being discovered in some way? After all, everyone feels guilty about something. Certainly if your child is lying to you, you are likely to feel angry, hurt, bewildered, let down. And maybe one of the reasons parents find it so difficult when children lie, is because it resonates with a real human fear – the fear of being found out. As Martin Amis, the British novelist, said, *"Everyone fears they are a joke which other people will one day get."* (1981)

> "I've been suspicious that my twelve year old has not really been going to his swimming club on Saturday mornings and now a friend has seen him in the shopping centre today. How do I confront him without going over the top?"
>
> *father of twelve-year-old Jason*

Managing secrets and lies

In discussion with both these parents, it became obvious that "going off the rails" or "going bad" meant taking a different route, choosing a different kind of lifestyle, than the parents would have chosen. You naturally want your child to value and enjoy the things you value and enjoy in life. What the tween is trying to do, is to discover what they want to value and enjoy. (Of course, one of the issues is that they often don't know what is "their own thing".) These parents were realistically worried about their youngsters' safety and their ability to trust them as they took the first steps into independence, but their anxiety was also an indication that they were finding it difficult that their children were beginning to develop a private life, highlighted by the coming transition from primary to senior school.

As soon as their children are born, parents are in the business of separation from them. Your main aim is to help them to grow up equipped in the best ways possible to leave home and lead their own lives, but this will not prevent you also feeling sad or even rejected as your children begin to be more and more independent. As a result, you may find yourself giving your tweens rather confusing messages. When I asked Tom and Marie's parents how they had handled these incidents, they gave similar replies, "*We pointed out that they need to grow up and be more responsible.*" Whilst we all know what the parents meant, both Marie and Tom thought they *were* being grown-up and responsible; sitting on a wall drinking cider is a grown-up image, as is being out after dark. Parents sometimes say "*Grow up*" when they mean "*Be good, behave.*" For it seems there is no greater public statement of bad parenting than if your child misbehaves in public. There is a sense in which your parenting is a public performance as the way children behave in public often feels to parents like "exposure". The difficulty with youngsters of this age, is that you, as parents, cannot help but expose yourselves and maybe what is most exposed is parents' ongoing fear that their children may "go off the rails".

- Accept that your tween needs to lie to you. This doesn't mean that you should encourage lying – "If you don't tell me then I won't know …" – but it does mean that you are going to have to tolerate a certain amount of lying.
- Decide the kind of lie you will need to confront and the kind of lie you can ignore. This will vary from family to family. In the mysterious ways families operate, in some families a tween lying about where they have been may be less worrying than them lying about whether they have showered or what they may or may not have eaten. As parents you need to decide between yourselves what you feel is important.
- Decide how you are going to manage the lie telling. Sometimes encouragements and incentives can be more useful than punishments – more on that in Chapter 6.
- Decide how you are going to manage the lies you ignore. You might decide to let the youngster know that you know they are

lying but that you are not going to do any more about it, e.g., "I'm pretty sure you haven't done your homework and I hope it won't happen again."

Sometimes tweens, and indeed teenagers, need permission to discuss issues with someone other than their parents. There are a number of ways that you can convey your permission. For example, if you suspect your youngster is having problems with friends, saying something like, "When Aunty Jean was eleven, she had a real problem with her friend, has she ever told you about that?" Or, if you felt there was a serious worry you could try something like, "Your behaviour tells us that you are unhappy and worried about something. We'd love to help but we understand you might rather talk to Aunty Jean about this. We're sure she'd love to help." However, I realize that this suggestion raises interesting questions, namely,

- What exactly is permission?
- How do you know when you've got it?

When they seem too good!

It takes guts to be a tween! Sometimes youngsters may feel it is all just too much. They feel overwhelmed by the physical and emotional changes going on inside them ... and their minds turn to finding a cure for it. Excessively good behaviour might be a tween's way of managing confusion and change. In a way, the tween who is "inappropriately good" can be thought of as saying, "I'm above all this, I've done it, I am grown-up already." So what they are doing is feeling superior to the turmoil other tweens are experiencing. Both parents and children may wish that growing up was instantaneous, avoiding the painful transitional stages. Many children dream that they can magically grow up as a solution to childhood difficulties. A friend recalls throughout an unhappy childhood that she always believed "everything will be alright when I'm fifteen". She considered fifteen to be very grown-up. She describes her bitter disappointment when she found on the morning of her fifteenth birthday, she was no more grown-up than she had been at bedtime the previous evening.

"My twelve year old seems too good to be true ... we are having none of the rebellions and difficulties our friends are experiencing with their youngsters ... should we be worried?"

Secrets in tween friendships

Nine-year-old Penny sobbed bitterly as she described the breaking up of a friendship she had had since she was five years old. Like many tween girls, the measure of a "best friend" was how many secrets were shared. When she shared a secret with her friend, she felt close to her, supported and comforted by her. The friend, for her part, felt important, excited and close to Penny. But keeping a secret can be a burden, a restraint, particularly for a tween who may be naturally gregarious and also competitive. It certainly seemed as though Penny's friend had betrayed her confidence mainly as a way of boasting to the other girls how close she was to Penny. But sharing secrets is a complex matter. Maybe the balance was tipped in this friendship because having a secret gave the friend a sense of power, whereas it made Penny feel dependent.

> "She was my very best friend, I told her everything, I told her all my secrets … and now she's betrayed me … I'm never going to have another best friend."
>
> *nine-year-old Penny*

What kind of teenager will I be?

"Boys pure in mind and heart, almost children, are fond of talking in school among themselves of things, pictures, and images of which even soldiers would sometimes hesitate to speak."

(Dostoevsky – The Brothers Karamazov*)*

How are you going to cope with the fact of your child turning into a sexual being? You may relate to this mother's attempt to romanticize her son's first steps into sexual relationships. Parents will freely admit that they are longing for this first girl/boyfriend stage to arrive – "*Oh, it's so sweet, it's so romantic … all that dreaming and sighing …*" Romance is the transition from innocence to experience. As a parent, you might find yourself sanitizing these boy/girl relationships as sweet and pastoral rather than the first steps into crude sex. This is partly because, as we shall discuss in Chapter 7, children's sexual curiosity seems to go

> "He's got a girlfriend, they go to the cinema together, I think there's a bit of kissing and pecking … it's so sweet!"
>
> *mother of twelve-year-old son*

underground between seven and nine years old, so you may have grown used to a picture of your child as "sweet and innocent". And tweens themselves perpetuate this image of wide-eyed innocence. The mother of an eleven-year-old boy was both slightly amused and concerned when her son arrived home from camp reporting that electric toothbrushes had been banned because "the girls were using them". She was touched by his innocence of the fact that an electric toothbrush might make a good vibrator but was also shocked that tween girls had made such a discovery! Similarly, an eleven year old girl reported a bewildering conversation to her mother. Several boys had said to the girls smirkingly, "*We know you use candles in the tent at night ...*" The girls had replied innocently, "*Oh, no we don't, we use torches ...*" Again, two ten year olds at a swimming party thought nothing of getting changed, albeit under a towel, in front of the boys present. All these behaviours are radically different to how a teenager in any of these positions would behave.

As your tween begins to think about sexu... tionships you are going to remember how it was for you ... We will explore this further in Chapter 7 but you are likely to find yourself either idealizing your own early adolescence and so feeling nostalgic about it or full of sadness for what you feel you did not have at that time.

> "I love watching this romance ... appreciating him ... is a real source of pleasure ... yes, I know I live through the kids ... it's a way of making peace with my own ghosts."
>
> *mother of twelve-year-old boy*

The tween's sexual tasks

Tweens are not teenagers and their first task is not to have to decide whether sexual intimacy in a relationship is appropriate. Primarily they need to:

- feel comfortable in their sexually developing bodies
- understand the emotional aspects of sex
- learn how to express sexual feelings other than in intercourse
- learn how to say "no" to unwelcome sexual advances
- learn how to say "yes" to welcome sexual advances

In order to begin to master these tasks, your tween needs to understand the link between the physical changes in their body and their emotions (see Chapter 2). They then need to have their feelings taken seriously.

Knowing the facts of life seems to have no bearing at all on the tween's insatiable curiosity about who does it, when, and how it feels. And this is not surprising as there is more to human sexuality than function. Many parents try to avoid the issue of sex education because, "*School deals with that*". Of course, in one way the school does "deal with it" – biological facts are true – but biological facts are just the beginning of the story. Sexual relations are as much, if not more, linked to our fantasies than they are to the facts. Sex is not so much about *what we know* as *how we understand* the facts of life and how we can link them to ourselves and our history.

An eleven-year-old boy surprised his mother when he suddenly asked, "*What's contraception?*" She clearly remembered a conversation with him when he was eight or nine in which he had asked the same questions and been given a clear, simple age appropriate explanation. He was now raising the topic as though he had never heard of it before.

Children's questions are interesting. At any age the words used to enquire may be the same, but the answer sought may be very different. As an eight year old, developmentally this child may have been vaguely curious about a word he had heard – "contraception". He may have been wondering what it meant, in the same way as he might wonder about the meaning of any other new word. A teenager asking, "*What's contraception?*" may very likely be asking for advice on what form of contraception to use. This eleven year old was showing how a tween, and anyone else for that matter, can only really learn what they want to know, and nowhere is this more true than in the area of sexual relations. He was certainly asking for more than the basic meaning of the word, but was not necessarily wanting information to act upon. The question for parents is how do they know what their child is ready to learn? Usually they don't! A twelve-year-old boy was telling his parents about his first school disco. He had clearly had a good time with no shortage of tween girls willing and eager to dance with him. He explained how he had managed to spend most of the time with his favourite "babe" but as the evening was drawing to a close, he had "… *asked Beth to dance because she was on her own and no one was really asking her.*" What an interesting picture of the difference between a tween boy and a teenage boy! It is unlikely that a teenage boy would want to be seen dancing with the school wallflower. The loss of "street cred" would have been just too much! In a later chapter we will consider how tweens are much more preoccupied with the romance of sex than engaging in sex. They are struggling to find a way of feeling comfortable with their bodies and sexual feelings and how to manage these two things in an age appropriate way.

For many tweens, flirting with sexuality means beginning to see the opposite sex as opposite, as a different, and potentially, exciting sex. "Going out" doesn't necessarily mean going anywhere. For many tween girls, "liking" boys may have nothing whatsoever to do with sex or even kissing. The same can be said for tween boys, they may often see girls as a kind of "girl-boy", a different kind of companion on the computer. An eleven-year-old girl came home from school and announced that she and Jason were "*going out*". Her father looked astonished, "*What do you mean 'you're going out',*

> "It's a leap into the great unknown ... I worry about what's going on ... in fact, there's nothing going on ..."
>
> *mother of twelve-year-old boy*

where are you going?"

"*What do you mean, where am I going?*" asked the equally astonished eleven year old.

"*Well, you said you and Jason were going out, where are you going?*"

"*Oh, I don't mean going out, I mean* going out, *you don't go anywhere, you walk round the playground holding hands and then you're going out.*"

A mother tells the story of her twelve-year-old son and his first girlfriend. He slept with a framed photo of her by the bed and had long phone calls with her every evening after school. "*Are you in love?*" she asked him. "*Mother,*" came the quick retort, "*I'm twelve years old!*"

Tweens may have friends of the opposite sex that involve some kissing and petting. Perhaps worrying your tween will get pregnant or get someone pregnant is a focus for the more general risks of sex. (Well, how can there be sex without risk and risk without sex? – see Chapter 8.) What do I mean by the risks of sex? Sex is an adult game, in the sense that the place where adults play is in the bedroom. So what do we know about games? Childrens' games can be

> "My biggest fear is that he'll get some girl pregnant ... I worry about it all the time."
>
> *mother of twelve year old*

thought of as in two categories. There are games like board games where there are definite rules, a definite goal and a definite winner. Imaginative or creative play, free play, is very different. There are no rules, there is no goal and there is no winner. The game begins, evolves in a life of its own and no one knows what is going to happen or what the outcome will be. Sex is the adults' version of imaginative play. You know it is highly unlikely that your tween may get someone pregnant or become pregnant, but you also know that they are fast approaching the age when this could be a possibility. In fact a pregnancy may be much more manageable for both you and your tween than the other risks involved in embarking on a game in which no one knows the rules or how it is going to end. As a parent, you are going to find it much more easy to talk to your tween about how to avoid the risks of pregnancy than any other risks involved in sex.

Your other worries around sex

I was surprised when I met twelve-year-old Jane. She was plumpish rather than heavily overweight. Her parents had been concerned about her overeating for some time and, from the depth of their anxiety, I had imagined a much larger girl. Jane talked openly about her "problem". She admitted to being greedy adding, "*I'm always hungry*". She would like to be slimmer but she was not unhappy about her size, and was not being teased by her peers. I began to wonder who had the problem – Jane or her parents?

> "Our twelve-year-old daughter is very overweight … we are worried …"
>
> *Jane's parents*

I explained that Jane did not present as a tween who felt she had a problem. "*But,*" exploded her father, "*look at Saturday!*" He explained Jane had been a bridesmaid at a family wedding. During the evening party, she had "hardly left the buffet", picking excessively, in her father's view, at food all evening. Interestingly, Jane's mother felt that whilst Jane appeared greedy, she had not been excessive. In discussion, Jane's father came to realize his extreme anxiety at Jane's appetite was his way of describing his anxiety about her other burgeoning appetite – her sexual appetite (of course, there is a link between these two appetites). If he couldn't control her eating, how was he going to control her sexual behaviour?

Whilst no one wants to encourage tween pregnancies, it is important to highlight here a marked contrast between the attitude of tweens and their parents at this stage. The tween is both anxious and curious about sexual relationships. Parents may be anxious and curious about how to delay them learning more! It is a time of challenge for both parents and tweens as friendships with the opposite sex begin to change and develop.

Should a parent read a tween's diary? Do you have the right to? Would you read another adult's diary? Diaries are usually an intimate record for the writer's eyes only ... and they are not usually left open. We could presume from the fact that this tween left her diary open she was hoping her parents might see what was written and offer her some help. On the other hand, tweens are impulsive and she may just have left the diary open in a moment of distraction. So how do you both respect a tween's privacy and offer them an invitation to talk about a worrying issue? Maybe the secret lies in the word "confront". To ask if you should "confront" your tween sounds more like a demand for them to account for their behaviour than an invitation to discuss or explore a worry. How are you going to justify or give an account of why you read her diary? It may be best to ignore the matter on this occasion but be alert to any changes in your daughter's behaviour which might indicate that she is worried about something.

"My twelve-year-old daughter left her diary open in her bedroom. I was very worried about something I read and am wondering if I should confront her about her behaviour with her boyfriend?"

Coping with life outside the home

Tweens are learning to rely on themselves, a heady process which confuses, excites and scares them. They may begin to practise their autonomy in a number of ways. Perhaps the most common are through indignation and self-righteousness. By now you are probably told regularly how all your tween's friends' parents are more liberal and understanding than you. Any thwarting of your youngster's wishes is likely to be met with indignation as they play hokey-cokey with their desire for independence. Parents will feel they are simply taking steps to ensure the tween's safety. The tween is likely to feel unheard, persecuted and unfairly treated. This sense of injustice may help them to flirt with the outside world by becoming passionate about good causes. High on the list is animal welfare; some tweens become vegetarian. They may be focused on and fierce about anti-drugs, anti-smoking, the environment and peace issues. They may organize little money raising events such as cake selling, white elephant stalls and sponsored events. They may well take risks in their ardour. Two ten-year-old boys decided to confront a drunken man abusing his dog in the street. "*We went up to him and told him we would report him ... and he was swearing and shouting at us*," they reported to their astonished parents. Tweens will be convinced that their way is the right way and often the only way. These fervours and passions are a way of testing what the outside world is like and also ensuring that they make the outside world safe before they enter it fully. It is a way of measuring their autonomy, of how much power they have outside home. Tweens believe intensely in their own private world. But this inner, private world is so intensely passionate that they are forced to bring their private world into the outside world.

"Going out" as a precursor to leaving home

Eleven-year-old Eve and her fifteen-year-old sister were packing their cases for a four day visit, without their parents, to some schoolfriends who had moved to another town. Whilst her sister prioritized packing cosmetics and clothes "for going out", Eve gave priority to Snoozy – her first and favourite bedtime cuddly toy and a favourite sweater, "*because I always wear it*". She also asked to take a "funky bracelet" of her mother's – "*because the beads exactly match the colours of the sweater*," and then added, "*... and can I take some eye-shadow and some blusher?*"

The contents of these suitcases are an interesting illustration of both the continuum and the distinction between teenagers and tweens. Eve's teenage sister was focussing on "going out", in every sense of the phrase because teenagers are thinking about preparing to leave home. For tween Eve leaving home is much more of a fantasy. As Eve's packing shows, tweens are much more focussed on how they will *cope* outside the home. Eve was looking forward to going out, she was clearly exhilarated when allowed to take the requested cosmetics, but she was also anxious, if not scared. We can see this from her packing "security" items from her childhood. She had always slept with Snoozy and needed to do so while she was away from home. At one level, borrowing her mother's bracelet was a grown-up act – Eve was thinking about fashion and colour and maybe also identifying with her mother as a woman. And the bracelet was also what Winnicott called "a transitional object" – a child's way of keeping linked to a loved one in times of absence.

Will I be able to make friends?

"*We only laugh,*" said Freud, "*when a joke has come to our help.*"

Many years ago I was working with a twelve-year-old boy, Gordon, who opened every session with a joke. He would thump on the door, bounce into the room and say, "Hey, do you know this one …?" This was a pattern for over three months, with the jokes becoming more and more feeble, and, needless to say, more and more crude. As he finished telling a joke, he would immediately laugh and say, "Good isn't it?" and thump me on the arm. I began to realize that the more anxious he was about the session, the harder he thumped me!

> "He seems to be under pressure, he seems to feel he has to come out with a series of jokes, whatever the place or time, and regardless of how they are being received."
> *Gordon's father*

Gordon was an interesting tween. Large, over-weight, rather ungainly and, whilst of average ability, not in the league of his very bright class-mates. Initially, he had been the victim of much teasing at school, for being "really stupid" and "weird, really weird". After a particularly inept act one day, he diffused the situation with his peers by declaring, "*Here I go, Mr Bean!*". From then on, any incompetence on his part, was greeted with an affectionate dig in the ribs, and a "Mr Bean". This was working well for him at school. He had become the class clown – who would rather be the butt of his peers' jokes than ignored and isolated. He was accepting his peers' assessment of him as "stupid and weird". His friends appre-ciated his initiating jokes against himself, and so we could think they despised him less and were more affectionate towards him. Gordon was also working very hard on his friends' behalf. Freud argues that we never really know what we are laughing about. We may be laugh-ing at one thing in order to avoid laughing at something else. If Gordon was the "Mr Bean" of the class, his friends could laugh, partly because *they* were not the Mr Bean of the class.

Gordon was finding it difficult to make happy relationships. He seemed agitated and anxious in social situations. Interestingly, his class teacher described his joke telling as "attention seeking", a behaviour which is so often described negatively as though there is something wrong with needing attention to one's needs. In a way she was right, for the child who is attention seeking is trying to get close to someone. Getting to know people is a risky business. Getting to know who we are may be even riskier. Gordon was using humour to "break the ice", to deal with the anxiety of establishing a relationship with me. But the jokes were fast becoming a wall for him to hide behind. When I commented gently: "*It seems difficult to get to know you*", Gordon replied quickly, "*But I know you like me ... because we laugh a lot.*"

Gordon was using my response to his jokes as a measure of my acceptance of him. He had to open every session with a joke as a way of checking at the beginning of every meeting that I still liked him. His anxious outpouring of jokes socially was his way of asking people, "Do you like me, am I acceptable?" Of course, he was taking a huge risk looking for such concrete affirmation as laughter. When he sensed people's irritation with his barrage of humour, he began to hide himself further and further behind the barrier. His mother was right, he was trying too hard but what is it that makes us want to try, to make an effort? Perhaps Gordon was equating trying with willpower. He seemed to feel that the more he willed something to happen, the more real it might become; unlike David earlier in the chapter, Gordon seemed to harbour the hope that he could *will* people to like him.

> "The problem is, he just tries too hard."
> *Gordon's mother*

"How will I know how to treat other people?" – dirty and racist jokes

Gordon presented both me and his parents with a problem. The risk was that Gordon could think I was agreeing with the views expressed in the joke. As he was using jokes as a barometer of the warmth of our relationship, how should I respond when his jokes were at the expense of other people, be it cruel jokes about friends and family, racist or sexual material? To laugh at these jokes would be construed as colluding with him, on his side against the world. The risk was that I could also be construed as agreeing with the views expressed in the joke. I was also anxious not to collude with his way of coping with making relationships. There is a difference between using humour to cope with a difficult experience (adults do it all the time, and interestingly, Gordon's parents had a very good sense of humour), and using humour to avoid acknowledging difficulties in an experience. Gordon's humour was a barometer of the warmth of our relationship but it was also his way of not developing a close relationship.

Gordon's mother described her difficulty when Gordon began a joke. The shock element of a joke is a real communication from a tween. You are riveted into paying the tween attention. You cannot ignore what the tween has said. So what is the communication in a shocking joke?

> "Sometimes, I don't realize it's a joke, I think he's being serious, telling me about something, and then suddenly it's a joke – it's a shock."
> Gordon's mother

Tweens like Gordon may use jokes to show their parents a shocking part of themselves, a part they are unsure may be acceptable. Gordon's parents learned to respond less to the joke – and more to the communication. The next shocking joke was met by a calm response from his mother.

"*That joke makes me feel I haven't been paying you enough attention lately ...*"

"*No, it's not that ... but dad never takes me to golf ...*"

It was true. The previous four months Gordon's father had been working away from home during the week, and had not spent the time at weekends with Gordon he had normally. Gordon was using shocking jokes to ask his parents for the time to listen to him.

Pushing the boundaries and learning more

Gordon's parents had less success when they changed their response to his more basically crude jokes. As he sniggeringly ended a joke, they said, "*Well, yes, but there are lots of funny jokes you can tell us, it doesn't have to be crude like that, tell us a better one.*" But Gordon persisted, often adding, "*Don't you get it?*" His repeated question, "*Do you get it, do you understand?*" was loaded with meaning. Maybe what he was really asking was whether or not his parents understood him; if they laughed they understood more than his joke, they understood him.

> "His crude jokes are revolting ... we just don't know how to stop them."

This may be particularly true of sexual jokes. Gordon's father recalled telling his own father a particularly crude joke after learning about menstruation at school, adding, *"I can't believe now that I said it, but I really wanted to know about it all."* Tweens may use such jokes as a transition from home and the outside world. They may be trying to discuss or introduce parents to issues which have been raised outside the home, whether in formal lessons, the playground, TV, etc. They are playing with ideas and notions, asking parents, *"What are your views on racism, sexism, etc?"* Again, the key lies in responding to the communication. Gordon's dad wanted his own father to say something like, *"Do you want to know more about periods?"* A racist joke may be best met with a casual, "What do you think about that? Do you think all Irish people are stupid?" etc., etc.

Can "a weirdo" find love?

Tweens are not only beginning to think about how they will cope with the world outside home, they are also toying with the idea of what life will be like for them when they have left home. Small children find the thought of leaving home frightening. It can be fun to go camping at the bottom of the garden or even to wander off on your own for half an hour but the idea of not living with mummy and daddy is frightening. Teenagers look forward to leaving home, often in a very idealistic way, i.e., all their daily problems will be solved when they are free of their parents. They may have anxieties about how they are going to cope but these are usually tempered by excitement. Leaving home is not the reality for a tween that it may be for a teenager, but it is becoming a possibility.

> "My eleven-year-old son is refusing to go on the school trip because he has been put in a dormitory with a group of boys he hardly knows. How can we encourage him to go?"
>
> *Mark's parents*

Until relatively recently, the time of leaving home could be predicted. There was the custom for children to live at home until they married. There was the custom for young couples to live with one set of parents in the early years of their marriage for financial reasons. There was the custom for some children to leave home automatically when they went on to higher education, aged eighteen. Now there are as many ways of leaving home (and returning) as there are families.

Mark was in a state; he was about to go on a school trip, involving two nights away from home, sleeping in a small dormitory. He was worried, and annoyed that he had been placed with a group of boys he hardly knew. "*They're real weirdos*," he exploded.

Of course, Mark was talking about a lot of issues – fear of the unknown, being liked, identity, who's in, who's out. But his perseverance on "weirdo", typical of his age, seemed significant. Until the dorm arrangements were announced he had been eager to go on the trip and seemed to be enjoying being quite secretive with his parents about details of it. He generally felt the whole project exciting fun, a time to be free from the restraints of home, and "little kids" (his brothers).

It seems as if the "*weirdo in the dorm*" incident highlighted Mark's ambivalence and anxiety about becoming himself with his own independent thoughts, ideas and preferences. There was a sense in which he was trying to become a *weirdo* to his parents; he didn't want them to recognize him as 'their invention', he wanted to be himself. But the other side of that longing was that if he did become a weirdo to his parents, would they recognize him when he wanted to return?

"The familiar strangers"

A friend tells an amusing story of being at home with her mother for the weekend when she was in her mid 40s. She was the eldest of three children, the youngest being a boy, Martin. Although the baby of the family, her brother had now, of course, outstripped his sisters in size and weight. During the weekend, she asked her mother if she could borrow some socks. "Oh dear", replied her mother, "I don't think I have any, there's a pair of Martin's in the airing cupboard, but they would be too small for you."

There were gales of laughter as the mother and daughter realized that the mother was still thinking of her children as being at primary school age. Her mother was desperate to see her as a six year old. She, at some level, was desperate to be seen as a six year old, but also as someone her mother had never met before. The tween's ambivalence is evident – let me go, let me become a "weirdo" to you, but recognize, love and admire me when I return for what I have become, not just for what you would like me to have gone on being.

Suffering from body ambition ...

Understanding the impact of their physical development

two

A primary school teacher overheard two little girls talking in the playground:
"I know how to find out how old our teacher is ... look in her pants!"
"Why?"
"Well ... mine says five to six years old."

This delightful little story sums up the tween's predicament about physical development. Children live in a world of relatively uniform bodies; some may be taller, some shorter, some fatter, some thinner but on the whole physical development marches in time with chronological age and there are relatively few significant differences across an age band. At the same time, looking in each other's pants satisfies curiosity about gender differences, confirms one is built the same as one's own sex and is relatively harmless. On the whole, your child will have felt safe and comfortable in their pre-pubertal body; all this is about to change because your tween is about to lose the body they know.

By eight years old, children are beginning to think about living in a pubertal body; they may still be pre-pubertal but will be aware of, curious about and looking at pubertal bodies and all that they signify (no nine year old would think it appropriate to discover their teacher's age by looking in her pants!) So we can think of tweens as experiencing a crisis of body ambition; what kind of body do I want? What kind of body will I have? How will my body compare with that of my friends?

Looking back

Nothing gives parents and children more pleasure than when a child achieves a milestone. Your child may well have just been doing what comes naturally but you probably found yourself knee-deep in a puddle of pride as they said their first word or took their first steps. In the same way, children are usually thrilled as they become more competent, mastering such skills as riding a bike or learning to swim and they all tend to do this around the same age. Now they are about to enter a new world, a world less to do with competence, and also including sexual capacity; it can be a frightening thought that one is about to become capable of making a baby!

They are also entering a world of differences; not only is their body going to lose its oval, childlike shape but it is likely to be going to do it at a different time and at a different pace from some of their friends. Nor will their own bodies develop uniformly or at an even pace. This mother was not the only one to be embarrassed. Her son felt awkward and self-conscious, "*I don't know what happens, it's like my arms and legs are on remote control.*" You will have noticed your youngster's limbs growing longer and that they are also fast growing taller and filling out due to a seemingly insatiable appetite. One mother described trying to, "*satisfy his hunger is like feeding strawberries to an elephant.*" Whilst you are counting the increase in your grocery bill, your tween may be struggling with a loss of self-image; their agile, co-ordinated, even graceful, child body is being replaced with one that is not only awkward and clumsy but also seems alien to them. Not only that, they may fear this embarrassing body will never change into the glamorous and sexy teenage bodies they see all around them. They know the facts, i.e., that their body is in transition, but they may experience a real sense of ambivalence and tension about this "transitional body". They may feel it doesn't really belong to them, they don't know what to do with it and may try hard to "dress it up" with teenage-clothes or return it to its comfortable

> "I'm sick of him galumphing about, knocking things over. He can't walk from one side of the room to the other without bumping into something or kicking it over. He lumbers round the house in such an embarrassing way."
>
> *mother of eleven-year-old boy*

> "He needs new trousers every week ... he's also got hollow legs."
>
> *mother of eleven year old*

child-like state by wearing inappropriately child-like outfits or a unisex uniform of tracksuits, jeans and t-shirts.

Boys who mature early

It seems particularly cruel that nature does not allow all children to develop at the same pace at an age when self-esteem is such a crucial issue. Boys who mature early may find it an advantage. They may be admired as more manly and, therefore, more attractive to girls. On the other hand, boys who are slower to develop may be seen as weak and puny. They may become anxious about "being a man" and sometimes show these anxieties in difficult and unco-operative behaviour.

Girls who mature early

Tween girls may be embarrassed by the early onset of menstruation or breast development. Whilst they know where babies come from, they may feel puzzled as to how this relates to their own bodies at this stage. They may try to hide the fact they have a period or mask the size of their developing breasts. One eleven-year-old described having run out of sanitary towels but, two days into her period, was "unable to find the right time" to ask her mother for more. We can understand this girl as illustrating how some tweens may not just feel bewildered by, but also disconnected from, what is going in their bodies. Their bodies are developing new signs and feelings (which we would call erogenous zones) inviting them to the new experiences of sexual relationships. Their capacity to feel comfortable and at ease with this new use of their bodies is going to depend very much on the relationship they have made with their bodies as they have been growing up. How they feel about their bodies is going to depend very much on how they have been taught to regard their genitalia. Picture the scene of a five-year-old boy in the bath talking to his mother. As he recounts a story he begins to play casually with his penis. The mother carries on with the conversation, seemingly unaware of what he is doing and taking no more notice than if he was playing with his leg. We can contrast this relaxed approach regarding sexual parts of the body as ordinary, good and as acceptable as any other part with the mother who may have immediately told her son to "stop fiddling with yourself".

Lance's mother had always wanted him to feel more comfortable in his body than she, or indeed Lance's father, had felt about theirs. She had grown up feeling that there were parts of her body so rude, unacceptable, distasteful and embarrassing that they could not even be named. Her problem was not so much that she was embarrassed about Lance's developing body but that she was embarrassed about her *own* body and always had been.

> "I'm just embarrassed by his body ... we were never even given a name for our private parts ... we just had to pretend they weren't there ..."
> *Lance's mother*

Psychiatrist Erik Erikson, writing in the 1960s, talks about children who are taught to regard their "private" parts as "too private for even them to touch" and such a child may grow up feeling that his private parts are even "not his private property". In order to feel that her body could be lovable and acceptable, Lance's mother had literally grown up having to pretend that her private parts were not so much "*not there*" but "*not their*" in the sense that, unconsciously, she had had to disown them. The risk for such a child is that when puberty begins they may find it difficult to associate warm close intimate feelings with sex or may feel guilty about doing so. Lance's mother didn't know how to feel good about her own body and so couldn't help him to feel good about his. (By feeling good I mean simply enjoying the pleasure of one's body and suffering the pain of one's body.) We will talk more about managing your own embarrassment in talking to your tween about sexual matters in Chapter 7.

Hot chicks and cool guys – friend or foe?

Tweens are aware that their bodies are becoming sexual. They are trying to connect themselves, i.e., the person they know they are, with the changes in their body and this raises for them the question of what it means to be a sexual person in their family and their world outside. Erikson equates this with a child learning to walk. The toddler not only has to practise the skill of walking, at a deep level they also have to master what it means to be "one who can walk" in their family and culture – "one who will go far", "one who will be able to stand on his own feet", "one who will be upright", "one who must be watched because he may go too far". In the same way tweens are both aware of and discovering the implications of having a sexual body. They are bombarded by media images and advertisers' products. The Lancôme Institute in Paris is not the only cosmetic company to target tween girls with grooming classes and make-up. Angela Lenci, the owner of The Parlour in London, argues that, "*Starting them at a younger age not only gives them healthy skin, it boosts their confidence*" (*The Times*, 6 April 2003). It could be equally well argued that if tweens need to "have their confidence boosted" about their bodies and appearance it is largely due to the media's promotion of the perfect appearance.

How tweens feel about becoming someone who can have sex is going to be influenced and affected by differing family cultures and attitudes to sex. A nine year old was shocked, puzzled and ashamed as she described an incident following a sleepover with a friend. In the morning the two girls had crumpled up tissues and pushed them under their t-shirts to make it look as though they had breasts. When they came down for breakfast, her friend's parents roared with laughter and her mother hugged her friend warmly and said, "You're just dying to be a teenager, aren't you?" Buoyed by their success, my client had then returned home still wearing the improvised breasts. Her mother greeted her with rage and disapproval, telling her that she was "disgusting to walk through the streets like that". We can see only too clearly the different messages that these two tweens were being given about their developing bodies. One was being told that this was admirable, attractive and fun. The other that this was embarrassing, rude and not to be shown in public.

Recent research shows us that physical changes are beginning at a younger age than ever before. Studies from the National Center for Policy Research for Women and Families in Washington, Penn State University, University of North Carolina and Great Ormond Street Hospital (GOSH) in London state that puberty may begin as young as eight years old for both girls and boys. Professor Peter Hindmarsh (GOSH) says that sex hormones, especially in girls, begin to increase gradually in the body from about seven years old (*The Times*, 28 June 2003). Oestrogen for girls and testosterone for boys begin to be produced at night until 4–5 a.m. Although the levels are not large enough to stimulate physical changes such as breasts or pubic

"Are they really developing earlier or is this being hyped up by the media?"

hair developing, they do affect the brain, causing mood swings. He likes the situation for the pre-adolescent child as not unlike that for a woman in the first three months of pregnancy who may feel awful but appears normal and it is not until the pregnancy is showing that she receives the sympathy she needs. Children get their sympathy when symptoms like acne, etc., begin to appear, which is unlikely to be as young as eight or nine years old.

Tweens are also bombarded with advice about what to do with their bodies! Magazines, such as the British *Pop Idol* and websites targeting this age group provide articles and advice on dress, cosmetics and sometimes sexual matters which at one time would have been the sole province of a late teenager. And of course, this is the age where many children are taught the facts of life in school. Such lessons now often include advice on topics such as sexually transmitted diseases and contraception. One eleven-year-old boy came home bemused after being taught how to put on a condom, clearly puzzled as to how this was relevant to his life of football and Game Boys. Other tweens may be ready to absorb this information and we need to bear in mind that as children develop at different rates there are going to be casualties when advice on sexual matters is offered across the board.

"Which hippie chick are you? ... a chilled out chick who likes to look glam and unique ..."

Pop Idol, June 2004

Why are they so moody?

Tweens may feel that it is not only their childlike bodies that they have lost; they also seem a stranger to their familiar and previously settled personalities. They may be as bewildered as you at their unpredictable responses and mood swings. They may be confused about their feelings. They know they are moody and irritable; they don't like feeling like they do but they don't know how to put it into words, let alone change it. "*Our moods don't believe in each other,*" said the American philosopher Emerson (Phillips). Tweens have very little control over their moods as they feel literally that they are a different person from mood to mood. An adult will understand the concept of "being in a mood". A tween feels they *are* their mood. They are

"... I don't know what's happened ... but I do know I used to sing around the house a lot and now I don't any more ..."

eleven year old

puzzled (even frightened) by their ambivalence towards you. They want to be close and they want to be independent. This mirrors their ambivalence and confusion about their developing bodies. What they need help to understand is that just as they are in a transitional relationship with their bodies, so they are in a transitional relationship with you. They are thinking about how they, as a teenager, can relate to you. They have a sense that teenagers relate differently to parents than children but as they are unsure of what kind of teenager they're going to be, they are left unsure how to forge this new relationship with you.

Why do they have to argue about everything?

Your tween is also beginning to change the way they think. Children tend to live in a black and white world where things are right or wrong, fair or unfair; their morality and sense of values is also likely to be what you have taught them. For most parents, teaching right and wrong is really a means of disciplining children! You may have believed you were teaching your children a morality but it would not be unfair to think that in teaching your child right from wrong you have been trying to mould them to your wishes. Young children tend to take language very literally, for example, the puzzled seven year old wondering how "a self-drive car" works, or the one who, on seeing a notice, "This Door is Alarmed" wanted to know what had happened to the door to worry it! By eight or nine children are beginning to develop the capacity to think abstractly, leading them to think about and question all sorts of issues they may previously have taken for granted. A seven year old may help to raise money for victims of the latest world crisis but a nine year old will be beginning to think also about the causes of the crisis and man's part in those causes. They are beginning to work out their own morality, what they believe in, what seems right to them, rather than what you tell them is right. They may become fervent about topics such as human suffering or animal welfare and try hard to convert everyone else to their views. There are risks here because your tween will not have a sophisticated sense of nuances and shades of grey and are consequently prey to being rigid in their views and carrying them to the extreme. For example, there is a big

> "Why should I tidy my room when the world is in such a mess?"
>
> *graffiti*

difference between insisting on eating only organic fruit and vegetables and refusing to eat any fruit or vegetables in case they have accidentally been sprayed by insecticides.

Excited as they may be as their brains buzz with ideas and issues, they are also going to feel they have lost the seemingly uncomplicated world of childhood in which parents know everything and could solve all problems. They may feel resentful or angry with you, feeling that giving one particular view on life was in someway a betrayal or even that you have double standards. A ten-year-old boy was both outraged and protective when his Christian widowed father began a relationship with a married woman. "*You said adultery was a sin … but then you're not committing adultery are you, she is … because you're not married now.*" In this one sentence he was poignantly both chastising his father and trying to keep him as the good and always right person with whom he had grown up. This mental state of "transitional thinking", moving from a "conviction" to a "repertoire" of ideas (Phillips) reflects the physical and emotional transition a tween is making from childhood to teenager.

How is it for you?

The tween has everything to hope for, the ordinary excitements of life are just around the corner: learning to drive, learning to drink, higher or further education, dating, first job, the list is endless. They are on the verge of everything new, just as you, as parents, may be beginning to feel life is slowly winding down. The tween is developing the capacity for sex and romance. Even at young middle age, parents are beginning at least to glimpse death and decrepidation.

When "cool and well wicked" tries to live with "sad and boring".

This sense of the passage of time is almost bound to colour how you manage your tween. Life today is still very exciting for parents and indeed grandparents. Gone are the days of pipe and slippers, twin-sets and knitting by the time you are fifty. But there is no getting away from the fact that, as one father described, "*The wind in my sails is just not quite as vigorous as it used to be.*" It is human to feel a tinge of envy at the exuberance of youth. A thirty-something mother was showing her girlfriend a new bikini explaining "there's something wrong with it, it just doesn't look right, but I don't know what." The bikini was certainly the right size, shape and colour for her. Her friend pursed her lips, "Mmmm, it's not right, is it?" The friend then tried it on herself and agreed it looked no better on her but neither of them could define the fault. As the bikini was cast aside on the bed, in walked her twelve-year-old daughter, "*Hey, that's cool, that's really cool, can I try it on?*" A few minutes later the daughter returned looking stunning in the bikini! The mother's eyes filled with tears and the two women exchanged glances, shrugged their shoulders and said in one voice, "*That's what's wrong with it!*" The tween gleefully ran off in her new bikini! Despite her sadness, this mother was able to admire her daughter.

Emerging sexuality

If there is one truth about parenting it is that your child's childhood will bring memories flooding back of your own childhood. We learn to parent from our parents and we pick up other ways as we go along. Most people want to do some things differently from the way their own parents did and most people are surprised to find themselves doing it the same. What your parents taught you about sex and their attitude to your sexuality is going to colour how you approach your tween and their sexuality. We will talk more in Chapter 5 about how parents always convey two messages to children. The first message lies in what they say, the second lies in what they feel. Add to that the fact that growing up is a process involving an extraordinary mixture of dependence and independence, parents may find a paradox, in that you devote yourself to helping your children to be close to you, to trust you to understand them with the sole purpose that they will one day be independent of you. Each milestone a child achieves, walking, talking, toilet training, reading, writing, etc., brings with it a change in family life. These may be subtle, almost unnoticed changes, described by one mother as, "*I suddenly realized that for several weeks now shopping trips had been easier. I didn't have to pack a survival bag with bibs, bottles and baby wipes ...*"

"I'm enjoying watching her blossom, I really am ... but why do I sometimes feel resentful about her fun?"

mother of twelve year old

Other changes are like dramatic alarm bells and none more so than when your child begins to swap their child bodies for adolescent bodies. As this begins to happen, you are forced to acknowledge that very soon your child will want something parents cannot provide, i.e., a sexual relationship. How you feel about this will affect how you parent and in turn will affect both your child's emotional and physical development. There is no way you can avoid your child's emerging sexuality speaking to you about your sexuality. The more comfortable you are with your own sexuality, the more comfortable you are going to feel about your child's emerging sexuality. It is also worth thinking about what your child's emerging sexuality says about you sexually. As your tween is looking forward to sexual relationships, are you feeling in a state of sexual neglect?

In the previous chapter we talked about how young children tend to view their parents as an extension of their own bodies. Starting school separates children from their parents' bodies and is a clear physical indication of the beginnings of independence. The next big physical sign your child is growing up is when their bodies begin to develop sexually. For the first time, their "private parts" may now be becoming private from you. You will find yourself having less contact with your child's body and this can feel like a huge deprivation.

Let's just think about issues around buying your daughter her first bra. Immediately a mother is going to remember getting her first bra. Do you want to have the same or a different experience? How do you arrive at the decision – by her bust size, social reasons such as closest friends are all wearing bras, simply on her wishes to have a bra, or on your wishes that she should or should not have a bra? Or a combination of reasons. In some families, buying a first bra is an exciting mother/daughter event celebrating this stage in a girl's development. Other mothers, through embarrassment or in an attempt to keep their daughter a child for longer, may go on refusing to buy a bra in spite of their daughter's body being physically ready. It is highly likely that the reasons you choose will be coloured by whether or not you were allowed a bra at the time you felt you needed one, physically or emotionally. And what of the mother who pushes her daughter to wear a bra when she herself is neither physically nor

"My nine-year-old daughter wants me to buy a bra. Her bust is barely developing but she says that all her friends are wearing them … what should I do?"

emotionally ready? Many small girls are now being drawn into mock bras, "crop tops", in preference to a vest. It is a cause for concern that some parents think (or is it unthinking parents feel?) little girls look sweet or cute in mock adult lingerie. The risk here is that these girls are being asked to think about (consciously or unconsciously) sexual matters long before they are ready to or capable of doing so. It also poses the question "What is sexual desire for?"

Dressing daughters, and in particular buying their first bra, raises interesting questions about bringing up girls. It is not uncommon for a pregnant mother to say she would, "... quite like a girl ... you can dress them up." There is an implication here that in having a daughter one is creating a spectacle, i.e., you are a good mother if your daughter looks "cute and pretty". Are you also a good mother later on if your daughter looks, "cool and sexy"? We talk of helping children "in and out of their clothes". Once a daughter becomes a tween, the script changes. Mothers help their daughters to dress with the implicit and explicit fantasy that someone else will be undressing them one day. This is a very different conversation from the conversations you will have been having with your little girl. It is also a different conversation from the one you may be having with a teenage girl, where the topic of sexuality may be much more explicit. How easily you can have these "transitional conversations" will depend very much on your fantasy of a good daughter. Is she a "walking, talking, living doll", an anti-depressant for men, or is she a living and developing personality who is now ready to engage with other people at all levels?

Fathers and daughters

Parenting a tween girl may be equally complicated for a father. Lizzie had always been a "daddy's girl" and he confessed to being charmed by her from birth. Although there were two younger children, both parents admitted Lizzie was, "*A bit special ... she's our first born, and, well, she's a bit special, she's pretty, she's bright, she's very entertaining and always has been ..."* Lizzie's mother had noticed that her father had begun to swing between being very indulgent with Lizzie, often inappropriately, to being quite intransigent, also often inappropriately.

"... I don't know what it is ... she just bothers me ..."

eleven-year-old
Lizzie's dad

"He used to be so good with her, she could always twist him round her little finger but he was good at being firm when he had to be. Now when she needs clear boundaries he gives in and when she needs a bit of spoiling, he digs his heels in." Lizzie's father was bewildered and dejected, feeling he didn't understand Lizzie any more and he didn't recognize himself as her parent any more.

The difficulties were not all of dad's making. Lizzie was also relating to her father differently; she was hostile, argumentative, defiant and derisive of him. She shrugged him off when he tried to be affectionate towards her. Above all, she had banned him from calling her by his nickname for her, "Daigy" (this nickname had arisen in infancy from the initials DSG, i.e., Daddy's Special Girl).

When I met Lizzie with her parents it was clear they were all very fond of each other. It was also clear that there were real tensions between father and daughter. Lizzie's father was struggling with his feelings as his "Daddy's Special Girl" was on the point of growing into an attractive, sexy woman. Being charmed by a child daughter is one thing, being charmed by a nubile young tween daughter may be more complicated. At a very deep level Lizzie was indeed "bothering" him. Unconsciously, he was warding off her desirability by being angry with her or hostile to her. Once he understood this he was able to behave less erratically towards her.

For Lizzie's part, now that she was thinking about what kind of teenager she wanted to be, she was finding her specialness to her parents a burden. (Indeed, for everyone, being special to someone is always a refuge and an obstacle.) Unconsciously, she saw being Daddy's Special Girl as a block to sexual relationships. She still wanted to be "a special girl" but not a little girl and not to her dad! Daughters have to get rid of their fathers if they are to be free to find a sexual partner.

It doesn't take a sage to show how crucial Lizzie's parents' attitude to her sexuality was in forming her own attitude towards her sexuality. If Lizzie's father had not been able to recognize the complication of his feelings he may have been like the father of another twelve year old who felt she had to accompany him to his weekly football match long after the time she would rather have been out with her own friends because, *"…dad wants me to go and I feel guilty …"*

This is an interesting illustration of a natural, unconscious boundary causing a problem in a family (see Chapter 5). This father is now seeing his daughter appropriately as a sexual person and yet he knows for him she is not a sexual person. She, on the other hand, is still enjoying an intimate and happy aspect of being a child in the family. A fully fledged teenager is likely to be seeking more privacy and may also have an unconscious sense that this was not necessarily an appropriate habit to continue on a regular basis. Equally, as sexual boundaries are so much more clearly defined in the teenage years such an incident may be much less complex. The whole family may feel more relaxed about such intimate matters.

> "My eleven-year-old daughter recently started her periods. I feel uncomfortable about her coming into bed with us on Sunday mornings and yet it seems harsh to stop her when her younger brothers are still doing so ...
>
> *Melinda's father*

We could think that there is no reason why either or both parents could not explain to Melinda how growing up involves losses as well as gains and help her to think of other ways she and her father could have special and close times. A parent's ability to have such a conversation will depend very much on what they were taught by their parents about menstruation. Is this a dark and dirty secret, not to be talked about? Or is menstruation seen as a celebratory rite of passage for a girl? Having such a conversation would also depend, of course, on Melinda's personality. A shy and embarrassed Melinda is going to be a very different person to talk to than a more open, confident girl who seems more at ease in her adolescent body (see Chapter 7).

Mothers and sons

Boys have similar and also different boundaries to negotiate. Both boys and girls begin life close to and identified with a female body – that of their mother. Tween girls are in the process of elaborating a female body and again we will think more about this in Chapter 7. Boys are in the process of learning how to be a boy separate from their mother's body.

> "My ten year old is obsessed with warfare and weapons ... is this normal?"
>
> *Max's mother*

Max's parents were of gentle, passive natures and were horrified at their son's intense interest in warfare and weapons. They felt he was becoming "uncouth and raucous", swearing, shouting and spitting. He had recently been accused of bullying at school. They felt they had "gone wrong" somewhere and seemed at a loss in a family meeting.

"*We just don't understand you*," said the mother as her son lolled angrily in his chair. "*I don't talk like that, I don't behave like that. You don't see me swearing and shouting and fighting ...*"

"*No*," burst out her son angrily, "*you made me think I'd be like you, and I'm not ... I'm the opposite of you ...*"

Max felt the only way to be a man was to be the "*opposite*" of his gentle mother. He seemed cheated that his mother had even allowed him to believe that he could be like her!

Boys integrate the aggressive, thrusting side of their nature with a more tender, loving side by being allowed to be aggressive, almost caricatures of the male persona. These usually appear as an exaggerated interest in dad's interests – sport, beer or whatever, as both a conscious desire to be like the man of the house and an unconscious rejection of all that is female as manifested in their mother. But Max's parents' interests were not clearly defined into male and female interests. They both enjoyed books, music and gentle outdoor pursuits. In a sense, their son had no exaggerated male identity to copy and so in an attempt to establish his "maleness" he was trying to be the exact opposite of his mother and a crude version of a man. In fact Max was not so much bullying other children as simply practising how to be a man (see Chapter 8). At the same time he raged against his mother because he had assumed their earlier closeness meant they were "the same".

Looking forward – "All you need is Maybelline"?

Tweens are not only in transition, many are confused! We are surrounded by images of bodies, the beautiful and sexy of both genders, and not only that, cosmetic and fashion advertisements would lead us to believe that a beautiful body can be instantly achieved by their products. They market the idea that there is a perfect, prescribed body shape that will provide both boys and girls with eternal success and happiness. The impact on youngsters who are already ambivalent about their changing bodies cannot be underestimated; in a sense, their pleasure is being spoiled. Many are cautiously looking forward to having more grown-up bodies but the media's demand to be sexy can feel a burden. Research (Hill and Pallin) shows that girls as young as eight are drawn to dieting to improve their self-worth and that they are strongly influenced in this by their mother's attitude to her body shape and diet. The research also shows that nine year olds associate fat body shapes with being "stupid and unpopular" and thin ones with being "popular, intelligent and kind". Increasingly, children are not being allowed to be in their own bodies and risk trying to attain a media dictated attractiveness. It is difficult enough for tweens to feel comfortable in their changing bodies without having normal differences in development highlighted and exaggerated to such an extent that they may set about rejecting their bodies before they have had an opportunity to get to know them.

"My nine year old says she is being teased at school about her hairy legs and she wants to shave them. Surely she's too young to be doing this?"

Like most adults you are probably discontent with some aspects of your bodies feeling there are lumps and bumps in all the wrong places. (It is worth thinking here about who you are comparing yourself with and from whose point of view you are looking at yourself!) Many adults would admit to spending time worrying about their appearance and also spending a good deal of money on clothes, cosmetics or even surgery in trying to enhance or change their appearance. Body ambition has always been the preserve of adults; it is an appropriate preoccupation for a teenager but it is an inappropriate worry for a tween.

Cordelia's mother was adamant that now that Cordelia was twelve years old discos were not the innocent fun they had been at eight or nine years old. She felt Cordelia was too young to be "dressing up ready for dating", and there had been a heated row over a new t-shirt Cordelia had bought with a friend. Her mother was surprised (surprisingly!) when Cordelia chose a black one, "*Black just doesn't suit her ... it's such a severe colour ...*"

"My twelve-year-old daughter has been invited to a friend's birthday disco and sleepover to which boys have also been invited. I think she's far too young ..."

Cordelia's mother

While Cordelia was at school, her mother returned the black t-shirt for a cream one, "so much prettier with jeans". Not unexpectedly,

Cordelia had been furious, refused to wear the cream t-shirt and her mother had eventually found it scrunched up in the dustbin. As this incident was related to me, I could feel the emotional temperature rising in the consulting room and decided to intervene as these two continued the argument. I asked Cordelia's mother, "*What does the colour cream mean to you?*"

She paused. "*Well, it can be very sophisticated … but it's fresh, innocent, it's more a young girl's colour …*"

"*And black?*"

"*Evenings, sexy, sultry.*"

She was a pretty woman who dressed attractively and creatively on a very limited budget. She had been a single parent for six years and was now feeling ready for another relationship. Unlike her two closest friends, she hadn't found "the right man" and admitted that she felt insecure about her own attractiveness and sex appeal. It was painful for her to begin to realize that her daughter was now becoming a sexual equal and rival. She was sad to realize that some of her strictness with Cordelia was because she feared that "… my own daughter will beat me to it …[*finding a partner*]." Her rivalry with her daughter was preventing her from treating Cordelia in an age appropriate way. It was also preventing her from enjoying helping Cordelia to develop into an independent and sexual personality.

But nature is also equally unkind to parents! It is likely that you have devoted the majority of your time and energy over the past years to developing a deep attachment to your child. The attachment between children and parents is not only deep, it is also unique, and now you are faced with the huge challenge of letting them go. How well you are going to survive depends on how well you can move from being the parent of a dependent child to being the redundant parent of a teenager. Until now, you and your child have been sharing the task of "attachment" – of being close to each other. Now your child has a completely different quest – the search for sexual relationships. You are really going to lose your baby. It may feel dispiriting … and wonderful. You cannot find a substitute but can you discover other passions to enjoy? The time has come for you to

"Mother nature is wonderful. She gives us twelve years to develop a love for our children before turning them into teenagers."

Eugene Birtin

plan for your retirement from parenting by developing work and leisure interests separate from your children. And will you feel disloyal to your children if you do? Or, does it feel as one mother said, *"He's getting a new body, but I've got my body back and I'm jolly well going to set it free."*

three

How tweens change families

As children grow up they wreak havoc in the family. Each stage of child development makes an impact on family life and demands that parents and children re-adapt to each other's changing needs; the differences between a nine year old and a twelve year old in a family highlight how frustrating it is that children's needs seem to change just as you feel you have mastered parenting! In this chapter we will look at the impact of tweens on family life and also some of the issues that may colour how you respond as a parent.

All stages of childhood are potentially stressful for parents! You will remember the havoc of the toddler years – locks on cupboard doors, precious ornaments on higher shelves, carpets permanently covered with plastic sheeting. You may have been exhausted, but you knew what was needed – mainly a watchful eye and constant reminders that this stage will pass! You could also capitalize on your toddler's innate desire to please you; and sometimes it was fun ... one mother described her frustration and joy at finding her twenty month old emptying the contents of her cosmetic purse onto her face, hands, clothes. "She's such a little pickle ... but she knew what to do with the stuff!" This parent had the sense of a child developing new skills. She was glimpsing the time when she and her daughter would share make-up tips ...

It can be so disappointing when that time arrives because the havoc of the tween years is different and less easy to manage. In

"Are the tween years automatically stressful for parents ... if so, why?"

some ways it may seem much more nebulous, vague … You sense all
is not well, your youngster seems to be racing ahead of their chronological age. In other ways it feels very concrete: you feel certain ten
years old is too young to have a mobile phone or to wear make-up
… and yet their friends seem to have all these things. You are
puzzled by the hostility; a previously friendly and co-operative nine
year old may now seem slightly strident and determined and, by
twelve, it is likely everything you do and say is wrong. Any attempt
you make to try and understand or set limits seems to make the situation worse. Indeed, at times you may feel your parent-child relationship is turning into a host-to-parasite relationship!

A tween challenges family rituals and traditions

Family life can be very idealized and romanticized and never more
so than nowadays and particularly by parents at the onset of the
tween years. The romance usually involves parents and children
taking an harmonious pleasure in each other's
company – all of the time! As it is as unlikely that   "Why doesn't the
this has happened in your family as in any other, it   family seem to
would not be surprising if you find yourself senti-   matter to our
mentally idealizing your child's childhood as it   tween …?"
begins to pass. You may find yourself remembering
only the cute and happy times. All parents want to feel they have
given their children a happy childhood and one of the ways of not
forgiving yourself for making it less than perfect is to join in today's
media presentation of childhood as care-free and adorable. Such
ideas about family life often tend to overlook the fact that everyone
in a family is trying to get their own needs met, i.e., getting what
they want for themselves. This is how human beings survive. You
know this only too well because you will probably have spent a
great deal of effort in the early years helping your child to learn to
share. (It is interesting that in order to survive, adults *have* to share,
and in order to survive, babies *must not* share.) Being a member of
a family means learning to balance our own needs with the needs of
other people in the family. Some children are better at sharing than
others but all tweens are beginning to become primarily preoccupied with their own needs. Family needs become less significant.

Family traditions and rituals may not only feel unimportant, they may actually feel constricting to the tween.

The importance of family rituals and traditions

How families adapt to each other's needs is always individual and sometimes painful but there is a constant process of adaptation as children grow up. One of the difficulties of parenting is that not only do children's needs change with their developmental age, but so do the needs of parents! As a parent it is likely you will have been immersed for the last few years in child-centred activities. Sex on a Sunday afternoon will have been replaced with a trip to the park, museum or a toddler birthday party! Now your tween's changing needs highlight your future: how is it going to be for you when Sunday afternoons are free again?

One of the tasks of parenting is to monitor not only the children's individual needs but also the needs of "the family as a whole". Family rituals and traditions will have helped you to develop and define the family. This is an important process which helps the children to consolidate the feeling of belonging to a family group. Sometimes you will have thought about rituals by deciding what you want the family to value. One family described a tradition of always having an elaborate special breakfast on any day a particular child had an exam or test at school. Other rituals will have evolved from the hurly-burly of family life. Either way your family rituals will have been highly influenced by memories of your childhood. "*I remember we always used to …*" or "*My mother always …*" are the reflections of all adults at times, whether the memories are good or painful.

Rosemary's family always had supper with granny on Sundays. Both grandparents were still working when she was born and in the mysterious way things happen in families, without any conscious discussion, a pattern evolved of them seeing her at Sunday supper.

One Saturday twelve-year-old Rosemary suddenly announced she had arranged to go to the cinema with a friend on Sunday evening. She became truculent when her mother protested, "*Granny will be disappointed,*" arguing, "*It's all arranged, Lucy's dad is picking us all up.*" Her mother insisted she shouldn't have made arrangements without consulting her parents and that she had to telephone her friend and explain that the family always went to granny's for supper on Sundays.

Rosemary's mother's view:
Rosemary's mother was shocked. This was the first time that
Rosemary had made arrangements contrary to a family ritual.
However she had a vague sense of unease about the
strength of her own reaction. She was certain   "She's so selfish
Rosemary should not make arrangements without   ..."
consulting her parents. She felt she had to set firm
limits or "... *it's the thin edge of the wedge ... we'll never know where
we are otherwise*" but still, she felt uneasy about her reaction and
wondered how else she might have responded.

Rosemary's view:
Rosemary didn't think she was being selfish. In   "I'm not selfish ...
fact, Rosemary didn't think! She had been with a   I think mum is the
group of friends when the idea of the cinema trip   selfish one. I see
was suggested and generally agreed on. Lucy   granny every
offered her dad as a taxi ... great! ... and Rosemary   week ... it's just
was sure her dad wouldn't mind collecting them   once I want to go
later. The girls were elated as they made their way to the cinema ...
home. None of them had considered how their   it's not granny
plans may have fitted in with the plans of anybody   who minds, it's
else in the family.   mum ..."

Understanding a challenge to family tradition

Rosemary was not open to thinking about the matter. As a nine or
ten year old, she would probably have been in the "I'll ask my mum
if I can go ..." frame of mind. As an older teenager it may not have
crossed her mind to mention the arrangement until the last minute
on Sunday. However, as a tween, caught up in the excitement of a
peer activity, Rosemary was left feeling her parents "*hate me having
fun*".

Rosemary's mother did want to think about her own strong reaction. She was hurt that Rosemary felt going to the cinema with a
friend was more important than seeing her grandmother. She realized that as this was the first time Rosemary had challenged a family
tradition she was "caught on the hop" and unprepared to deal with
the confrontation. She also realized that perhaps now granny needed
to see Rosemary more than Rosemary needed to see granny. She

feared this was the beginning of a disintegration of the family life she had carefully nurtured throughout Rosemary's childhood.

When Rosemary and her mother were offered an opportunity to talk about this incident, several issues became clear.

Rosemary understood:

She should have consulted her parents about arrangements for the cinema trip rather than presenting them with a *fait-accompli*.

Rosemary's mother understood:

She realized that as Rosemary began to practice her independence family rituals were going to be disrupted. She was disappointed Rosemary was choosing not to spend time with her family and reacted to her disappointment by becoming rigid with Rosemary, insisting that the *only* solution was for Rosemary to cancel her arrangements.

A happy compromise?

At the end of the discussion, both Rosemary and her mother agreed there were several ways they could manage this incident. Rosemary could phone her grandmother to explain why she wasn't coming to supper. Or, Rosemary could phone her friends to say she could go to the cinema but her father couldn't collect; this way she wouldn't lose too much face with her friends and her father's evening wouldn't be disrupted. Finally, they both had to accept that mother and granny were going to be disappointed by Rosemary's decision.

Managing a challenge to family traditions

Change can be difficult to manage. All change involves loss (we lose the thing we do not choose), but change also brings opportunities. In this family, it was likely that increasingly Rosemary would prefer to spend time on Sunday with her friends rather than her family. There was now an opportunity for the family to make new rituals, more appropriate to the growing youngster's needs. Maybe Rosemary and granny could have some quality time on a week night or granny could spend Sunday in Rosemary's home where she would have "casual access" to the children as they went about their own activities during the day.

- Hold in mind this is a time of transition; Rosemary is now saying friends are more important than family, this doesn't necessarily mean that family will never be important to her again.
- There is a difference between a family falling apart and a family changing; when changes happen in a family it may feel as though the family is disintegrating but this is simply a sign that a big transition is occurring.
- *"But this is the way we've always done it ..."* doesn't mean there isn't another way of doing it just as well.
- Embrace the opportunity to establish new family traditions and rituals appropriate to your child's developmental age.

Moping in their bedroom

Bedrooms are an interesting symbol of children's changing developmental needs. During infancy and childhood, parents and family bedrooms are to some extent a shared space. Parents and small children will feel free to wander in and out of each other's bedrooms. However, bedrooms also represent each family member's need for privacy and individuality. Just as there are things you want to do in the bedroom without the children present, by six or seven years old your child will be beginning to have secrets in their bedroom. Gradually little notices such as "Private please knock" will appear on the door. For a nine year old, their bedroom is often a club room for friends with all kinds of shared secrets going on behind a firmly closed door. By the time your tween is eleven or twelve years old the bedroom will have become an intensely private space (much more than that of an older teenager because it is likely that by the teenage years your youngster will have established the right to a private life); going into your tween's bedroom to clean or collect dirty washing is likely to be regarded as a gross intrusion of their privacy. It is also true that at this age, the parents' bedroom begins to take on a different symbolism for children. You may have noticed that your tween comes into your bedroom less ... and they know why they should keep out!

"He slopes off whenever he can and spends hours in his bedroom ... the thing is, he does nothing in there ... it's just a waste of time ... or is he depressed?"

Even though families may not spend as much time together now as they did even twenty years ago and even though from the early years many children have televisions and computers in their bedrooms, you may be puzzled as to what your youngster does in their bedroom. They seem to do nothing but lie immobile on their bed for hours at a time, conserving energy whilst listening to music so loud that the very foundations of the house seem to shake. At other times, there seems to be a suspicious silence emitting from the bedroom.

"Feeling what I want to feel ..." – the tween's view:

Being a tween is hard work! You may feel irritated by the waste of time "doing nothing" in their room. Tweens are not, in fact, "wasting time". They may not be meditating upon the finer points of the great philosophical thinkers, but they are practising being independent in many ways. Most important is their need to *"feel whatever I want to feel"*, to have time and space to find meaning for their welter of new feelings and experiences. Listen to what they say:

"*The trouble is my family take it personally ... they think I don't want them ... my brother doesn't understand, even if he's sitting on the bed doing nothing, he's irritating me ... because this is MY SPACE.*"

"*I go to my bedroom to get away from my family.*"

"*I go to my bedroom when I'm sick of my family ... I go to my bedroom to be angry.*"

"*I go to my bedroom when I've nothing to do ...*"

"*I go to my bedroom when I can't be bothered ...*"

"*I love my bedroom ... I don't know why because it's 100% mess, but I just love it, it's my space ... sanctuary ... I lie on the bed mostly and listen to the radio ... and I can feel whatever I want to feel. Nobody can ask me, 'What's the matter?'*"

"She's locking us out ..." – the parents' view:

However, there is no denying how rejected the family may feel by having the bedroom door locked or slammed in their face. Listen to what parents say:

"*She doesn't seem to want to be with us any more ... it can't be good for her to spend so much time up there [in her bedroom] all alone*".

"I get suspicious, there is always the sense that he's up to something up there. If I call or knock on the door, I always get the feeling he's hastily hiding something he doesn't want me to see ..."

"It's really difficult to keep any semblance of family life going. It would be much easier to let them just go off into their individual cells."

Understanding the closed bedroom door

Distance and proximity in the family

Adults should understand about private space as it is something everybody seeks. Like everyone else in the family, tweens are negotiating constantly how close and how distant they want to be from other members of the family. One way of understanding growing up is to think of it as a gradual distancing from our parents' bodies. As dependent babies, we are in constant physical touch with our parents as we are fed, bathed, changed, nursed, carried around, etc. As your child learns to walk, talk, feed themselves, they begin, literally, to lose touch with your body. Tweens may fluctuate between enjoying cuddles and "sluffing off" any affectionate gesture. They are likely to lock the bathroom door to ensure privacy; for parents, especially for mothers, the beginning of the loss of easy physical intimacy is a huge deprivation. It seems so less natural than it does with the older teenager who is physically fully sexually developed. Tweens are quick to sense they are depriving their parents of something, and equally quick to feel guilty about doing so. (I will explore this theme more in Chapter 4.)

For the tween, spending more time alone in the bedroom is the beginning of practising separating from the family. We can think of the bedroom as a transitional "womb" between the relative safety of home and the exciting unknown of the teenage world outside. But tweens are not *just* between worlds, they also have their *own* world. For many this world is represented physically by the four walls of their bedroom.

The importance of time alone

Winnicott has highlighted how growing up involves developing both a capacity to be alone and to be together with others. He talks of how initially a baby believes he and his mother are the same person – not surprising as the baby's every wish is seemingly magically met on demand, be it feeding, changing, cuddling. Gradually, the baby learns he and his mother are separate people and being alone may feel frightening as the baby's sense of self, i.e., identity, is precarious and he needs the reassurance of a mother constantly there to bolster him. A baby strengthens his sense of being a separate person by practising being alone in the presence of his mother, for example, by eight or nine months a baby may play happily with toys as long as he can see or hear his mother in the same room. This then extends to him being able to cope for short periods with mother out of the room until he slowly learns to be alone as well as together with other people. The tween years bring a return to this stage of developing "who I am". The tween needs to be in touch, in all senses of the word, with other people but they also need time and space to be alone. A nine-year-old boy returned from a visit to Granny's. Recounting his day he reported, "... *and then Granny and I had a really companionable read* ..." His mother presumed Granny had been reading to him but what he meant was that he and Granny had read their individual books separately – and together. His story illustrates how tweens are beginning to experience a different kind of separateness from you; a separateness out of which sexual desire can grow. He felt free to be alone in the presence of his Granny (and his mother). How free do you feel to be alone in the presence of your child?

"*The word alone carries overtones and undertones of 'all-one'*", said psychotherapist Robert Hobson. He went on to highlight how aloneness and togetherness are interdependent. He argues that to be an individual with an identity and to be a member of a community is only possible if, "*I can only be alone insofar as I can be together with others. I can only be together with others if I am able to be alone.*"

Who is shut out and who is shut in?

Closing the bedroom door may be a two way communication from the tween. On one hand they are practising "shutting the family out", being independent in their own world. On the other they may be illustrating their anxiety that you will "slam the door" on their childhood, lock them out, so they will never be able to return to the safety of childhood. Your tween wants to lock you out of their world but they also want to ensure they can return to you safely when they so desire or need. They need you to know that they are *practising* being separate from you. This may have a different quality to the teenage desire to *be* distant from you.

I remember one young mother describing how, at times, she used to go and sit in her car, just to have "*some space that was mine*" away from the demands of the family. In any work situation, people need their own space, even if it is only a desk. A secretary was telling me how outraged she felt because her boss had gone through her desk drawer while she was away. She could accept the reality that he was entitled to do so, but, "*I felt violated*", she said, "*that is my space*". Shutting your boss out is one thing. Feeling shut out by your child is quite another and it happens in so many symbolic ways; one mother was very upset when her ten-year-old son decided he wanted to keep his towel and wash things in his bedroom rather than in the family bathroom.

Managing moping in the bedroom

- Remember, this quest for separateness and privacy is part of a process. Your tween won't always be as hostile and you won't always feel as rejected as you do now. It may feel as though the family is disintegrating, but have faith that it may well integrate again further into the future.

  "How can I ensure we have some family time together ... surely that's important?"

- There is all the difference in the world in saying, "*I want to be alone*" and saying "*I don't want to be with you*". Sadly, in families these two are frequently confused.
- Try and get them to suggest how they would like to spend family time and be prepared to have to do things that you might not necessarily have chosen.
- Claim them! Your tween will welcome some demands to join in family life. They may not show you that they do, but they will!

The battle of the bedroom – *is it worth fighting?*

Bedrooms are interesting places in the home also because they are a symbol of power and freedom. Over the years you will have been in charge of what does and does not go on in your child's bedroom (in the early years, at times they may have been in charge of what went on in your bedroom!). You may have allowed them to play in the bedroom, you will have had rules about such as things paint, glue, sand, food and drink. You will have done your best to prevent them from drawing on the walls. Now that your tween's bedroom is becoming an area of potential privacy, it may also become a potential battleground.

"I have to clear up my mess everywhere in the house ... that's their rules ... in my bedroom, my space, I do what I want, my rules ... it's nothing to do with them."

Ben, aged twelve

Younger tweens may not want you to clean their room because they are keeping it private in a rigid order. Older tweens will share with teenagers the idea that bedrooms are a place to sleep, store dirty linen and crockery, dream dreams and pretend to do homework. However, as Ben shows us, tweens also see their bedrooms as a place where they can practise making their own rules and decisions.

Professionally, I am still puzzled why so many parents take on this battle of the bedroom. It is a cause hardly worth fighting, so why do so many parents try? Appeals to St Jude (Patron Saint of Hopeless Cases) are more likely to result in your tween tidying their bedroom than any appeal you make to their better nature, or any threats, bribes or punishments you proffer. You may genuinely want your tween to clear up the mess in their bedroom. You also know it is unlikely to happen in any satisfactory way, and yet the argument goes on endlessly. Could this be because the battle is not so much over the mess as over your feelings of rejection and loss of power? You know you can't stop them going off into their bedrooms, you know the time is coming when you will be unable to control what they do in their bedrooms, but still you feel hurt and rejected. Feeling rejected and powerless can make us feel angry and for some parents the attempt to control the mess in the bedroom is an attempt to stem the tide of their increasing powerlessness over their children.

Managing the mess in the bedroom

Ben had a point – his bedroom was a place where he could practise making his own decisions and rules. Ben felt that "*this is my room and I can have what I want on the walls. If they don't want to see it, they don't have to come in.*" Fine ... and as his parents pointed out, he also has to practise taking the consequences of his own decisions and rules. Both parents had taken exception to a poster on his wall saying, "*Rugby players do it with odd-shaped balls*." However, his father (who initially seemed to be suffering from severe amnesia about his own dominant interests at Ben's age) eventually laughingly acknowledged "at least I had the sense to hide my dirty magazines."

A happy compromise?
Ben and his parents agreed:

"But how do I cope with the mess?"
Ben's mother

- Once a month he had to clear everything away or into a pile so his mother could clean the room and change the sheets.
- His mother would only wash washing in the laundry basket. Any clothing left lying on the bedroom or bathroom floors or anywhere else, he had to wash himself or wear dirty.
- He was allowed only three dirty mugs in his room at any one time and would be fined per mug if extra were found. This rule was not solely for hygiene purposes; it was also to ensure that the rest of the family could occasionally have a drink!

I am not sure that these rules lessened tensions in the family – Ben irritated his mother even further by wearing dirty clothes – but as she said, "it does make us feel there are some boundaries on the mess."

On being sad your children are growing up

Many parents feel sad about their children growing up. Your tween is beginning to be somewhat outside your orbit. You may have the idea that your children being within your orbit is good, whereas for them to be outside your orbit is both bad and dangerous, and yet at the same time you will be exhorting your children to be "grown-up and independent". It is not surprising that you feel sad as you become aware that you know less and less about your youngster's daily life and that they will confide in you less as time goes on. You may feel afraid that you are losing your youngster and that you are losing control of your youngster. You may also be afraid of your own sadness. Children have to work very hard to make themselves private. At some level they know how sad it is for you.

"I just feel I'm losing her and I can't do anything about it ... my baby's going ..."

Penny's mother's view:

Penny's mother was upset, "*We used to be so close … it's a shame … she never tells me anything, we used to be so close and now I feel I've LOST her.*"

"I hardly know anything that's going on now …"

"*Do you know exactly what it is you feel you've lost?*"

"*Well, I've lost HER, she doesn't confide in me any more, she doesn't tell me her secrets. We used to be such good friends.*"

Had Penny's mother really "lost her" or was Penny simply practising her independence by not confiding in her mother? Her mother felt that if Penny had secrets with her friends, it in someway reduced her relationship with her. But there is a difference between a relationship being "reduced" and a relationship reorientating. She may well have lost her very dependent small child – a painful experience – but she had not lost her tween. Her task now was to find a way of being close to Penny, who was struggling with her desire to be both close to her parents and to hurt them. Being close to Penny now was directly linked with being able to tolerate the fact that, for the time being at least, she may no longer be Penny's prime confidant. Being close to Penny may also mean understanding that, as part of the transitional process, she may not *feel* close to Penny. Paradoxically, feeling "not close" to Penny may in fact mean that she was deeply in touch with how Penny was feeling, i.e., "Let me feel not close to you so I can be independent."

It's okay to feel resentful

"I've spent years pouring everything into her … and now she's going … and she'll take it all with her when she goes away …"

Penny's mother admitted that sometimes she felt resentful. As tweens begin to keep secrets from their parents, they highlight something which is always true in parenting but which is often masked in the hurly-burly of daily life, i.e., that parents know their children very well – and not at all.

The impact on siblings

It doesn't take a sage to understand that these are challenging days for parents and tweens alike. But other children in the family may also be struggling with difficult and painful changes. Families are a system in the sense that a family is comprised of a set of people connected to each other, and consequently a change in one person will resonate a change in everyone. When the balance in a family shifts it is not only parents and tweens who will feel the impact; tweens' siblings also have to accommodate the change.

> "Ben used to be my friend ... but he isn't any more, now he's got into grown-up things ..."
>
> *Ben's brother*

Sebastian's view:

We can sympathize with Sebastian, Ben's younger brother. Two years apart in age, they had always been "good companions" (which included the usual sibling spats and quarrels). But now Ben was trying to find a place in the family as a teenager.

> "Ben just doesn't like me any more."

Sebastian was both desolate and angry. "Ben just doesn't like me any more." This was a marked contrast to their younger years when Ben had shown a brotherly concern for him. In particular, Ben had a favourite miniature computer game and whenever Sebastian was really distraught, Ben would say to him in a warm brotherly fashion, "*Come on, Seb, come and sit on the stairs and I'll let you play with my Game Boy.*" Everyone in the family found this change painful. Sebastian, feeling angry and rejected, would bang on Ben's bedroom door trying to be let in, which led to screams and fighting on both sides. However much their mother tried to persuade Sebastian "*to leave him alone*", or Ben to "*just let him in for a few minute*s", the explosions continued. It seemed as though Sebastian felt that if he couldn't feel close to Ben, at least he could make an impact on him by enraging him.

Ben's view:

Ben and Sebastian's story raises an interesting question, "What are siblings for when you're a tween?" A full-blown teenager may be irritated by younger siblings, even hostile to them, but they are likely to have benign moments when they can enjoy being "adults" to them. For example, a twelve-year-old boy was delighted when his sixteen-year-old brother offered to help him chose new clothes for a disco. Older teenagers, with all their insecurities, have more confidence in their place in the family as aspiring adults and so can afford to be companionable, if only now and then, to younger children in the family. For a tween it is different; at times, they will still "enjoy" childish things. They may even envy younger children in the family who still play unashamedly when they are having to "say goodbye to all that". The tween may deal with these feelings by being superior and denigrating to the younger child. They may feel they risk being cast in the role of a child by any close association with younger siblings. Ben's hostility had less to do with whether or not he liked Sebastian, it was more about what Sebastian as a younger child in the family represented for him. Ben may have been afraid that if he did "give in to Sebastian" and enjoyed playing with him, then somehow the child in him whom he was struggling so hard to relinquish, might become dominant again.

"Sebastian messes up my stuff and invades my space."

Ben knew how upset his younger brother felt, but was powerless to move from his own position, "... *it's not personal!*"

The role of the tween's older siblings

Teenagers are tweens' first chosen role models. You can learn a lot about your tween by observing the way they relate to teenagers who, of course, represent their possible future. Your six or seven year old may observe your teenager, enviously wishing they too could drive the car, go to the pub, etc. For your tween this is rapidly becoming a reality, as it won't be long before they can do these things. So we can think of tweens as both admiring and resenting their older siblings and they may be impossibly anxious to be treated as equals with them.

Managing sibling relationships

- As parents you may have to accept that however you handle such a situation, one or other child will accuse you of taking the other's side!
- Sometimes, finding space in a more quiet moment to talk to your children about how *you* felt about *your* siblings at the same age can help create some understanding in the family.

- You may succeed by pleading to your offsprings' better natures – on the other hand you may not! Tell your children it is okay not to like each other but they have to respect each other.
- Because Ben and Sebastian can't get on together at the moment, it doesn't mean that they will never ever get on together again.

Issues influencing how you respond as a parent

In Chapter 1 we talked about the fact that it is likely you never were a tween. Some of the anxiety of parenting this age group is that you cannot fall back on your own experience at the same age. As the mother of a ten year old said, "*I was playing with dolls and reading comics, she wants glittery crop-tops and a mobile phone ... it terrifies me.*" However, you *were* a teenager, and how your parents managed your adolescent years, and how you felt about the way your parents managed your teenage years, is almost bound to influence how you approach the onset of adolescence in your own children. Let us look at two different scenarios:

"Why does remembering my own teenage years seem to make it more difficult to manage ..."

Martine and her parents

Most parents want to give their children the things and opportunities they never had – and are equally frustrated when the children do not seem sufficiently grateful! (Why do parents want to do this? What makes them think children might want the things they never had?) Martine's parents had got into some confusion. She had been referred to me because she had been found smoking and drinking at school on several occasions. Martine's mother had missed out on the carefree teenage years, "big time", as she put it, because of her parent's strict discipline and emphasis on academic success. Martine's father had had a wild adolescence. Both parents were determined to be liberal with Martine and to enjoy her tween years "at her level". Her mother saw her chance to have her own "unlived tween years" through her daughter. Her father, on

"My parents were so repressive, so out of touch. I always felt different ... sensible shoes, etc. I couldn't go to parties and things because I hadn't got the right clothes. I'm going to make sure she never feels like that ..."

twelve-year-old Martine's mother

the other hand, was hoping he would be able to "stay young", i.e., hold onto his teenage years, through Martine. Her parents were falling into the trap of both anticipating and scripting her teenage years. Instead of helping her as she struggled to decide what kind of teenager she wanted to be, they were misreading her tween desire to play at being grown-up as a teenage desire to be allowed to be grown-up.

"It's no fun and they're embarrassing ..." – Martine's view:
I asked Martine why she continued to smoke and drink at school when she knew that it would get her into trouble.

"*Well, my parents let me at home*", she volunteered in sulky defiance.

"*If your parents let you at home, why take the risk of doing it at school?*"

"*Well ... it's ... more fun ... once my mum caught me and my friends and she wanted to join in ... it was really embarrassing ...*"

Martine's parents couldn't understand why she needed to flaunt school rules when they would have let her smoke and drink at home. In Chapter 8 we will think about the joys of delinquency; suffice it to say here that from a tween's point of view, there is little fun in being delinquent if your mother wants to join in. And, of course, the last thing Martine wanted to do at the moment was go to a disco with her dad. She was finding her own risks and excitement by breaking school rules. This behaviour led her into trouble at school but it also provided her with the space to be a tween.

Ruben and his parents

Ruben, aged eleven, reacted rather differently to a similar situation with his parents. He had always been a lively and engaging child, but recently his teachers had become concerned about him; he had become quiet and withdrawn and seemed reluctant to join in social activities.

"How can I remain cool and at the same time not embarrass my tween?"

I met Ruben with his parents, an attractive and vivacious couple, who had had Ruben when they were still in their teens. They were puzzled, rather than worried, by his behaviour. They seemed rather embarrassed by Ruben's lack of social contact and at one point described him as "*middle aged*". They explained they were both "*very outgoing and loved to socialize … the house is always full of people.*" They had tried to encourage him to bring friends home, adding, "*Our friends are always round …*"

"*And you are always getting drunk …*" interrupted Ruben angrily.

His parents denied the charge but he persisted with resentful accusations about their "*bad behaviour*" ending,

"*… it's really embarrassing … it's really embarrassing if my friends come round …*"

"*Just when your friends come round?*"

"*No, all the time, they think they're really cool … they're just embarrassing.*"

"*Maybe somebody else would like to be the cool one in the house?*"

"*Yes, it's like cool to be my age, but not like thirty … like there's no point …*"

Ruben's view:

You may sometimes feel that your tween is more grown-up and sensible than you! Ruben felt helpless, and somewhat hopeless, about how to be a tween. He didn't know whether to rebel against or to identify with these "cool" parents who seemed to be mimicking teenagers. This gave him a dilemma because he wanted to be a teenager but he didn't want to be like his parents. As a young tween he was still developing his own morality, his own rules about how people should behave. Had he been a full-blown teenager he would have wanted to tell his parents to "*get off my back*" and let him experiment with the drinking and socializing. As a tween he was looking for the chance to be "*the cool one*" supported by parents who were appropriately "*sad and boring*". He wanted to be cool but also in control so he could change at any moment to enjoying a more child-like activity. He wanted to find his own way of being cool rather than complying with his parents' notion of socializing combined with heavy drinking, of which he disapproved since he was learning the dangers of binge drinking at school.

> "There's no space in the house for another cool person."

Both Martine and Ruben's parents were confusing tween behaviour and teenage behaviour. Both Martine and Ruben wanted an opportunity to be a child in the home as well as to be a teenager in the home. Both sets of parents had mistaken their youngster's "playing at being adolescent" talked about in the first chapter, with actually being adolescent. Consequently, Martine felt pushed into extreme behaviour and Ruben just didn't know how to be a tween.

Josie and her parents

"I was wild by fourteen, my parents couldn't do anything with me. I would lie to get out anywhere. There's no way she is going to take the same liberties with us ... we'll always be one step ahead."
mother of twelve-year-old Josie

Josie and her parents came to see me after her teacher had become worried that Josie was eating so little at school that she was "on the verge of an eating disorder". This quotation from Josie's mother illustrates how your own adolescence can hinder your parenting. She was determined to be strict with Josie because she was acutely aware of the desire to take risks and to enjoy taking risks. She knows Josie is going to take risks because of the pleasure she herself had from taking risks. She also knows how frightening risks can be and how a tween secretly longs for parents to be in control. But, of course, Josie is not her mother.

Josie's parents' view:

Josie's mother had lost her virginity two days after her fourteenth birthday – to a boy she was sure she loved and after having drunk several cans of cider in a park with friends. She had lied to her parents about where she was and had also smuggled out some of her mother's cosmetics to wear for the evening. At the time, it was all great fun. It was only as she grew up she realized the risks she had run. She was determined to have more control over her daughter than her parents had managed to have over her. She was adamant that Josie could not wear make-up yet. She felt she was far too young and that "*it gives out the wrong message*". She realized many of Josie's friends did wear make-up but that she felt she had "*a responsibility to protect Josie from herself*". Her father seemed somewhat battle-weary! Whilst he agreed in principle with his wife, he also felt "*no*" was her gut reaction to any such request from Josie.

"I realize now my parents were frantic with worry all the time. If they'd known what I was up to, the risks I was taking, they would have been desperate ..."

Saying you will be more strict than your own parents is a way of saying, "*I wish my parents had been more strict*". Home is the best place to learn about taking risks and a too repressive approach not only scripts your child's tween years, it may also give the message that everything is dangerous. For the tween this only makes everything more desirable.

Josie's view:

Josie didn't consider her requests outrageous. There is always going to be a complication when parents forbid something. You forbid your youngster to do something in order to protect them from something. However, by forbidding something you make that "something" interesting to the tween. Both things need to be done because tweens need to be tempted into the world *and* kept safe.

When what your parents did isn't helpful – a happy compromise

Josie's mother began to understand the impact of her own liberal adolescence on her parenting of Josie. She could understand that she was being too strict a parent with Josie but didn't know how else to respond. As she said, her own parents would never have known that she wanted to wear makeup; she would simply have bought or borrowed it and put it on after she had left the house, meaning she was unable to use '*what my own mother might have done*' as a resource to help her parent Josie. She also began to understand that in a sense Josie was trying to share with her in that she wasn't putting the make-up on after she had left the house. She realized that she would rather help Josie to wear light make-up appropriately than to be excluded from her daughter's important rite of passage.

"I feel like I'm in prison ... it's not like I want to wear make-up to school or anything ... just some eye-shadow and stuff like everyone else at the disco. She just says 'no' all the time and I know she's going to say 'no' so I'm angry when I ask her, then she tells me off for the way I speak."

Josie had to understand that trying to control what went into her body, i.e., what she would eat, was not going to control her mother. She felt she had so little freedom that she was trying to gain freedom in an inappropriate area. Whilst there might have been nothing wrong with her trying to control what she ate, it wasn't getting her what she wanted. We will think more about eating disorders in Chapter 8.

The influence of your older childrens' adolescence on parenting

"We won't make the same mistakes again. We learned a lot with his sister at this age ... we're not going through that again ..."

(parent of ten year old)

"It's such a shock. We were really worried as his brother approached his teens, anxious how we would manage it ... but he was a doddle. There was the odd spark now and then ... but this one ... it's a permanent smouldering bonfire."

(bewildered parents of twelve-year-old boy)

Being a member of a family is a messy business because it is unpredictable: there are no blueprints for being a family member. How your eldest tween behaved will inevitably influence how you manage your younger childrens' tween years. The impact of the older child may be useful in alerting you to the risks and pitfalls of parenting a tween, but every child is an individual. And indeed, as psychotherapist Adam Phillips says, "Every child is a bit of an experiment". What works with one tween may not necessarily work with another. Just as parents will often perceive the same child differently, there is a sense in which every child in the same family has a different parent. As parents, you will need to hone your skills at muddling through, tolerating the fact that you will make mistakes but not letting the preoccupation with "getting it right" prevent you from having the courage to risk "getting it wrong".

Who has all the fun? – feeling envious of your tween

It had long been their custom for ten-year-old Aiden and his father to mow the lawn together at weekends. Dad would mow, while Aiden wheeled away the cuttings. On this particular day they were about to begin when they heard the phone ring. Dad went into the house to answer it and was amazed when he came back to find Aiden had started up the mower and begun mowing.

"Sometimes I feel jealous of my tween ... is that normal?

Aiden's father

"I yelled at him, I thought I was yelling because it was dangerous. But I wasn't, I was yelling because I hadn't realized he was old enough to do that, that I could end up having to wheel away the cuttings!"

He went on to compare this experience with the time Aiden had learned to read. On a long car journey one day, Aiden was demanding that they stopped for a drink. They fobbed him off with a half truth that there were no cafés on this road. They were completely thrown when after about ten minutes, Aiden leapt up in the back seat shouting, *"Look, look, stop, it says 'teas'!"*. The moment when a child learns to read can cause a shift in the balance of any family!

Aiden's father was quick to recognize the source of his rage, i.e., partly anxiety as to whether it was safe or not for Aiden to be mowing alone, but mainly, his recognition that *"My boy is fast becoming a man"*. When asked what that meant to him, he replied, *"Well, if my boy becomes a man, it means I'm the grandparent."*

Understanding the obsession with mobile phones

A particularly cool grandfather received this message from his eleven + year-old grandson who was about to spend three weeks in France with his family. (For the less cool reader, it translates: "It's child abuse. Can't take my mobile phone on holiday! HELP!") Tweens often seem married to their mobile phones. Girls, in particular, seem to be permanently on a telephone of some kind or other. If challenged, they are likely to toss their heads and snarl, *"We're doing my HOMEWORK. MY HOMEWORK."*

Jason's parents were highly irritated by his constantly using his mobile phone. They had decided, in the interest of the family, to have some quality time together on holiday and, having some peace, Jason was not going to be allowed to take his mobile phone with him.

Jason was not only furious, he was panic stricken and appealed to his grandfather to talk to his parents. He couldn't bear the idea of being cut off from his friends for *three weeks*. He felt he would

"ts chld bs! Cnt tk mbl n hldy HLP!"

"It's constant, meal-times, watching TV, out for a meal, in the cinema, wherever we are, 'Bleep! Bleep! And he has to deal with it at once, not only pick up the message but reply at once ... and it's trivia – see you in five minutes sort of stuff."

have "*no one to talk to*" and that he would "*miss out on everything*". He ended his appeal to his grandfather with "*Just tell them I NEED my mobile phone.*"

This good natured grandfather tried in vain to find some compromise but the parents were adamant, "for three weeks Jason can just be part of the family." Jason was equally adamant that he was not going to be part of the family! Friends were what mattered to him.

Being in and out of touch – the tween's view

Mobile phones are an interesting symbol for the tween years. They give the youngster the opportunity to practise being in and out of touch with their parents. They represent dependence and independence. In case of need, parents can be contacted at once, but the phone can also be turned off, preventing parents from making contact! Mobile phones help to link two worlds – the world of home and the world outside. No tween is likely to admit it, but they may feel much safer in the outside world carrying a mobile phone as a "transitional object" between home and the world.

"Transitional objects" is a phrase coined by Winnicott, in the 1960s. He explains how very young children may well become "addicted to some special object ... a blanket ... a rag doll". The object first becomes important around the first birthday and will be crucial to the child at times of transition such as sleeping and waking up, going out of the house, being left with a babysitter, etc. It may be taken everywhere all day or it may just be used at bedtime. The object is extremely important to the child who will become immensely distressed if it is lost or misplaced, in spite of the fact that it may become dirty and smelly through constant cuddling or sucking.

What is happening is that the child feels that the object is part of both the mother and themselves. The child feels safe to explore the world because he feels he is holding part of his mother. By five years old, this obvious object has been relinquished in the face of the excitement of school and the general outside world. Tweens and toddlers have much in common!

And did Jason survive?

Yes, he did – and so did his family. He reported to his grandfather the holiday had been "*fine*". He'd missed his mobile phone, he'd missed his friends, but he had had a *"fine time"* with his family. What then emerged was that the holiday home had Sky TV and so *"it being the holidays, they let me watch TV more ..."*

Knowing his own son's views on television watching, granddad was rather surprised to hear this – *"So did you all watch more TV?"*

"No, but I did ... they [the family] were usually doing something else." Granddad laughed. Jason had found a way of "not being with his family" on holiday.

Friends are much more important to tweens than family; however, Jason's story shows us how, sometimes, tweens may enjoy being claimed by their parents for a while.

The rewards for parenting a tween

Parenting is more than a full-time job. It is twenty-four hours a day, seven days a week for eighteen years with seemingly no salary. So what are the rewards? What recognition do you want from your children? Are people right to expect to be rewarded by their children? When a child succeeds in the ordinary tasks of childhood – walking, talking, coping with school, etc., parents feel rewarded. Your pride and pleasure in your child is your salary for parenting. So what are the rewards of the tween years, when it may feel difficult to feel much pride or pleasure in your youngster's behaviour and when most of the time they seem to hate you?

As this mother went onto say, *"However negative it feels, I know we are helping him to build a future."* At this stage the early rewards for parenting are suspended; your reward for parenting lies more in your acceptance that your child is becoming him or herself. Your life can be enriched by someone who is very different from you, and yet part of you.

So, yes, Penny's mother is right: as Penny leaves she will take away with her all that her parents have given her. You have to let them go, so they can bring so much of their own back. One mother compared it to helping her son learn to ride his two-wheeler bike without training wheels. The

"It reminds me of weaning him ... I remember when he began to bite the breast and I knew I had to wean him ... and it hurt but of course I knew it had to be done ... and it's the same when he's horrible to me now ... a sort of emotional biting of the breast ... I know I have to let him go ... but it hurts an awful lot more ..."

time came when she had to let go of the saddle and stop running alongside him! She explained how she didn't want to because she knew he ran the risk of wobbling and falling off. She realized that this could be a bad experience and he might not want to get back onto the bike. But if she never let go of the bike, her son would never gain the sense of *"getting his own balance"* or learning from his own painful experiences. By letting go, if things go well enough, your reward will be that there is more space in your relationship with your tween. As a mother said, *"I'm able to enjoy him more because I don't have to be busting a gut to run alongside him all the time."* There are enormous freedoms for parents in children growing up. It may be useful to think now about what you need more space for in your relationship with your tween.

On keeping your sense of humour

To anyone on the outside of the family, tweens are very, very funny, "comical" as one grandparent described. It also seems to be true that in the daily barrage of hostility and cynicism, parents lose their sense of humour about tweens. *"I can take a joke … when it's funny,"* cried one father.

"Get over it, mum …"

The tween years are a difficult but passing transitional phase in a family. The family is reorganizing itself to embrace adult to adult relationships. So what can parents do to help them survive this rite of passage?

- You will need a sense of humour to survive!
- When you begin to lose your sense of humour with your tween try to think about what other situations make you lose your sense of humour.
- Don't expect too much, these are not the years in which you are going to feel best rewarded as a parent. Think more of this time as laying down foundations for a more stable future relationship … and be there!
- Trust in your own parenting skills. With a bit of knowledge, understanding and a lot of muddling through, you and your child have got this far and there is no reason why you should not complete the journey.

This twelve-year-old boy, renowned for his toughness at school, summed it up: spending time with someone is a clear message you like and value them. However, for parents, spending time with a tween can be a daunting task. One minute they no longer want to be read to, or played games with, they don't want to be seen out with you. The next moment, they seem content to be with you and involve you and be involved in childhood activities. As one mother said, "*She just likes me there in case ... I'm like a bag of potato crisps, she dips into when she feels like it ...*" And that's it!

"I hate it ... my mum goes out when we're in bed and I hate it ... I know I'm usually asleep ... I hate knowing she's not there ..."

Quality time with a tween may mean just being around in case they need you – for support or abuse!

four

Cool or mateless ...?

Too many feelings in search of an identity

"A long settled childhood personality can fragment into tears and moods and sulks and rows and daft (and sometimes dangerous) behaviour. Out of the shards grows someone, not only large but usually more impressive."
(Anne Fine – programme notes for "Book of the Banshee")

Eleven-year-old Casper peered at me with a puzzled brow over his ill-fitting spectacles as he told me how unhappy he was at school. *"You see ... when everything works out and everyone's partnered up ... I'm always the one left ... because I'm mateless."* He could never imagine himself being otherwise. *"I'll never be in the cool group ..."* he said sadly, feeling his peers had labelled him for life!

"Cool or mateless ... what do you mean, is there anything in between? You're cool or mateless, that's it!"

At any age it is important to children to be popular with their peers; for a tween it begins to be crucial to be "in the cool group". Their desire to be seen as "cool" reflects their growing struggles with their self-image and identity. Many eight and nine year olds will be taking a keen interest in their looks and appearance and certainly by eleven or twelve, tweens are becoming preoccupied with who I am and am I acceptable.

In middle childhood there are always children who are left out and not as popular as other children but on the whole this is a relatively kind period. It is a time of games, rules, gangs and groups. A significant change takes place in friendships at the onset of the tween years. Firstly, friendships are less likely to be orchestrated by parents; certainly by eleven years old your youngster will be making friends independent of the family's circle of friends.

Most nine year olds have one best friend and are aware of shades and degrees of friendships. Indeed, we should be concerned about the nine year old who does not have at least one close friend. This girl was aware of the subtle nuances of difference in the kind of friend who gets invited round to tea and other friends.

> "I get invited to the parties but nobody asks me round ... like for tea or anything"
> *nine year old girl*

The nine year old who feels "mateless" may still be confident in their identity as a child. They know what it means to be a child, they know what children do, they've been doing it for a long time. The "mateless" teenager may lack confidence in their identity as an adult wondering, "How do you be a cool adult?" The "mateless" tween is unsure of their identity as a teenager and like Casper they are susceptible to "buying an image" from their friends. Recent research from University of Leeds School of Medicine (Hill and Pallin) shows us that young primary school children very quickly label their peers. Fat body shapes are equated with being "stupid and unpopular" and slim children are regarded as "popular, intelligent and kind".

The "mateless" tween may be desperate to be liked by others. Parents may begin to worry about their tween's self-esteem or "lack of confidence" as they see them trying to win friendships by being either over-eager to please or aggressive with their peers. Others may be reluctant to try and make friends. Kit showed his insecurity in his feeling "*well, if they wanted to see me they would phone me*".

> "He's always pleased to accept invites but he'll never phone a friend to come round ..."
> *eleven-year-old Kit's mother*

The tween years are a transition and whilst some tweens may have poor self-esteem we must remember a lack of confidence is almost a necessary phase in the process of a transition. For "being in transition" involves suspending what we know so that we are free to learn something new and move on.

What is self-esteem?

Self-esteem is composed of two separate but inter-twined aspects:

> "Am I me and therefore lovable or am I lovable and therefore me?"

- Self-concept – the way we see ourselves
- Self-worth – the basic belief we are worthwhile and valuable as a person

We learn to value ourselves according to how we understand the way other people value us. An eleven-year-old girl won a music scholarship to a prestigious specialist school. She shrugged off congratulations from family friends with, "*I mean, it's okay, but like music isn't rocket science, is it?*" Coming from a highly academic family, she felt less value was placed on her talent. She was under-valuing her own skills and abilities because she felt only intellectual talent was valued in the family.

Small children will describe themselves by physical characteristics. "*I'm Rosie and I've got red boots.*" Older children will widen the scope to include family relationships, friendships and educational abilities. "*I'm Rosie. I've got a little brother. I go to school. My best friend is Joan and I'm good at reading.*" Tweens are beginning to be able to put into words how they see themselves as a person and so will describe themselves in much more qualitative ways – "*cool, mateless, sad, a boff*". They also may begin to describe their beliefs and values. "*I'm Rosie. I like to be kind and I am vegetarian. I think it is cruel and unnecessary to eat animals.*" They will also focus criti-cally on their appearance – a nose too big, teeth not straight, hair that is "so not fair." There is a risk that they will begin to feel they are defined by their physical faults – a birth mark on the right arm must mean "*no one will ever want to date me*"; and they have real doubts about their abilities, worrying about their weaknesses – a big nose will always cancel out beautiful eyes.

You are likely to find your tween's self-criticism both poignant and painful. No one wants to see a youngster unhappy and missing out on the fun. However, sometimes "feeling ugly" is more about self-protection than self-confidence. For some tweens, growing up is something that can't happen soon enough. For others, it is a worrying process. They see teenagers portrayed in the media as sophisticated and silly, amusing and weird, reckless and vulnerable and, above all, sexy. The prospect of turning into one can be exciting and very scary. Perhaps Ruth is telling her parents she doesn't yet

"Our twelve year old says, 'I'm too ugly to go out' – how can we give her confidence?"

Ruth's mother

feel ready to be launched into the wider world and is saying, "*I'll go out slowly and gradually and in my own good time*".

Ruth's parents may do best not to argue with her when she says she's unattractive. They don't have to agree with her! But trying to persuade a tween to your point of view can be a fruitless task. Ruth might be most helped by her parents supporting her and encouraging her to broaden her social circle in places which feel familiar and safe to her, such as home and the homes of her friends.

The development of self-esteem

Good self-esteem, the belief that we are lovable and valuable simply because we live, is rooted in our infancy. Winnicott talks about the importance of the baby experiencing from birth "a stable, continuous, dependable and loving relationship" with permanent parents or parent substitutes. He stresses the importance of parents enjoying "a rewarding relationship with each other". This may seem idealized but, of course, such an ambiance in a child's life does not preclude there being difficulties within the family; being a human being is a messy business and there is nothing which is guaranteed to make a good life. The quality of our first relationships with our carers influences and colours the way we approach all future relationships – friends, teachers, sexual partners. The child who feels they have been loved from birth "irrespective of ... sex, appearance, ability or personality" will presume the wider world will also love them. The child with a less solid foundation may be more cautious.

Showing your baby that you love them probably came easily and spontaneously through tender physical care, hugs and kisses. It is interesting, however, that from birth, children are praised and admired mainly for two aspects – their appearance and their achievements. The former is completely beyond their control and so it is interesting that looks continue to bring such congratulations. Equally, in the early stages achievements are simply stages of development which all children will achieve at roughly the same age given a satisfactory environment. I remember being present in a family when a nineteen month old took her first steps. Her parents could not have showered more praise and adulation if she had climbed Everest. I remember reflecting at the time that if all this child's achievements were greeted with the same rewards, then she was guaranteed a good life. For praise and recognition not only help children to develop a sense of self-worth, they also encourage children to identify with the adults. Praise for small achievements encourages young children to strive to achieve grown-up skills such as reading and writing.

Is this unconditional love?

You may well feel that you love your youngster unconditionally. Winnicott talks of parents' love being given "without expectation of, or demand for, gratitude". Maybe that is so. Or maybe the idea of unconditional love is a solution to all of our longing for such love, and our disappointment and our fear that maybe it does not exist. For as children grow up it does seem more difficult to praise them spontaneously. Why should this be?

"I am the product of my mother and my father. I am their way of expressing what they really feel and what they would have liked to have been."

Tomasina, aged twelve

During pregnancy you will have dreamt and talked endlessly of your hopes and expectations for your coming child. Of course, during pregnancy you could only have unreal expectations of your child as there was no real child on which to formulate your expectations until the birth. When you first saw your baby you immediately modified many of your expectations. (A blatant example would be if you were convinced you were expecting a girl and were delivered of a boy.) But at an unconscious level, it is likely that many of your hopes and expectations were still present. Children are born into a world of expectations, and parents and children spend the rest of their lives trying to extricate themselves from each others' inventions. The older your child becomes, the more you are likely to be aware of the difference between what you would like them to be and what they want to be. Maybe your praise and encouragement becomes less spontaneous and more a method of moulding your child to your expectations. This is natural; you are likely to reward and praise your child for achieving in the areas you value, be it education, sport or the arts. At this point, it may be worth asking yourself what would be the risks for your child if they didn't grow up to be like you, or like you want them to be? And what will your child's life be like if they do grow up to be like you or like you want them to be?

What is a confident tween?

Self-confidence is discovered in all sorts of ways. There must be as many ways of being self-confident as there are tweens. We could think of a confident tween as being sure they are loved and lovable, i.e., they presume that people will like them and they will like other people. They are likely to have some ideas about their goals and the direction in which they want their life to go and may have a realistic enough idea of how they can achieve their aims. Other signs of self-confidence we might look for are being able to talk about their feelings and behaviour, how they behave towards other people and how other people behave towards them. We would also hope that such tweens are assertive enough both to say what they need and to express their opinions in such a way that they are taken seriously and valued.

The importance of the group

In the tween years, being accepted in a group becomes crucial and the aim is gradually to relinquish groups of friends, and find one particular group to which you can belong. Between eleven and twelve years, some chopping and changing of groups takes place but by twelve years old, a youngster is unlikely to switch groups easily. Friendship groups tend to centre around a common interest, such as a pop star or a sport. For both boys and girls, it is important to be "in" and not relegated to the perimeters or outside the group. However, there are general differences between girl groups and boy groups.

"Why have friends suddenly become so important?"

Secrets, clothes and size

Girls' sharing often centres around an interest in fashion, make-up and weight leading to sharing confidences and anxieties about appearance and desirability. I talked in Chapter 1 about how intimacy is measured in girl groups by the extent of secrets shared. The more secrets shared, the closer the friendship. Tween girls, unlike teenage girls, may well be sharing confidences with you but sharing secrets with friends will have

"You can't say who you are to your mum and dad."

twelve-year-old girl

become much more important and much more a focus than earlier in childhood. Groups may also form around a passion for a particular good cause or to raise money for a charity or disaster fund.

The World Cup, jokes and girls

Boy friendships tend to form around sport; unlike teenage boys who are out to win, tween boys are more likely to enjoy the process of being in a team. Being good at sport is always an advantage to a tween boy, but most important is to like sport and to participate. Humour is to boys as secrets are to girls. A boy's status in the group may well depend on how much he can make the others laugh. Being funny is very important if you want to be popular.

A tween boy reported an interesting insight into boys' popularity. He explained how at primary school a boy's popularity depended very much on his popularity with the girls. If the girls thought a boy "*funny and could make them laugh*" then they would like him, giving him "*street cred*" with the other boys. If a boy wasn't popular with the girls, "*I mean even if you liked him, you wouldn't hang about with him because … well, you just wouldn't.*" It was also interesting that if the boys launched an attack on a particular girl, "*even if it was just teasing*", the girls would rally to the victim's defence and turn on the boys. However, when the tables were turned, and the girls launched an attack on a particular boy, "*none of his friends would like to defend him in front of the girls*".

"Your parents have known you all your life and you feel under pressure if they make critical judgements when you change. Friends don't know you (like your parents) and so they can accept you as you are."

eleven-year-old Tomasina

At his single sex senior school the boys felt much freer to form friendships on the basis of whom they themselves perceived as fun. Maybe this gives us something of an insight into the different natures of girls' and boys' friendships. It is possible that girls' friendships are based on communicating with each other, whereas boys are much more preoccupied with competing with each other.

Practising identities

From a very early age children model on or practise being their friends. Maisie, a well behaved four year old, greatly admired her

friend Joe at nursery school. Joe threw outrageous tantrums whenever he was thwarted. Suddenly Maisie reverted to having temper
tantrums and after several days, her parents were growing desperate. "*What is the matter, Maisie, this is just not like you?*" declared her
mother. Maisie stopped crying, drew breath and replied, "*I'm being
Joe,*" and then proceeded to cry again. Her mother kindly and
firmly informed her that she could be Joe for the rest of the day and
then tomorrow she wanted Maisie back because she was missing
her! In a similar way, in the tween years the peer group becomes a
place where tweens can experiment with being different versions of
themselves.

Eleven-year-old Ryan discovered that experimenting with being
a different version of himself in the family may be hazardous. He
was a quiet and fastidious child who formed a close holiday friendship with Jock on a campsite. Jock had not discovered the joys of
opening his wash bag, let alone cleaning his teeth on holiday! Ryan
was captivated by him seeing him, in one sense quite accurately, as
a great risk taker. Ryan's behaviour became more slovenly, evading
washing, not clearing up his sleeping bag, etc., etc., much to the
anger of his mother. When Jock left the camp a few days before
Ryan's family, Ryan reverted to his usual more compliant behaviour. (He did, however, volunteer to a relative later that he often just
stayed in the bathroom and didn't actually shower or clean his teeth
if he thought he could get away with it.)

Why do they all have to be the same?

Friendship groups also provide the tween with a place to practise
being one personality consistently – a personality likely to be somewhat different from the personality expected by
parents. A teacher reported an interesting incident
he had observed in the playground. At the end of
the day, a group of eleven-year-old girls were about
to leave school when it began to pour with rain.
One girl didn't have a coat. As they set out in the
rain, somehow she managed to persuade all her
friends to remove their coats, announcing in a satisfactory tone, "*Yes, now we all look the same.*" Not looking different
was obviously vital to this girl. The compliance of her friends indi-
cates that "*looking the same*" was very important to them.

> "I don't want to be
> like my parents ...
> not without
> exploring every
> other option!"
>
> *twelve year old*

What is being "the same as" a solution to?

Friendship groups provide an important bridge between home and the outside world. In order to separate from the family we have to establish our identity as a distinct and unique person in our own right. "*Being the same*" provided the girls with a corporate identity. "*We are all the same*" can be a solution to the fear "*I don't know who I am*". I know I am me, i.e., identifiable as an eleven-year-old girl in my coat because everyone else has a coat. But if everyone else has a coat and I don't, then I may be forced into the anxiety of wondering who I am. In this sense, psychotherapist Valerie Sinason has described the group as giving the youngsters "a second skin" in which to experiment with personalities. As one twelve year old described, "... *because you're always trying to live up to their [friends] standards. I mean, even if they're lower than your own ... I mean, it's competing ... no, well, it's you have to be the same ... so you know who you are ...*"

> "I feel lonely at home because my mum and dad don't want me to change but I can be different with my friends because we're all the same."
>
> *eleven year old*

Feeling special in the group

Being part of a group may make a tween feel they belong but it may also reduce their sense of being special! Eleven-year-old Rav had always been top of his class in his primary school. He was also an outstanding sportsman. He carried extra "value" by being the only Sikh in his school. His worry about secondary school centred around the fact that he had heard there was bullying and he was afraid he would be targeted because "I'm different", by which he meant his turban. He was afraid he wouldn't have any friends, even though a large group of children from his class were also going onto this school. I listened as his parents tried to reassure him by pointing out that there would be a much larger Sikh population at the new school. This idea seemed to increase his distress.

> "My eleven year old has begun to suffer from panic attacks. He says he is dreading moving on to senior school ... how can we help him prepare?"
>
> *Rav's father*

"*Rav,*" I asked, "*how do you think you will be special at the new school?*"

"*Well, I won't be, will I? I won't have any friends ...*"

Rav was confused. He had enjoyed his celebrity status as a distinguished star in his primary school – and who wouldn't? But he feared his friendships were based on his "specialness". He was afraid he would not stand out in the same way at senior school and would therefore be friendless. He also admitted to some ambivalence. He wanted to go on standing out as unique and different, even if this meant his not having any friends. So in one sense, the thing he feared was actually the thing he desired. His task now was to work out exactly *for what* he wanted to be liked and loved.

"Sad geeks and outsiders" – when they have no friends

At times, most tweens will complain of having no friends or of feeling left out of a group. Feeling lonely is part of the human condition. If we believe we are all individual and distinct personalities with our own unique viewpoint and important things to say, then at times we are going to feel isolated from everybody else. One of the tasks of parenting tweens is to help them to tolerate feeling alone; to bear the sense of being a little removed from others. (Trying to cheer them up with positive facts may be missing the mark!) Many adults find loneliness difficult; tweens may feel desperate. However, complaining they have no friends may be a complex communication from your youngster.

"I don't really have any friends. It looks like I have lots of friends ... but that's because I ask them. I'm the chooser, I never get chosen."
eleven year old

Friends are so important to tweens that they may fear that it is impossible to enjoy any activity alone. The less gregarious tween who may enjoy solitary pursuits or the company of one or two friends may feel different or odd because they do so. As one ten-year-old boy replied to his mother encouraging him to have friends round when his one best friend was on holiday, "*You are always trying to make me something I'm not ... I don't want other friends round. You just don't like me the way I am.*"

"I can't do anything, can I? I mean I can't go out or anything because I haven't any friends to go with ..."

On being desireable

Twelve-year-old Sky had always been a tomboy. She eschewed all out-of-school activities, such as ballet, that could be considered "girly". However, at home she loved bubble baths, expensive shampoo and feminine underwear. She had a large collection of "pots and potions" in her bedroom. Whilst she rejected lipstick and nail polish, she collected face creams and body lotions. Other children found her "quirkiness" appealing and she was an averagely popular girl. Now she was clearly pubescent but continued with her boyish sense of fashion.

"Our twelve-year-old daughter has always been a sociable girl but now she's often in tears that no one likes her and she has no friends ..."

mother of Sky

Her parents sought my help because they felt she was depressed. She had recently dropped many of her out-of-school activities. She refused to have or to go to sleep-overs because, "*No one likes me.*" Her parents had tried everything from a firm nagging "*of course you have, now get on with it*" approach to trying to encourage and persuade her to accept social invitations.

It is interesting to wonder whether Sky was saying, "*I haven't any friends,*" or saying, "*Sometimes I worry that I'm not lovable because I have a darker side to me*". She could have been afraid that there were aspects of her that would be exposed in tween friendships that had not been exposed in childhood friendships. Asked one day:

"*What would be different if you felt you had lots of friends, that you were a really popular girl?*"

"*Well, people would like me ...*"

"*And how is being liked worrying?*"

"*It's not, but, well, like, just it can be scary.*"

Being loved and liked is closely linked with being desired. Sky's fear of not having friends was also her way of expressing her fears around her burgeoning sexuality and desirability. She had always been a tomboy but she admitted to continuing as one because she was frightened of being seen as the attractive, feminine and desireable youngster her "pots and potions" indicated she could enjoy being. We will think more about the tween's anxieties around sexuality in Chapter 7.

Managing a tween who feels they have no friends

- It is best not to argue with tweens when they say they have no friends. You are more likely to open conversation by saying something like, *"Well, that surprises me.What is there about you not to like?"*

The skill is then to help them to think about their negatives in a positive way, e.g., Sky eventually moaned, *"I'm too bossy, I always want to be the leader ..."*

"How can we help when she says she has no friends?"

- Her parents helped her to think about her "bossiness" by rephrasing it as, *"Bossy is about having good ideas; perhaps we can think of ways you could show people you have good ideas other than being bossy."*
- When tweens are able to see their negatives as possible assets, they are able to think about changing their behaviour.

On dumping parents

Elaine was a much adored only child of relatively older parents. She was intelligent, attractive and very personable. However, she had always preferred one or two close friends to being part of a group. The family culture expected her to go to boarding school at twelve and she had reluctantly accepted this but made it plain she would prefer to remain at home. She was placed in a four-bedded dormitory with two girls from her primary school and another. She seemed to settle in well until the end of the second term and by the beginning of the third term, was phoning home several times a day and asking her parents to remove her.

"Our twelve year old settled happily into her boarding school but is now complaining that she has no friends and she wants to come home ..."

Elaine's mother

It is always interesting, and sometimes significant, to try and pinpoint exactly when a youngster's troubles began. After some unravelling, we realized that Elaine had become unsettled at the time she had to choose who she would like to share a double room with in her second year. Interestingly, her parents remembered that she had become even more distressed around that time when a friend wrote to her in the Easter holiday inviting her to spend part of the summer holiday with her family at their summer home in France.

Elaine was confused. She had initially been dependent on her dorm mates for company but had then made a best friend outside this group. She now wanted to share a room with her new friend. She explained, with both guilt and distress, that she found her new friend much more companionable and she felt she had more in common with her than with any of the other three whom "*I didn't really choose as friends, we were just put in the dorm together ...*" She then went on to list the boring qualities of these girls. When I suggested she maybe didn't like these girls any more she quickly retreated.

"*Oh, no, I like them, but I like Eni better.*"

"*If you didn't like them, what would you do?*"

"*Well, I'd feel bad, I mean they were my friends and I can't just dump them.*"

Growing up involves understanding that we don't have to like everyone and everyone won't like us. It also involves realizing that it is possible to like some aspects of our friends and not others and that some people will not always like all of us. We have to learn that we may grow out of friendships – and our parents!

Elaine was also confused about whether or not to accept the invitation to France. She was struggling with an ordinary tween problem – how do you dump your parents without hurting them or yourself? Of course, you can't. Elaine was trying to solve her confusion by changing schools; she felt then she wouldn't have to choose between her friends and she wouldn't be leaving her parents all alone.

"I mean, I want to go but I don't like to leave my parents all alone, they always try to take as much time off as possible to be with me in the holidays ... but, it's just a bit boring ..."

If tweens are going to be themselves, then they are bound to hurt their parents. To find out who they are tweens have to experiment with being someone other than the person their parents would like them to be. The problem is that most tweens have a very unclear picture of the person they are, let alone the person they wish to become.

Helping them to dump you

Sometimes tweens will provoke a crisis in order to test the adults. Elaine was struggling with two major issues and she may also have been trying to find out how much her parents wanted her home. She was anxious about leaving them and she was also anxious about them leaving her. Elaine needed her parents to:

- Encourage her to have a good time away from them
- Tell them about the good times they had when she was away (she is not their *only* friend!)
- To reassure her that life is very different at home without her

When your tween is sidelined by their friends

Charles was rude, aggressive, foul-mouthed and a bully. At primary school he had been eager to make friends but did not fit in. He became distressed and truculent. His mother describes how she felt hopeless in the face of his pain and would snap, "*Well, what do you want me to do about it?*" when he complained that no one liked him and he had no friends. She wanted to help him but didn't know how. His father took a "be a man" line – "*If they hit you, hit them back.*" Charles had become more and more aggressive and was now on the brink of being suspended from school.

"Our eleven year old has never fitted in ... he wants to make friends but is being pushed more and more to the sidelines ..."

Charles' father

He came into my room unwillingly, declaring he was "*not a nutter*" and that I was sad to spend my days seeing "*nutters*". I agreed he was not a nutter and pointed out that people did not come to see me because "*there was something wrong with them*". They came because they were confused and I tried to help them to understand their confusion.

We came to understand Charles' aggressive opening to me as an illustration of his confusion. If he couldn't make people like him, he would make them frightened of him. I pointed out that in a sense there was nothing wrong with what he was doing but it just wasn't working for him. He was making sure people remembered him by his behaviour, but he was left feeling people didn't like him very much.

"*No, they don't,*" he said, "*and so I always say the horrible thing first.*"

Managing the sidelined tween

Elaine was trying to find out how to deal with people when one doesn't like them. Charles was struggling to understand his part in people not liking him. Both sets of parents were in danger of taking precipitous action, which may or may not have helped their children.

- Charles' parents practised trying to *think* with him about situations with his peers rather than just *reacting* to them. So when Charles came home and said the other boys were saying that he was no good at cricket, his mother was able to respond, "*Well that doesn't make it true*", and then help him to try and think why the other boys might be being unkind to him.
- Perhaps one of the hardest aspects of parenting tweens is tolerating not knowing what to do, not having a clue of the best course of action to take. Try to resist your tween's pressure to make you *act*, to panic you into *doing* something. In the long term, it may be more productive to stick with trying to help your tween to understand what they are feeling. When Charles understood that he felt *hurt* by his friends' rejection and that he turned his *hurt* into *anger*, he was freed to think about more constructive ways of behaving.
- For the tween, sometimes just knowing that someone is trying to understand, is taking their feelings seriously, and is trying to make sense of their chaos, is enough to deter them from even more rash behaviour.

When they have no friends

Feeling you may have no friends is very different from being afraid to have friends. Damian's father had left home when he was two years old and there had been little contact with Damian and no financial help for his mother since then. Engagingly, she described herself as "always shaking the shillings", by which she meant that she was always struggling to balance the household budget. However, she had also always been anxious that Damian should join in any out-of-school activities that she could possibly afford. However, he had always been reluctant to do so. She had

"Our eleven-year-old son has always been a quiet and reserved child. He rarely invites friends home and seems unhappy and worried."

Damian's mother

become increasingly worried about him in the last year. He was complaining he had no friends but was also refusing to allow his mother to help facilitate any arrangements.

The reality was that Damian felt he was not worth having friends. He couldn't see why anyone would want to be his friend except out of pity. He felt different from the other boys. Why would anyone want to come to his home, so lacking in the most up-to-date technology in computers, videos, etc? He felt he didn't fit in because he didn't have the necessary designer clothes. Damian did have poor self-esteem but he was also extremely angry and envious.

> "I know other people don't have dads ... but I'm less, it's like I know my mum tries but there isn't enough money ..."

"*I wouldn't see my dad if he came now ... he doesn't care about me, it's too much trouble to see me, so I wouldn't see him.*"

We came to understand how some of Damian's solitary behaviour, though not all, was a solution to his rage at his father abandoning him. He had never learned how to express the anger in a healthy way. As he became more aware of other childrens' material possessions his anger became fired with envy. He avoided other children because he didn't know how to be friends with them without "*blowing into bits*", i.e., his anger and envy taking him over. By being solitary he felt he was protecting other children and also convincing himself that he did not possess these powerful feelings. His mother had never encouraged him to talk about his father, "*because it just upsets us both*", and so gradually Damian had pushed his feelings further down inside himself.

Managing the tween who feels unworthy of friends

Tweens need spells of being withdrawn and solitary but parents need to be alert to the time when "*struggling through the doldrums*" becomes a permanent way of being; such a youngster may be depressed. Children like Damian need to be helped to face reality or they risk distorting their development and so making a good life impossible. For example, a four year old at a family gathering announced, "*When I grow up, I'm going to sing grand opera.*" Everyone smiled good humouredly and her father replied, "*Of course you are darling. You will sing grand opera splendidly.*" If she repeated this ambition at seven years old, her parents may respond along the lines of, "*How exciting. And what do you think will be fun about singing grand opera?*" If this ambition were again repeated at eleven or twelve years old, then her parents might respond with a serious discussion about training, opportunities, what the youngster needed to be doing in the present to prepare for such a career. However, if at fifteen she is still carrying this burning ambition but shows no talent for singing at all, cannot even hold a tune very well, then her parents would have to help her to face reality. As parents you have to tailor your response to meet your tween's developmental needs. It would have been cruel to do anything but encourage her as a four year old, but even more cruel to encourage her as an untalented fifteen year old.

- Youngsters like Damian need to be helped to face the reality that friendship is based on more than material possessions.
- He needs to be helped to talk about the things that were making him angry and resentful.

"*I felt liked crumpled paper*" – when they *are* different from other tweens

Sometimes youngsters not only feel different, they *are* different from other youngsters. Oliver had moved with his family from the country to an inner city. At the end of his first academic year, he was mocked and bullied by his classmates because he came top in every subject. Without entirely realizing it, he had moved from a school where most pupils made some effort with their work to one where "swots and boffs" were derided. Help was at hand in the form of an excellent teacher who contained the group's aggression. The teacher was able to help the group understand that because they were afraid they could not do well academically, they mocked the youngsters who did achieve. He was able to help them to see that maybe there were other solutions than trying to pull this boy down into their abandonment of academic work. Perhaps they could think about what it was about him that helped him to succeed and whether or not they had the same qualities? However, no one really expected Oliver to fit into this environment easily; his task was to learn how to cope with being

"Oliver is different from other boys, other boys enjoy football, he really enjoys academic study, but, of course, that leaves him isolated."

father of twelve year old

different from his peers. It was not going to be easy for him to be helped to find common ground with his classmates but it was not impossible. He needed someone to understand how painful feeling different is as a tween and also to understand any part he may have in provoking aggression from the other boys.

The child who is easily led

So what do we mean by "bad company"? Are there grades of bad company? For example, would you worry more about bad company leading your tween into alcohol abuse than shoplifting? Of course you worry about friends who influence your youngster into taking risks. For the first time in your child's development, you are having to compete with their peer group for influence over your youngster. For the very first time in their lives, tweens have a choice of listening to their parents or listening to their friends. Ryan's parents had good cause to worry. His group of friends had recently been in trouble with the police for trying to break open a slot-machine. Ryan had not been arrested but he was with the gang.

"How can I help my twelve year old to make better friends? ... at the moment, he is getting into bad company."

father of twelve-year-old Ryan

We should not presume that being "easily led" is necessarily an indication that a tween is lacking confidence. It may be so, and certainly the less sure a tween is of their ability to be loved, the more they are likely to try and earn acceptance and praise from their peer group by doing risky and silly things. In thinking about Ryan, it is clear that there are other factors to hold in mind about "easily led".

"He's never had much confidence. He's never been particularly strong willed ... and I think he's just going to do whatever these boys tell him to do."

- We can think about Ryan's relationships with his classmates. Why were the older boys so attractive? Had something happened to alienate him from his peers? Was he being excluded or bullied? Had a clique formed in his class around a particular interest he felt unable to share?
- We could think about Ryan in a family context. By choosing friends so very different from his family, he could be understood to be experimenting with different versions of himself. Maybe he was experimenting with being a mildly delinquent teenager?

Ryan was making an impact on his parents with his current behaviour. In a sense, they were reinforcing his activities with the older boys by being so disturbed by them. Maybe what Ryan needed was for them to be highly disturbed, i.e., excited, by other activities he was involved in.

Why is bad company so attractive to tweens?

Ryan tried to explain why he liked "bad company". He thought these boys were "cool" because "*they are darers; my mother thinks I'm not a darer, but I am …*"

"*You are a darer?*" I asked this quiet, rather withdrawn youngster.

"*Yeh, I'm a darer … but I don't do dares …*"

A darer who doesn't do dares sounds like a contradiction in terms! Ryan was always well behaved and reserved but longed to be able to express a more daring, a more naughty side of himself. He was fascinated and intrigued by these boys who behaved in a way he didn't dare. Unconsciously, he was trying to find out with the gang if it was okay to be a bit delinquent and rebellious.

- Maybe you would rather blame bad company for your youngster's behaviour than accept they may have a side to them you dislike or don't approve of and you fear you can't control.
- Bad company may be a tween's way of disowning versions of themselves unacceptable to parents.
- There is a fine line between monitoring their friendships and choosing their friends for them! Of course, the more you moan about a friend, the more attractive that friend becomes to your tween.

Talking about "bad company"

"My eleven year old always defends her friends, even though they are in trouble with the police. How can I persuade her these friends are bad company?"

Communicating with your tween may be much more important than what your tween thinks is "right or wrong". Ryan's parents focussed on asking how he *felt* watching, how he *felt* when the police arrived? They told him how they *felt*, rather than what they *thought*, e.g., "*We were really worried when we knew you might have been involved* …" By keeping the conversation on "sharing feelings" you avoid your tween having to prove their position or defend their friends.

However, it is also important to explore your tween's reasons for supporting their friends but you will need to do this more in the spirit of curiosity and interest than interrogation! Discuss where they would draw the line, e.g., in Ryan's case, breaking open a slot machine, shoplifting, stealing from friends and family, bank robbery?

Sometimes it may be important to stand firm on your beliefs and spell out the consequences of delinquent behaviour. You may have to accept your tween will then close the conversation.

Helping yourself

Over-anxious parents make anxious and worried youngsters and when youngsters are anxious they are less able to think clearly. So relax! Trust your youngster to make a good choice in the first place and trust them to be able to pick up the pieces if they make destructive choices.

- Explore your "worst case scenario". Then explore how you would manage it. Fear and imagination go hand in hand and it is amazing how much less frightening a worst case scenario can seem once it has been explored and discussed.
- Enlist the help of your youngster's teachers. They are likely to know the "bad company".

Understanding the constant rows

The volcano rumbles
The row has started
The cracks started to open
The shouting begins
As the thundering voice is let out
Dad shouts, I squeal
Lava bubbles.
There's tension in the air
The flaming rock shatters
Outrage is now poured out
The lava flows
Emotions are running smoothly
As all dies down
And feelings become calm.

Harriet Mathams (aged eleven)

Not all aggression is bad. Being angry with someone, having a row with someone can be a way of getting to know them. Do they crumble, give as good as they get, confront your aggression … what? Tweens are slowly developing their own opinions and values. For the tween, part of the process of understanding, "What do I believe in?" is answering, "How valuable is what my parents' believe in?" Many of the seemingly unfathomable rows provoked by your tween are an attempt to see how firmly you will stand up for what you believe. However hard they may push the boundaries what they really want is for you to stand firm. In this way, your beliefs become a framework or even a foundation for their own.

> "I get mad at my mum for nothing, I just get mad."

How much do you want your tween to change you?

> "My dad used to think men shouldn't be nursery nurses, he said it was very suspicious. But I talked to him about gender stereotypes – he was very interested and said, 'Well, I guess things are changing …'"
>
> *twelve-year-old girl*

Tweens also use rows as a way of checking how much their presence is felt in a family. Growth brings change and change is usually a two way process in relationships. Tweens may not hope to revolutionize their parents, but they do hope to see they make a difference – and have enormous pleasure when they do so. We will think more about managing rows in Chapter 5.

Disappointment is part of life

> "How can we help our eleven year old who flies off the handle when things don't go as he wants?"
>
> *Leo's father*

Eleven-year-old Leo had left home very excited that morning. His class was being taken to see a Mediaeval battle re-enactment. He returned home in a temper and berated his mother all evening. His class teacher had been taken ill and the trip had had to be cancelled. It was hardly his mother's fault! Tweens can be so bitterly disappointed by seemingly minor events, one eleven year old was plunged into misery because her local shop had run out of her favourite chocolate bar. They tend to show this disappointment as anger – anger with someone else or with themselves.

There is nothing wrong with wanting things, be it a teenage magazine, invitations to *all* the parties, an expensive item of clothing, or your divorced parents to get back together. But nobody has everything in life (any more than it is true that there is a time and place for everything) and everybody has to learn to negotiate disappointment in a constructive way. In fact, it can be argued that disappointment is essential for a good life. However, it is not necessarily a good idea to encourage children to be too keen to accept disappointment for fear they construe it as accepting defeat.

Disappointments highlight our limitations (I realize now I will never be a prima ballerina!) and show us the limit of our powers. We are then not only consoled, we are freed and strengthened to aspire to be our best. In this sense, disappointment helps us to face reality. Disappointment is part of life and not catastrophic. In an age that promotes the notion that every one can have everything (and is indeed entitled to everything), it may be a difficult task for parents to help tweens accept and negotiate disappointment as a fact of life, but it is an essential task.

How parents can help to build self-esteem

You can help your tween most by doing what you are doing, i.e., thinking about your tween and trying to find some meaning in what seems like meaningless behaviour. You may protest that you bought this book out of desperation, at your wit's end, having run the gauntlet of your parenting skills. That may be true, and the fact that you are willing to buy a book (if not a library of such books), shows your readiness to believe that tweens are worth some time and effort. Believe it or not, at some level, your youngster will sense that you are trying "to get it right" – and in a way that may be more important than getting it right. Of course, there are better and worse ways of responding to a tween but perhaps most important for parents is to be able to tolerate not knowing what is going on. Emotionally, your tween doesn't know what is going on inside all the time so nobody else stands a chance. You may also have to accept that at times your tween does not want to be understood.

Balancing comfort and confrontation

Tweens are most critical of their parents for being critical!

It may be helpful at this point to think about three things you were most criticized for by your parents … and did their criticism make you change your behaviour?

Learning to cope with criticism is part of growing up. It is a difficult task made more palatable if your youngster feels the criticism is just and fair, and not phrased in such a way that they are left feeling all their good points are being ignored or cancelled out. It is easy to lose sight of the lovable in tweens. They can be exasperating and, like many parents, you may fall into the habit of listing their failings and shortcomings to any other adult who listens. Being constantly negative about your tween may lead them to feeling unacceptable just at the time they are struggling to find acceptance as themselves. It is worth trying to find some praise or comfort within the confrontation. There is all the difference in the world between these two statements:

"*Tomasina treats us like we are dirt, she's so contemptuous of us*,"
and
"*Tomasina is a lovely girl and we love her dearly but she does sometimes treat us with utter contempt.*"

If you attack, your tween will defend. "*You always leave your room in such a mess*", is likely only to lead to an argument on the definition of mess. A request to tidy your room by picking up the clothes and removing dirty mugs may not be met with a winning smile and a prompt response but it does at least tell the tween exactly how to be helpful. It implies less that the tween is behaving badly and more that there are certain daily jobs to be done – boring as that may be.

"Just jobs" – replacing *but* with *and*

Darren has a point. Parents often have the idea of putting praise first and then adding a "but" criticism. The problem is that the Darrens of this world only hear the criticism. As he says, "*As soon as she says 'but', I just feel 'Okay, I got it wrong again.*'"

Substituting *and* for *but* may help. "Well done, you've cleared up your room *and* could you shut the wardrobe doors" is somehow heard more positively. Perhaps this is because it recognizes the

"My mum is so sad – she's so sad, she's full of 'just jobs'… just do this, just do that, and I never do it right. She says, 'Ok, well done, you've cleared up your room, but'… like you haven't shut the wardrobe doors or something."

Darren, eleven years

effort that the tween has made, however inadequate. They may not do things to your standard and they often fail to complete activities but they are going to be much more encouraged if you can grit your teeth and highlight the positive in what they have done.

Check that you really are praising!

It is interesting to wonder whether this was true of Mr and Mrs Greenfield! What matters, is that that is how they made their daughter feel!

Parents and children communicate in many ways. There is always what you mean to say, are aware of saying, i.e., your conscious messages. Then there is what you haven't thought about saying, what you didn't know you were saying, the *unconscious messages* in your conversations. It is a sad truth of life that we cannot pass on emotionally what we have not experienced emotionally. The mother of eleven-year-old Sandy who was referred with poor self-esteem was distraught. "*I've always encouraged her, I've always told her I love her and believe in her. I've never pressurized her, always said that all that matters is that she does her best, she doesn't have to win or be top.*" Her daughter, who had been silent in our consultation to that point, suddenly interrupted angrily, "*You don't think I can win – you think I'm a loser because you're a loser.*"

"Everything I did was applauded, all the trivial milestones of childhood were celebrated."

Professor Susan Greenfield, first female director of the Royal Institute of Great Britain

This mother was brought up by strict parents whose demands for high standards made it difficult for them to praise her. She was left feeling inadequate and never believed she could produce an attractive, capable, confident child and so her messages to her daughter had a hollow ring. She, in turn, sensed her mother's lack of confidence in herself and therefore in her as her daughter. "*She's right,*" said her mother, "*I was always secretly surprised when she did well.*" Consciously, Sandy's mother was saying, "*You can succeed in anything you want.*" Unconsciously she was saying, "*I can't believe a child of mine can really do well.*" Sandy was picking up both messages.

It is every child's fate to deal with the impact of the unconscious messages they receive. Children always have choices about how they can respond to parents' messages. A father was describing how his family went bankrupt when he was twelve years old, and he had to change schools. He was bullied and teased mercilessly in the first few weeks, "*But then, I just thought I would show them ...*" and he went on to describe how he not only came top in almost every subject but was also an admired sportsman. He did this in spite of the bullying, and in spite of earlier messages from his parents. "*My brothers both went to highly academic schools. My parents knew I would never cope with that and so I went to a much smaller place. They really despaired when I had to transfer to the large school ... they didn't think I had a chance.*"

Accept you will be worried

Every child is a bit of an experiment and all experiments involve risk and risk involves anxiety ... on somebody's part. Perhaps one of the most difficult aspects of parenting a tween is carrying anxiety for the tween. They often use disturbing, disruptive or bizarre behaviour as a way of communicating their anxieties about growing up. This is worrying for you but it is also par for the course as your tween struggles with too many feelings in search of an identity. At times, both you and your tween may feel they are, as Churchill once described Russia, "*... a riddle wrapped in a mystery inside an enigma ...*"

"That's so not fair ..."
Boundaries and discipline

"Children nowadays are tyrants. They contradict their parents, gobble their food and tyrannize their teachers."

(Socrates)

Children need to be told what to do. They don't need to be told what to do all the time, but being told what to do is one of the things children need. Also children *want* to be told what to do (they may also *not want* to be told what to do) and this is a secret both parents and children share.

"*What that child wants is a good smack,*" said an elderly woman watching a distraught young mother struggling with a four year old in a temper tantrum. A good smack may have suddenly shocked the child into temporary silence but in the long run, if not immediately, it would only have made her more angry. But if we translate "a good smack" as "a boundary" then the older woman was absolutely right. This child was desperately seeking a boundary, her belligerent behaviour could be understood as her asking, "*How far can I go, where is the boundary?*" So whilst it is slightly comical to think of a child *wanting* "a good slap", it is all too true that children *want* boundaries, they *want* to be told how far they can go.

The first boundary – children and parents are different

Children and parents are different, and the differences between children and parents are in themselves a boundary. For example, adults can make choices, (they may not always be the best or the most sensible, but they are able to make choices), children are growing into choice-makers. Think about it, most of the choices you have given your small child are not choices at all – "*Eat up your supper or go to bed*," is the equivalent of saying to your partner, tired at the end of a long day, "*You can make the supper or vacuum the stairs.*"

- So the first natural boundary you will enforce is to acknowledge that you and your children are different.

(You may not go as far as the teacher, determined to teach an unruly class, who began by saying, "*Right, I'm fifty-six and you're eleven. I know a lot, you know nothing. So I'm going to talk, and you are going to listen*" ... but you understand the principle!)

Children set boundaries

Children also enforce a natural boundary by separating from you as they grow up: they become more in themselves, i.e., more boundaried. You can understand your tween's thoughts and feelings about independence by measuring how easily they are separating from you. The more naturally separate your tween is becoming from you, the more they are ready to have adventures and this seems relevant throughout the spectrum of the tween years. Many nine year olds may need encouragement to go out alone, others may be in an impulsive rush. Some twelve year olds are able to take responsibility for themselves, others maybe need to be encouraged into more independence. Children show they are becoming separate from their parents in many ways – having secrets, developing a life outside home, and, at the onset of the tween years ... arguing.

In Chapter 2 we thought about how tweens experience a rapid growth in intellectual development and, in particular, their capacity for abstract thought. The toddler asked to put on his raincoat because it is raining responds, "*Why is it raining?*" Toddlers think concretely in the same way as a five or six year old told to "pull their socks up", may literally bend down and pull up their socks. Tweens and teenagers are able to see beyond the literal to the shades and nuances of answers and meaning. Tweens' questions are not so much a thirst for knowledge as a means of practising a new realization; the realization that adults, especially parents, are not always right. Tweens may have a strong sense of what they believe to be right and wrong and, at the same time, may be ambiguous about their beliefs. They sound out their beliefs to themselves by delighting in practising their newly discovered skill of arguing with adults. They will be quick to detect the slightest flaw in your reasoning and endless, seemingly inane arguments can ensue.

"You can't go out like that, it's raining."

"So?"

"You'll get soaked ... put your raincoat on ..."

"I won't get soaked, the rain's not heavy ... heavy rain soaks you."

Tempted as you may be, you can no longer demand they put their raincoat on "because I say so". Now is the time for both you and your tween to practise negotiating skills. And cheer up! What better place is there for your youngster to learn to argue than in the home? Hopefully, home is where we can make the most ridiculous arguments and yet still feel accepted and admired without too much loss of face.

"Why should I ...?" – the purpose of boundaries and rules

The purpose of the rules and boundaries you set is going to depend very much on what you are hoping they will achieve.

"Did you hear about the group of anarchists who tried to set up a commune but no one would obey the rules?"

- Are you setting guidelines or prohibitions?
- Do you want to reinforce current ways of behaving?
- Do you want to change something? If so, exactly *what*, and/or *who*?

How well you can enforce rules and boundaries will depend very much on the history of your relationship with boundaries. By that I mean how well or otherwise you feel your parents managed boundary setting and how easy or difficult you have found it to manage your child so far. It stands to reason that if you and your tween established clear understandings in early

"Now she's a tween do I have to change my methods of parenting?"

childhood then the setting of new rules and boundaries in the tween years will be part of a continuum. If on the other hand, for whatever reason, you and your child have never had much success at establishing firm boundaries, then managing the tween years will exacerbate the struggle. All parents have to learn new skills at this stage, but especially, perhaps, parents who have relied on a rigid and inflexible enforcement of rules and boundaries in the early years, relying overly on the phrase "Because I'm your parent and I say so."

Rules incite risks

It is worth bearing in mind that rules incite risks, i.e., when someone produces a rule, it provokes someone else to break it! Ask yourself whether the rule you are trying to impose is aimed at helping to keep your tween safe and to develop a sense of who they are and what they should be doing ... or whether you are just seeking peace and quiet! Of course, there is nothing wrong with simply seeking peace and quite, it is something everyone needs at times.

"Parents are not interested in justice, they're interested in peace and quiet!"
Bill Cosby

"My twelve year old has started coming home late without phoning ..."
frantic mother of Lou

"I don't know how to manage Lou any more. The third time she was late in I grounded her. I telephoned all her friends and told them she had been grounded ..."

"I've told her, 'I just need to know you are safe ... I need to know where you are and who you are with. I need to know how you are getting home, and when you are coming home ... how do I know when you are not safe if I don't know you are safe?'"

Lou and her mother were both having to learn new skills. They were struggling with a new relationship in which Lou had to discover how to manage independence with responsibility – no small task. Her mother's task was equally daunting, not only did she have to cope with her ambivalent feelings about letting Lou loose in the world, she had to find a new way of talking to Lou about rules and boundaries.

We can all relate to Lou's mother's desperation and it may be interesting to reflect on what you would have done in her position. Grounding tweens is a complex punishment because what it really means is that you, the parent, have to put up with the tween hanging round the house in the worst possible mood! Lou was no exception. She was angry and humiliated by her mother's behaviour. Like all tweens, she was adept at driving her mother to extremes of anxiety and worry. In such a state, parents may lose track of whether they are trying to discipline, or to devastate their tweens.

Why rules and boundaries?

Boundaries help to keep us safe – from the dangers of other people and the dangers of ourselves. When you say, "this far and no further" to your tween, you are helping them to understand they have to respect you as your own separate person, with your own thoughts, wishes and ideas. Intrinsically, this conveys to them that they too have a right to develop a sense of privacy, a sense of self respect. You are modelling for them how to "put boundaries around themselves" in terms of the way they will allow other people to treat them. Boundaries show us how to respect ourselves and other people and help us to develop a sense of independence with responsibility.

... Boundaries are a way of both creating and solving a problem ...

Sometimes making rules can seem like a kind of magic. We turn to rules and boundaries at times to try to solve something, to keep something under control, to try to make something happen. For example, some parents use strict rules to try to ensure a sense of emotional togetherness in the family. There may be rules such as "everyone has to be together for everyone's birthday". In Chapter 3 we thought about how this is one of the ways families develop traditions in the early years. It is natural, as you begin to lose intimacy and closeness with your tween, to try and legislate about emotional closeness; and indeed, there is a sense in which boundaries can control. In this case, you can make your tween be present for family birthdays but what you can't do, is control the atmosphere they may create by their presence! So there is a sense in which we all need to create a relationship with boundaries.

The drawbacks of boundaries

- Boundaries may make us feel lonely and cut off. They may make us feel different from other people. This is the other side of privacy.

John "let slip" they were going to watch a horror video, two days before the sleepover. This was particularly provocative as John knew his fourteen-year-old brother had been refused permission to see the film at the cinema. John's father immediately said that John couldn't go to the sleepover. He was also wondering if other parents knew about the video and whether he should inform them. He suggested to John that he phone the host parents to check whether or not this was a vain boast. John was incandescent at their suggestions, "*You'll make me look a wuss ... you're so stupid ... everyone else in my class has seen it.*"

"My eleven year old wants to go to a sleepover to watch an X-rated movie. We know the violence will be too much for him ... how do we stop him going without humiliating him with his friends?"

John's father

John understood his parents' behaviour as robbing him rather than protecting him. It did not help when they offered him a choice; they would phone the host parents to assess the situation or they would offer an excuse to get him out of the evening. John chose not to go over the risk of being seen as a "wuss" by his peers. But John's behaviour was interesting. He must have known that if his parents knew the video was being shown then they would forbid him to go. So why did he "let it slip"? This is a simple example of how the tween wants to be both beyond, and within, their parents' control. Maybe a part of John was anxious and wanted his parents to forbid him to go.

Check that they do know what you really think!

John's story also raises interesting questions about what parents can assume tweens know about their views. You probably underestimate or overestimate how much they understand what you think. It can be useful to begin conversations by making it explicit to your tween what they do know, e.g., "*John, you know our views on that video and you watching it. We are not discussing that, we are discussing how we are going to handle Saturday night.*"

The difference between boundaries and barriers

In one sense, boundaries are a fantasy for us all. By a fantasy, I mean a way of thinking about something that may or may not be related to reality. Psychotherapist Michael Balint illustrates this by posing the question, "Is the fish in the water or is the water in the fish?" So sometimes, we tend to talk about boundaries in parenting without always thinking what a boundary involves. We all know a boundary on a map, but recognizing a map boundary does not necessarily help us to understand boundaries between people. Attached to my consulting room is a door, which leads into my house. This door has a coded lock. Some youngsters see this door as a barrier – the fantasy is that my "real life" takes place in my home on the other side of the door. Others see it as a boundary – no one from my home can come into the room while they are there ... for their time, they are the "special person" in my life. I experience the same issue around my answering machine. Some clients see it as instant access to me; they can leave a message at any time. Others experience it as a barrier which prevents them from speaking to me personally. This raises interesting assumptions about both my, and other people's, availability. It is likely that your tween will feel you should always be available to them and that anything which causes you not to be is a frustrating barrier.

Most tweens feel that rules are there simply to spoil their fun. Rules and boundaries are almost bound to be a frustration for tweens but they also may feel contained and relieved by them. Fun is not a simple issue, fun involves excitement and one of the things tweens want to be protected from is the risks of their own excitement. And there may be a grain of truth in their argument. Many parents will admit to a vague sense (usually in the face of the most outrageous behaviour), that tweens deserve to be punished.

"*I won't let her get away with it*", insisted Pippa's mother talking about Pippa's rudeness and uncooperativeness. "*I come down really hard on her. She needs to be stamped on.*"

Pippa had a different view, "*Mum's really tough. I don't like her. She thinks she's winning but I just get really angry and think I'll get my own back.*"

In the face of Pippa's disobedience, her mother felt a natural anxiety she was losing her ability to control Pippa. One of the tween's tasks in life is to practise being beyond their parents' control, so Pippa and her mother raise interesting questions.

Pippa certainly seemed to believe life would be better without rules – making her mother and I reflect on the question of "What would

"My eleven year old accuses me of making rules to spoil her fun. She reckons as soon as she says she wants to do something, I pass a law against it."

Pippa's mother

life be like without rules?" I asked Pippa's mother what it said about her if Pippa broke the rules. *"I'm a bad mother"* she replied, meaning she would be perceived as not "making her child behave properly". So what does this say about a parent if their child *doesn't* break the rules? They may be seen as being good parents; they may also be seen as repressive parents. Perhaps sometimes we should be more worried about the child who doesn't break the rules than about youngsters like Pippa who feel able to make a bid, albeit inappropriately, for independence.

Pippa, like many tweens, felt asking for advice, or accepting help, was diminishing or in some way childish. It is rather like the two year old who will get angry if you intervene to help them in a struggle to master a task, as though your very offer of help highlights their lack of skills. Older teenagers gradually learn to respect and even to seek advice from adults (although this may be more likely to be from a grandparent, uncle or teacher than from a parent!) They can do so because they have developed more confidence in their ability to be independent. They are more sure of who they are outside the family and so can afford to develop a new kind of dependent and interdependent relationship with the family. Until your tween reaches this stage, you may have to accept that both you and your help are essentially nothing but a major embarrassment. Confrontations, arguments and battles over the most trivial matters may be the stuff of daily life.

Enforcing rules and boundaries

"Young women especially have something invested in being nice people, and it is only when you have children, that you realize you are not a nice person at all, but generally a selfish bully."

(Fay Weldon, Independent on Sunday, *5 May 1991)*

Rules and boundaries are difficult to enforce because of how both parents and children feel about saying no. (You may just like to pause and think about how it feels to say no to yourself.) Even when conscious that saying no may be in a child's best interests, many parents will admit to feeling that saying no is:

- aggressive towards their child
- spoiling fun for their child
- withholding something from their child
- likely to provoke an argument!

The first skill parents need in enforcing rules and boundaries is the confidence to say no in a firm, but kind way. If you say no anticipating an argument then, unconsciously, you are inviting your tween to argue. The skill lies in your confidence in knowing that, give or take the odd bad day, you will withstand your tween's arguments.

Enforcing rules for tweens is difficult because your approval is no longer first on their list. The young child's self-image is dependent upon the praise, recognition and admiration they receive from adults. They are concerned with curing adults in that it is in their own interests to sustain adults and make them feel better about life whenever possible. They do so because they are so dependent on adults for their own survival. Tweens are much more anxious to have praise, recognition and admiration from their peers. Feeling the same, fitting in, being "cool" with their friends are what matters now. Indeed, you may well have become exactly the kind of person they don't want to be!

> "My eleven-year-old son turns the simplest request into a declaration of war. Why is it so difficult to get him to obey the simplest of rules?"

Rules are difficult to enforce when the rule presents the tween with an impossible contradiction. Hattie was bullied mercilessly by her thirteen-year-old sister. It was very difficult for her to follow the family rule, "you must be kind to each other and love each other" when her sister was making her life a misery. Hattie's mother could not *make* her buy a present. Of course, she could purchase something on her behalf but what would that achieve? By not giving a birthday present, is Hattie trying to bully her sister into not bullying her? Or is she finding a way of putting boundaries round herself, saying, "*I can't do anything about you bullying me but I can do something about the way I respond to your bullying.*" It may be less important on this birthday for the girls to exchange gifts than to be given some help to talk about the difficulties in their relationship. At times like this, parents need to think about two important points:

> "My eleven year old is refusing point blank to buy her sister a birthday present. Should I make her?"
> *mother of eleven-year-old Hattie*

- Who did you learn your favourite rules from?
- Where did you learn how to make those rules work?

Of these two, the most important is where you learnt your methods for enforcing rules, for how you learnt to enforce rules will colour your understanding of what it means to enforce a rule. Does enforcing a rule mean:

- Letting your tween off a rule every now and then?
- A form of negotiating?
- Laying down the law, i.e., "*I know best, you do this, and this will happen and I will ensure it happens.*"

On being fair

Treating children equally does not necessarily mean treating them the same. No two children are the same; they all have different needs and abilities and so "being fair" may mean treating them differently. Times change as children in the family grow up and parents have the right to feel free to change their minds. Of course Lena's sister may be outraged but rather than trying to avoid a conflict, her parents may need to say something like, "*You can be as cross as you like, but the rules have changed ...*" Changing your mind is sometimes difficult for parents because it challenges your image of yourself as a consistent parent; consistent means "compatible" as well as "not contradictory".

"Our twelve year old wants her ears pierced now like all her friends. We made her sister wait until she was fifteen ... how can we be fair to them both?"

Lena's mother

Parenting styles

Richmal Crompton, best known for her *Just William* stories, wrote an adult novel, *The Family Roundabout*, a fascinating study of two families dominated by two very different kinds of mother. Mrs Fowler is described by her daughter, Judy, as having "a suggestion of loving, uncritical understanding ... never inquisitive about one's affairs ... content to give all and demand nothing in return." We read of her as a mother who shrank from bringing pressure to bear on her children in any way "and so ... suspected ... she had often failed them".

Mrs Willoughby, by contrast, "expected, and received, implicit obedience." She dominates her children, interfering in their lives to the point that the only child she considers to be "satisfactory" is the one who never rebels – "the downtrodden and repressed Cynthia". The novel traces the development of these two families, and the reader finds their allegiance switching from one style of mothering to the other, depending on the success and happiness of the children's lives. Mrs Willoughby's autocratic style is usually held up as the way not to parent. Such parents tend to be inflexible with fixed opinions and rules.

Naughtiness is very much a matter of the way a child's behaviour is construed. In Mrs Willoughby's home, to argue for a change in a rule, or to flaunt a rule, was considered disobedient and disrespectful. Parenting was regarded as a kind of battle, which either Mrs Willoughby or her children won. In the short term, such parents may feel they "have won" in that the children seem to be obedient.

Tamsin was such a child. Her friends had swapped their sensible childhood fashions for the tank-tops and mini skirts of the tween. Here parents felt such fashions simply served to encourage the sexualization of children. On the surface, Tamsin seemed to accept their views, and wear clothes of her parents' choice. Imagine their distress when they discovered she had been seen in the town wearing clothes lent to her by her best friend! In the face of absolutely no negotiation, Tamsin felt she had to rely on more and more underhand methods to get her needs met.

> "My eleven year old wants to wear teenage clothing. Are we right to put our foot down?"
>
> *Tamsin's mother*

The authoritarian parent

Mrs Willoughby's approach, the authoritarian one, has a valuable place in the tween years. Tweens need simple, clear rules stated in a kind, but firm manner. Pushing the boundaries, arguing, defiance are all ways of driving you mad, but they are also ways of finding out what you are made of, and what you really believe in. Total inflexibility can sap their confidence and undermine their resourcefulness. Youngsters may become passive and timid or they may become rebellious and obstreperous, seeing life, as described by a twelve-year-old boy, "*That when there are two, one has everything, and the other has nothing*". Such a tween may never witness the gently shifting balances of power that go on in successful adult relationships. They believe that the only way of empowering themselves is to render someone else powerless, i.e., to behave in a way beyond the parents' control.

The permissive parent

One of the tasks of being a tween is to begin to have a sense of what it is like to rely on yourself. When your baby began to walk by holding onto the furniture, it is likely that you made sure the furniture was close enough together to allow the baby to stagger from one piece to another. You wouldn't have removed all the furniture, all visible means of support, in an attempt to make the baby practise walking unaided! And so it is with tweens learning to rely on themselves. They need the support of boundaries. Learning to be autonomous can be confusing and frightening and too much freedom too soon may leave your tween floundering.

> "We don't give her a time to be in, so there can't be any problems. If you give them a time to be in and they are late, then you are always nagging."
>
> *Cora's mother*

Cora, aged twelve, was in serious trouble at school. Her teachers complained of her "lack of motivation and ambition, and her breathtakingly flagrant disregard for school rules". Cora's mother was clearly concerned by her school reports but was also highly critical of the school in front of Cora. She felt Cora was a bright girl who was bored at school because she was not being "stretched intellectually". As she talked about the school, she tossed her head and wore a sulky, rather more angry expression than the concerned look one might have expected. Cora, on the other hand, sat hunched in her chair looking resentful, dejected and squirming with embarrassment. It began to feel as though there were two unhappy tweens in the room. The conversation continued. Cora's mother went on to say she didn't think Cora should be "nagged" about doing her homework. She saw her as an able girl who would do enough work to pass her exams as and when she needed. She described how her autocratic parents "made my life a misery over exams". She had been considered of "average ability", and her parents realized she would have to work hard in order to achieve. "But it just made me

> "My parents were far too strict ... I just want Cora to have some fun."
>
> *Cora's mother*

stubborn," said Cora's mother, "after all, they could shut me in my room but they couldn't make me do it [the homework]."

Cora's mother was now in full flight as she described the differences between her relationship with her parents and Cora's relationship with her. She felt that she and Cora had a close, open relationship in which they could talk about anything. At this point Cora exploded, "*I don't want a mum that sits up all night with me talking about my boyfriends – I want a mum that says, 'Here's your tea …' I don't always want to talk about it … I just want her to make me do it.*"

Cora was begging her parents to treat her like a tween, a twelve-year-old girl, not a late adolescent. Her mother was clearly shocked to hear Cora say she wanted her to insist that she did her homework – "*Sheila [Cora's friend] isn't allowed out until she's done her homework – her mum really cares.*"

Growing up involves establishing our own goals, our own sense of purpose, but youngsters need to practise this first of all by working towards and achieving goals set for them by the adults. In this sense, clear boundaries help us to define not only who we are, but also what are appropriate tasks for us to be doing at any given age.

- Permissive parenting may so often leave children without a sense of drive or healthy ambition. Like Cora, they may interpret their parents' lack of control as lack of care. They feel they "don't matter", and consequently, nothing matters.
- Permissive parenting may give tweens responsibility beyond their age and ability. It is also confusing for youngsters.

Cora wasn't old enough to decide for herself what time she should come in. She said she often felt "*lonely and isolated*" at the end of a gathering with her friends. "*They all have to be in, and they rush off, so I'm always left at the end, and I go home because I know it doesn't matter.*" She was actually envious of her friends' mad dash to be home "on time", "*because when I get in no one will check.*"

Cora's rule-breaking at school was also an interesting communication and we will explore this more in Chapter 6.

It was now Cora's parents' turn to "feel at sea". In a moment of insight, her mother volunteered she

"It's like they want me to play a game but they won't tell me the rules, so I have to make it up as I go along, and so I keep getting it wrong."

Cora

had developed her parenting style partly as a way of showing her own mother how wrong she had been in her parenting. Her own unresolved tween battles with her mother were getting in the way of her being a "good enough" mother to her own tween daughter. She was so anxious to have a good relationship with Cora, that she found it hard to deny or disappoint her.

Tolerating them hating you

Parenting can be relentlessly exhausting. You know that and I know that and yet, when you decided to have your children, you did so, most likely, because you thought it would be fun. So what has to happen for fun to turn into exhaustion?

"How do you stay calm when your eleven year old is screaming abuse at you ...? I feel she hates me ..."

Children of all ages will pitch their behaviour against yours. You may not be able to avoid exhaustion at times but there are ways of not exacerbating it. There is nothing more exhausting than going on trying to enforce rules and boundaries in ways that simply don't work. So if you find yourself powerlessly repeating yourself, then it may be time to find some energy in a different way of management.

It may also be helpful to hold in mind that a little rebellion is no bad thing. It is easy to become a permissive parent through "battle fatigue". It may seem easier just to give in to your tween's demands, and, on occasions, there may be no harm done. But as a long term strategy, it is fraught with potential difficulties.

You are going to have to be able to tolerate your tween hating you. In the tween years, it is much more important to be a hated parent than to be a cool friend to your tween. They have plenty of cool friends who won't enforce rules and boundaries; being hated is integral to making boundaries. So why do we feel it is so awful to be hated? Well, you probably feel rejected, unwanted and not needed. Nothing could be further from the truth.

Responding to the battles in spite of yourself!

Just as tweens are likely always to see boundaries as barriers they may also see rules as arbitrary. It may well feel to them that you will permit something one day and not the next. One tween couldn't see the difference between being allowed to go to the school disco with an older group of teenagers and being allowed to go to the pub for the evening with them!

Tweens will go on and on pestering in their own way, probably in the most derisory manner. As one mother commented, it is extraordinary how tweens think that the more rude they are to you the more likely you are to give in to them. And of course in one way they are right! If they don't push you into being a permissive parent, they are likely to push you into at least one of the three following very human reactions.

- The "stressy" parent
- The "do it your own way" parent
- The yelling parent

More hurt than angry – the "stressy" parent

At some time, most parents will resort to assuming an air of combined disappointment, hurt and enduring tolerance in the face of their tween's behaviour. David christened his mother "the stressy mum" because of her frequent lament that his behaviour caused her such stress she couldn't sleep or she felt ill. The true "stressy parent" will consistently, albeit unconsciously, try to make their tween feel guilty. David felt guilty, and he also felt angry. He felt he couldn't "get it right".

David's parents didn't understand his bewilderment. They felt they always allowed him to make a final decision on any matter. They talked through courses of action and encouraged him to decide "the right thing" to do. David had a different view, "*They're always saying it's up to me, I must make my own decisions, but when I do they get stressy. Then they start saying, '... so and so does this ...' and '... so and so does that...'*" He felt that whatever decision he made was in some way "wrong".

"They're always saying it's up to me, I must make my own decisions, but when I do they get stressy. They start saying 'so and so does this' and 'so and so does that' ..."
David, aged eleven

"How do I cope with our sulky son? We always talk through decisions with him and let him make up his own mind ... but he behaves as though we've forced something on him!"
David's parents

• Stressy parents leave a youngster confused. They rarely get angry, are always sweetly reasonable, leaving the tween, as David said, *"banging my head on a duvet"*.

"Do it your own way" – the "shrugging their shoulders stuff" parent

If you feel you "just can't get it right" with your tween, then, it can be argued, you are in a good place. Firstly, this may show you really understand part of your tween's predicament, *"I don't know how to get it right, i.e., I don't know how to be me."* Secondly, it may be evidence that there is a living, growing, developing relationship between you and your offspring. You are not assuming that the tween you spoke to yesterday is the same tween you are speaking to today – because often a tween isn't the same person from hour to hour, let alone from day to day! This may be all very encouraging on a good day with your tween, the rest of the time it is enough to make any parent throw their hands in the air and abdicate parental responsibility with, *"He'll just have to learn the hard way"*. Of course, this is partly true, your tween will learn most from their own mistakes. It can also do no harm for them to see now and then that they have exhausted your resources for the moment. Indeed, it may help them to see you as a human being for a split second! However, Martine's mother had fallen into the habit of abdicating. Firstly Martine knew, and took some pleasure in, the fact that if she hounded her mother long enough, she would shrug her shoulders and say, *"Do it your own way"*. *"And then,"* said Martine, *"she just walks out of the room and won't talk about it."* So secondly, Martine was extremely anxious. Her battles with her mother were her way of trying to discuss the pros and cons of any decision. But her approach was so confrontational and derisory that it was difficult for her mother to be aware of this fact! Martine was adept at taking her mother's arguments apart and making her feel foolish. By shrugging her shoulders her mother was secretly punishing Martine for disagreeing with her.

"She drives me to distraction ... I just end up shrugging my shoulders and telling her to do it her way ... What's the right way to handle arguments?"
Martine's mother

"The secret seems to lie in giving them enough rope to play with, but not to hang themselves."

"*She'll have to learn by her own mistakes*," is tantamount to saying, "*I know she's going to suffer, and I'm glad, and it's all her own fault.*" At the very time Martine needed her mother to stand firm alongside her, she felt abandoned by her.

- The "do it your own way" parenting gives tweens the message, "*Do it my way or I'll abandon you.*"

The yelling parent

Minty's mother was feeling low and had gone to talk to her own mother about the stresses of raising Minty. She wasn't comforted when her mother shrugged her shoulders and said, "*Well, I don't know ... in my day, we didn't have time to be stressed ... I was far too busy bringing you up.*"

Many parents feel stressed raising children today. Is it true that previous generations suffered less stress or were the stresses as great, but described as "too busy to think about"? Parenting nowadays is certainly very complex and the demands on parents in both the home and the workplace seem to have increased. No one is immune from stress and maybe this is why the word has become so popular. Was Minty's mother stressed by Minty's behaviour or was it that she felt angry and frustrated about her seeming lack of power and resource to cope with Minty? It is always a useful question to ask yourself when feeling stressed, "*What am I anxious/angry about at the moment and what can I do about it?*" Just asking the question may help you to realize that you have some resources to regain a sense of competence.

Many parents will relate to this desperate cry from Minty's mother. In the twinkling of an eye, or so it seemed to her, she had moved from knowing, give or take the odd hiccup, exactly how to manage her daughter to having no idea at all. "Yelling back" can quickly become a habit mainly because you feel so frustrated.

Parents should not yell at tweens but they do! And they're likely to feel guilty about it. "Yelling" seems an inevitable part of parenting and is therefore worth some thought.

> "There's got to be a better way than just yelling back at her ... but that's how it always ends up with us, I get so stressed."
>
> *mother of eleven-year-old Minty*

> "How come when she was ten I knew everything and now she's eleven, I know nothing?"
>
> *Minty's mother*

There may be good reasons why you yell. Minty felt as stressed as her mother.

"*She gets me real stressed, I don't know how to persuade her I'm not a baby, I'm grown-up now,*" she moaned.

"*Do you think a first step might be to try not to yell at her, to talk to her quietly?*"

"*Well, she yells at me …!*"

The risk of yelling back is that you are not modelling for your tween what they want and need – a way of managing their frustrations. For them, frustration is an important developmental tool. They become frustrated at one thing in order to get another. One of the tasks of parenting a tween is helping them to bear frustration. Minty was making her mother feel her frustration so she could help her to express it and if not to get her own way at least to negotiate a compromise with her parents.

Managing the yelling

- Take a deep breath, say something like, "*Look, we're on the same side …*" This may not only take your tween by surprise, but it will help you to calm down and think of how you can help your tween, rather than *confront* your tween at this moment.
- You could try saying something like, "*Look, we're both yelling which means we are both frustrated and we both feel powerless. We're not going to get anywhere right now … let's talk about this again later.*"

The sophisticated art of negotiating with tweens

A rather harassed young father was trying to get his two-and-a-half-year-old daughter to go to sleep. He had run the gamut of his parenting skills. She seemed to have an endless list of reasons why she needed to be downstairs with him and not upstairs asleep! She eventually appeared asking for a different pillow because this one was "lumpy". Exasperated her father replied, "*Alright, I will change your pillow on the understanding that I am not coming upstairs again and you are going to go to sleep.*" The two and a half year old stared at him. "*Daddy, I'm not negotiating.*"

The father collapsed into gales of laughter as he recounted this charming story. So why is this story so amusing and negotiating with a tween so often anything but amusing? Of course, this father wasn't really negotiating with his little daughter, he was persuading her. What's the difference?

Teenagers are often better at negotiating than tweens. They may well have learnt the subtle difference between persuasion and negotiation, though I would agree they are often more likely to try and persuade you than to negotiate with you!

It is unclear exactly what is going on when people are negotiating; how people manage to agree and disagree is a mystery. Think of the last time you negotiated with an adult, what were your main aims? In any adult negotiation there is the implicit understanding that:

"After two or three attempts I just feel furious, I just feel like hitting him. And then I say something I can't believe I've said! I think how on earth could I say that? It's not only that I'm losing him, I'm losing myself at times."

- compromise is a possibility
- agreement is a possibility, but not a necessity
- negotiating implies a deal is possible
- negotiation involves tolerating frustration

Negotiating with a tween is different from negotiating with an adult.

- you and your tween are not equals
- compromise is rarely what a tween is looking for!
- negotiating with a tween may be more about living with disagreement, than reaching an agreement

When you begin to negotiate, you do so from the standpoint that you have a duty of care and control towards your tween. They have the sole task of persuading you to give them what they want! However, the problem is that your tween may not know what they really want from the conversation. Let us think again of John and his horror video.

The argument seemed to be about letting him see the video. It wasn't clear whether John really wanted to see this horror video or not. This may have been the main purpose of his argument with his parents, to find out for himself what he wanted. So, keep in mind that your tween may be trying to draw you into an unnecessary confrontation.

Limiting the confrontations

You may help yourself to resist being drawn into confrontations by holding in mind three important points:

- you are not here to argue
- know and be prepared *not* to know your baseline
- remember it may be more important to say what you feel than to present a united front

Lana, aged twelve, and her mother were arguing about whether or not she could go on a camping weekend with friends. Lana became increasingly angry and frustrated by her parents' request for more detailed information. She had just got to the defiant, "Well, you can't stop me", when her mother had what she later described as a "moment of inspiration".
"I said to her, '*Lana, this feels like a fight.*'"
"*Sure ...*" nodded Lana.
Before she could add any further attacks her mother added, "*I don't understand that, Lana. We're not here to fight, we're here to try and work out how you can have a fun weekend.*" Lana looked shell-shocked! It had not crossed her mind that this could be negotiated without an argument. Try to hold in mind that you are here to listen, to hear and then to decide.

Knowing and not knowing your baseline?

Before entering any discussions on any matter with a tween, you would do well to be clear of knowing and not knowing your own bottom line. Whilst it is useful to have a sense of what basic rules you are going to insist on, you will find that your bottom line keeps shifting. It may be, "she can't go to the party", or "she can go to the party if ..." but you need to be clear at what point you would be immovable. Otherwise, you are prone to being tossed about on a sea of tween's persuasion and resentment.

"How can I manage to stick to my baseline ...?"

- Try to state calmly and clearly what you need from your tween in the discussion, e.g., "*I need to know exactly whose house you are at, and I need you to phone at nine to tell me you are leaving.*"

The argument may well continue but it is important to remain firm, perhaps repeating something like, "*I'm afraid I'm immovable on this, can you suggest a compromise?*"

As psychotherapist Adam Phillips says, "*A repertoire might be more useful than a conviction, especially if one keeps in mind that there are many kinds of good life.*"

Present a united front?

If tweens feel they can play parents off one against the other then they are likely to do so. You are going to find it much easier to negotiate a sudden, new crisis if both parents agree on the basic rules of the house. (It is equally important to remember that the advantage of having two parents is that you get two points of view on the world.) One of the things your tween is trying to discover is where their parents agree and disagree, i.e., "Where are the boundaries between my mother and my father?" What matters is how you present your differences to your tween.

"What do we do when my husband and I disagree about a rule or boundary ...?"

There will, of course, be fundamental things that as parents you will disagree about and that can't be presented to your tween without their sensing the conflict. In such cases, the only thing you can do as parents is to live out the conflict and this may not be all bad; for there is a sense in which it is important that children can learn not only that they cannot split their parents but that they can expose differences in their parents. Differences between couples are a fact of life. Exposing differences in a family may not split a family apart but it will help people to find out who they are in the family, i.e., "I am me, and this is what I think" as opposed to what anybody else in the family may feel or think.

Children learn to manage conflict by observing how their parents deal with conflicts and other relationship issues. We could argue that parents who are able to expose their conflicts and diffi-culties leave a child more secure than a couple who have a weak relationship but try very hard to cover up the difficulties, leaving the risk that the tween engages upon the hopeless task of trying to keep the couple together.

And if they don't calm down?

No one can negotiate effectively in a state of anger. Your tween knows that, and that is why so often discussions may end with a dramatic flounce from the room and a bedroom door slamming. As one tween said, "*I lose it, because I know I've lost it.*" When you feel both sides are getting heated, it may be helpful to suggest a "five minute breather" while you both calm down. You may need to be firm on this, remember your tween wants this *sorted now* – explain neither of you want to make a bad decision in anger. This is different from giving your tween the message that being calm is reasonable and being angry is unreasonable. Maybe these two are equally valuable, but different, sides of the same coin. Remember how aggressively David experienced his parents' calm reasoning? Being calm can be a way of being aggressive if you think about it. Your tween has every right to get angry about matters they may feel are of life importance, even if they feel very trivial to you! If you give the message that being angry is unreasonable, they will interpret you as devaluing the importance of the issue that is so important to them. In quieter moments, you can explain that calm isn't necessarily better than excited but it is a better state of mind in which to negotiate.

"How do I calm down my eleven year old when she just stands there giving me cheek?"

Sometimes you will lose your cool

In which case, don't collapse! You can later make it clear to your tween that retaliation is as important as containment. By contain-ment I mean your ability to bear your tween's aggression towards you. By retaliation I mean their need to try and show you that they are more powerful than you.

- Make it clear to the youngster hurling abuse at you, that this is an inappropriate way of talking to you and that you are not discussing the subject further until they change their tone and attitude to a more respectful one.

Are you really listening?

How do we know when we are listening or when we have heard something? The effects of really listening to children are very unpredictable. Listening can make us feel and think all sorts of things, thoughts we want to have and thoughts we don't want to have. Really listening to children can give us surprising, stray thoughts and so we listen to children at the risk of surprising ourselves. Being heard and understood, i.e., being taken seriously, is more important than whether or not people agree or disagree with us. So in any confrontation with your tween it's worth asking yourself, "What would have to happen for her to know that I am really listening to her?" How would you know that you had really listened to your tween?

How much does your family listen to each other?

How well you and your tween can listen to each other now will depend on the foundations laid in early childhood. How much do you think about things that go wrong, for example, if there is a row, what happens afterwards? Is it ignored, people pretending it never happened? Do the people involved briefly apologize and then carry on? Or do people try and talk over the disagreement, see how it arose, and try and make some reparation?

How much power does your tween have in the family?

How would your tween know they had some power in their lives and in the life of the family? When was the last time your tween would know that they had influenced a family decision in the life of the family? Although everybody in a family does not have equal power, it is very important that everyone feels that at some time they have some impact on decisions being made within the family.

It is both a huge responsibility and a difficult task for you as a parent to decide how much independence your tween should have and when they should have it. The word "power" is interesting. Parents often see this stage of child development as a gradual transition of *power*; words like "*independence*", "*self-reliance*" and "*autonomy*" somehow describe so much better the natural process that you and your tween are trying to negotiate. Sadly, transitions can very quickly become power struggles.

Are you really hearing?

"I know you believe you understand what you think I said, but I am not sure you realize that what you heard is not what I meant"

graffiti

- Don't assume that what you are hearing your tween say is necessarily what they are saying!
- Check by saying something like, "*It sounds as though you feel angry because you think we are being unfair by saying so and so.*"

This will not only help you to verify that you are hearing accurately, but it will also help your tween to distinguish between what they are *feeling* and what they are *thinking*.

- Remember your tween can be upset by things that adults may regard as too trivial to be of consequence in the discussion.
- Your tween is entitled to their own point of view.

One aspect of listening and checking is respecting your tween's thoughts and feelings however much they may differ from yours. There is no reason why two people should ever have to think in the same way. Sometimes, saying something like, "*Well, I know we can't agree about this and …*" will help your tween to stop trying to persuade you to their point of view and help them to listen to the negotiation.

- Sometimes, getting on with your tween is more important than understanding them. The purpose of this book may be more to enable you to get on with your tween than to understand them.
- Knowing your own base-line means also being prepared to let your tween suggest their own rewards and punishments, e.g., a father was despairing of the fact that his twelve-year-old son had been offered generous pocket money each week if he remembered to make his own bed and keep his room tidy for five consecutive days. "*I can't believe it, he did it for a couple of days and that was it. He just didn't seem bothered about the money.*" This father was rather surprised when I pointed out to him that there may be lots of things that he wouldn't do for money. The situation changed (for a couple of weeks at least!) when the boy was allowed to suggest his own reward for keeping his bedroom tidy. If they can't, or won't, then you may be able to offer an area of compromise, but if the conversation goes nowhere it might be best to point out it's time to stop now, but perhaps you can talk about it later. Your tween needs time and space to think and

assimilate what you have said and to consult with friends how next to try to persuade you. It may be difficult for them to bring the conversation to a close without feeling they have lost face!

Punishment vs. encouragement

With all possible respect to Jake's father, if punishments make no difference then maybe Jake is telling you that what you are doing simply isn't working and you need to risk doing something else!

It is surprising, but true, that punishing children simply doesn't work. Punishment is a way of not thinking about children and what they need. By this I mean, maybe Jake's father is *reacting* to his defiance rather than thinking about when, how and why it arises. It may seem quick and effective to try and "stamp out" Jake's defiance with a swift punishment but it does nothing to help Jake and his father to understand what is going on between

> "My ten year old has become extremely defiant and punishments seem to make no difference in the long run. What can we do?"
>
> *Jake's father*

them. Why does Jake need to be consistently defiant? Is it over everything or over specific issues? Is he more defiant with one parent than another? If so, why? Constant defiance can be a tween's way of asking parents to re-evaluate the rules. So we could wonder if Jake's parents are insisting on rules that were appropriate in childhood but perhaps not for a tween. Or maybe Jake feels he just doesn't have enough power and control in his own life and has to fight for any sense of independence.

Punishments set up a power struggle and allow your tween to feel the victim!

> *"... I am the fish that always gets caught,*
> *I am the door that always gets slammed ...*
> *... I am the ant that always gets stamped on,*
> *I am the food that always gets eaten,*
> *I am the chair that always gets sat on,*
> *I am the runner who always gets beaten.*
> *When will it be my turn to be the fisherman,*
> *Or be the slammer, or be the pro, when will it*
> *Be my turn to do all the stamping ... I don't know.*
> *from* "Angry I Ams", *by Michael Parkinson (aged twelve)*

It is fascinating how quickly people can get into the habit of enjoying being punished and punishing. We could argue that the more Jake is punished, the more of a victim he may begin to feel, the more powerless he may be feeling and the more defiant he might become! Equally, there is the risk that Jake's father may begin to enjoy punishing Jake in the sense that he may begin to enjoy exerting power and control over Jake. Parents put boundaries and rules into place as a response to their childrens' behaviour. You make a rule when your child does something you didn't expect them to do.

Right and wrong vs. behaviour and consequences?

Jake's father's predicaments highlight an interesting question about rules and boundaries. Is teaching your youngster right from wrong more helpful than talking about behaviour and consequences? Punishments can work if they are understood by the youngster as being a legitimate consequence of their behaviour. For example, Jake wanted his mother to give him a lift to his friend's. She asked him to do several jobs such as making his bed and loading the dishwasher before they left. When it was time to go, Jake had not attempted any of his jobs. Previously, his mother would have refused point blank to take him to his friends. On this occasion, she quietly explained that these jobs had to be done and that she would now have to do them which would mean they would be leaving later and he would have less time with his friend. Jake was sullen and furious. But his mother insisted quietly that he could speed things up by helping her to do these tasks.

Privileges motivate

Tweens like Jake are much more likely to be motivated by privileges than by punishment; a privilege should be a privilege not a necessity of life for a tween, such as pocket money. When Jake was offered the reward of getting to his friend's house earlier by helping his mother, he shrugged his shoulders and said, "*I'm not bothered.*" His mother made no attempt to argue with him, shrugging her shoulders and saying, "*fine,*" as she went off to do the chores. It was interesting that she was soon followed by Jake …

In enforcing rules and boundaries, consistency is what matters. And consistency is different to rigidity. Rules are made to be bent and broken! Parents have very good intentions and there is often a huge gap between a parent's aspiration and what actually happens. From time to time you are going to be inconsistent and that doesn't matter, because the project of parenting is not to manage your youngster perfectly.

Keeping a sense of humour!

Negotiating with a tween may make you feel that you've lost the fun in family life. Gone are the days when you may have been able to quickly avert potential conflicts with a chirpy choice such as, "You eat up your fish fingers and then we can all go to the park." But tweens will often respond to genuine humour, i.e., laughing *with* and not *at* them. A moment of humour may divert a tween. They may not respond with a laugh or even a humorous retort, but they may temporarily give up the fight. One mother expressed her surprise when, after persistently nagging her ten-year-old son to go and tidy his room, she suddenly yelled, "*Right, go now, do not pass go, do not collect £200, go straight to your bedroom.*" Her son laughed spontaneously and in that moment, temporarily gave up the fight.

The risks of over-protecting your tween

Rules and boundaries are the most obvious ways that you care for your children. We can argue that there are both advantages and disadvantages to being cared for sufficiently as a child. Children who are nurtured and cosseted through childhood may find the hurly-burly of the outside world more demanding than the child who has to fend for himself to a small degree. The American novelist, Maya Angelou, has expressed her view that affluent children raised in a culture where materialism and appearance are the most important aspects of life may experience difficulty in growing up. Such youngsters often think they are growing up when, she says, they pass their driving tests, they go to college, they marry, they have a family but, she argues, "*They are not growing up, they are just getting older.*" Children who are more exposed to a reasonable level of risk may grow up more quickly and be more ready to get on with life than the child who has always experienced an adult ready to protect them. Of course, this is a matter of balance, the child who experiences too little care may be just as disadvantaged as the child who is overprotected. However, tweens need to experiment and they need to make mistakes. There is no point in trying to rule out their doing silly or even dangerous things or their getting hurt. At such times you have to be, in Shakespeare's words, "… *a candle holder and look on* …" (an observer who sheds light). Balance this thought with the knowledge that parents are allowed to make mistakes. "*We serve them most when we fail them,*" said Winnicott of his patients. And this is also true of parenting for it is when you make mistakes that you and your tween are forced to examine and re-evaluate what is going on between you.

Keeping a head in school

six

"Learning about something is essentially learning about ourselves."

(Coren)

School is your child's first significant contact with the world outside home and the first main influence on them after home. It is the first place they are likely to experience values and opinions which differ significantly from those you have been teaching them. Home and school are always together in a child's mind: not only are they balancing the differences in values and opinions but at a deep level all children are concerned about what is happening to their parents whilst they are at school. That said, young tweens will feel they are experts on school, they've been going for a long time and it is a familiar world. You are also likely to think of yourself as an expert on your young tween's school, you may even still be a daily visitor, you will know all the teachers and most of the children and probably many of the parents. A huge change is about to take place.

In Chapter 1 we thought about how sexual curiosity goes underground in the middle years of childhood. On the whole, nine and ten year olds enjoy school because younger tweens are curious about the outside world. School and learning will become a focus for their curiosity and an exciting resource for discovery; they can explore the world from the safety of the classroom. They may throw themselves at school enthusiastically, eager to learn not only facts but also about morals, rules, social and environmental issues. This is also a time of solid friendships. All in all, by this age school is a habit but it is a habit which is about to become serious.

School is serious for older tweens because the scene is very different. They are preparing for, or experiencing, one of the biggest changes in childhood, the transition from the primary to the secondary school just at the time huge changes are taking place in their bodies. Older tweens are returning to being preoccupied with their own bodies and what is going on inside them; they are curious about what kind of teenager they will be and may be ambivalent about many of their models. As they are thinking about how they will cope in the independent world outside, school may come to symbolize that outside world and be a place to focus and to negotiate their anxieties and ambivalence. So in this sense, the transition from primary to secondary school is a symbol of the tween years, i.e., the transition from childhood to teenage. How well your tween is coping with school may well be a barometer of how well they are coping with the onset of puberty. (We need to hold in mind that some tweens will be bursting with the wish to be older and can't become teenagers fast enough, whilst others may be more cautious and wish to stay a child for longer, although many tweens will fluctuate between those two positions.)

Tweens are becoming aware of differences. They are not only learning new facts, views and opinions; they are also discovering how social differences such as family income can affect them, illustrated in Britain by their becoming aware of the two kinds of school on offer – the State System and the Public (private) System. Some may take this as an ordinary part of everyday life. Others may become hostile and defensive in their belief that public school children are all "posh and snobs". In turn, state school children may be seen as "rough and aggressive". Again, school acts as a symbol for this wrestle with comparisons.

Transition to secondary school

Colleen was describing vividly how going to secondary school marked the end of an era for her. From the comforting feeling of knowing and being known by everyone in her primary school she was beginning to feel frighteningly anonymous in this large new institution. She missed the security of having one familiar teacher for the whole day and lived in fear of "ending up in the wrong room". She struggled to remember the teachers' names declaring,

"*They've got names but no faces ...*" The size, the noise and above all the strangeness of the senior school can feel overwhelming. The transition from primary to senior school reminds tweens of the first time they left home, i.e., the day they started primary school. Each transitional stage in growing up will remind your child of their experiences of a previous transition, and all transitions are prepared for with echoes of previous ones. Their memories of that day, their excitement and their trepidation, will echo with a terrifying intensity as they also realize that at the end of secondary school they may be leaving home for good.

From major to minor ...

They will have been seniors in their primary school, some will have had positions of responsibility such as being a prefect. At the senior school, they are the most junior. The older children may seem much older, much bigger and much wiser. The changes in tweens' bodies which may have been masked by the security of the primary school become highlighted so that they arrive in this new place feeling clumsy, moody and self-conscious. They may be accompanied by friends from the old school but will also have to negotiate making new friends and, possibly, in a much wider social circle. Some tweens may have to think about cross-cultural and cross-racial friendships for the first time. Differences such as these all tap in to the question a tween is asking themselves, "Where do I fit in?"

"... and there is just so much to remember ... I have this mega timetable and I have to find the right room and remember the teacher's name and have the right books ... and my bag gets real heavy ... I hope you're listening because I have to talk about this to anyone who will listen ... it's really serious."

eleven-year-old
Colleen

How are you coping at secondary school?

It is not only the children who experience a huge change as they move from primary to secondary school – so do you, the parents. Senior school may symbolize your tween's increasing need for a private life. You are likely to be less involved with the physical building of your child's school, you may even feel unsure how welcome you are to visit.

"I don't even know my way round the building ... let alone any of the teachers."

mother of
eleven year old

You will have noticed a change in the way your youngster involves you in their life at school. On one hand they may appear very teenage, keeping school life as private as possible. Then suddenly you may get surprise bulletins about how they are managing. They may become quite child-like in needing help with a project or a particular piece of homework or a crisis with friends. They may suddenly begin talking about a piece of academic work as a way of introducing a crisis. When it comes to school, as with so many other things, tweens want to have it both ways with patches of teenage and patches of very young behaviour.

Until children go to school parents may, to a large extent, control what they learn; you could teach the views and opinions you value, you could censor TV programmes, books, films, etc. It is relatively easy in the early years to persuade your child to your point of view because, most of all, your child wants to please you. Once at school, your child is exposed to a whole range of experiences and opinions, including those of the state, the teachers and their peers. This is true at primary school level, but it is even more true at secondary school level and this is a time when you may begin to feel panicky about your diminishing influence over your child. You are likely to have decided views on how you wish to see your child's mind develop and these views may or may not be consistent with some of the views being taught. Parents and teachers can easily get into unconscious rivalry which can leave parents feeling, as one father said, "*After all, it is a battle for our children's minds.*" Your attitude to your youngster's schooling is going to be coloured by how you feel about them growing up and losing some of your influence over them.

"Who decides what my child shall learn?"

Managing the transition

- Don't presume your tween knows what to expect!

"How can I ensure that my eleven year old's transfer to secondary school goes smoothly?"

This is a major trauma for most tweens, both physically and symbolically. They know something enormous is happening, but they don't know what it is and, symbolically, the transition to senior school is often more powerful than a youngster can understand.

- This is an important time for listening and talking.
  It may seem obvious, but an important place to begin is the beginning – explain to them, as far as you know, how they will spend their first day and how the general running of the school is going to be different.
- Tell them how it was for you ...
  Tweens often feel they have a monopoly on angst. Tell them about your experience of going to secondary school, how you felt, what was fun, what you found difficult, and what helped you to negotiate that difficulty.
- Listen to them ...
  The first weeks may be full of moans. Moaning is a tween's way of expressing bewilderment. They may revert to "childish" behaviour as a way of coping with stress and anxiety. Resist the temptation to tell them to "grow up" and allow for the fact that in a transition, we are allowed to go backwards as well as forwards.
- Celebrate them!

What is school for the tween?

Parents and teachers are likely to share a common view on the purpose of school. Children attend school to increase their knowledge on a range of topics, to then be examined on what they have learned in order to gain qualifications for a "good job" so that they may live a successful life independently. (And every parent will have a different idea of what a successful life is for their child!) School is also meant to provide children with an opportunity to practise and extend their social skills. For you, "doing well" in school may mean your child succeeding in both these topics. Your tween may experience this as a complex demand. In order to learn we have to admit there is something we don't know. We also have to admit that we are dependent on someone else to teach us. Tweens are becoming ambivalent about needing adults; they are practising being independent and self-sufficient and having to study and learn tells them that they are not, they still need other people. Psychotherapist, Michael Eigen, has talked about children having "a different curriculum" to that of the school. This raises the question that if studying is about curiosity, looking and finding out, then what are tweens wanting to find out about? They may be ambivalent about studying because *their* curriculum – what it is like to be a teenager – is not on the school curriculum, although of course, they are suddenly exposed to a world made up entirely of teenagers in all sorts of shapes, sizes and with differing ways of behaving – a fact which may increase their confusion and ambivalence.

The tween years are a time when children begin to wonder about what they want to learn. They are becoming aware of who they are and what they do and do not like and consequently,

"My twelve-year-old daughter will only work at subjects she likes …"

what they do and do not want to study. Consciously, they may be thinking, "I am better at mathematics than I am at English." Unconsciously, they are beginning to have a sense of where their interests lie, i.e., who they are. It is important that parents recognize and validate these emerging identities and this will mean taking seriously comments like, "I know I'm good at French but I don't like it and I don't want to do it any more." Such a comment may say more about what your youngster is feeling about their identity than about studying.

School symbolizes adult demands

School forms a large slice of a tween's life and is the first place in the outside world they can claim as private. However, as tweens are not teenagers school life cannot be completely separate and private from other places in their lives. The school is a potent symbol for this age group and we are now going to think about some common difficulties that can arise because of the symbolic nature of school. For a tween school may symbolize adults' demands and expectations:

- To study and do homework
- To collaborate with others in a community spirit
- To attend school regularly

The demand to study and do homework

This generation of children are more tested and under more academic pressure than any before. Schools may be kinder places than they were for past generations but children feel under just as much pressure to learn. Many small children are worryingly aware of this pressure but, as public exams become clear on the horizon, in the tween years the need to succeed becomes a serious reality. Let us think first of the paramount demand, the demand that your child learns to read.

The importance of being able to read

Amongst my most treasured possessions is a small card written by a nine year old, saying simply, "*Thank you for teaching me to read.*" Learning to read seals the fate of a child's academic future. All further study depends upon it. Becoming self-reliant, finding our own way in the world, is also dependent upon it. By seven or eight, most children have mastered the skill and so

"Now I can read, I'm a person."
ten-year-old girl

the tween who cannot read is seriously handicapped – and not only in their ability to learn. Their self-esteem and general curiosity may suffer. Reading provides children with a fascinating entry to the wider world and in so doing stimulates their curiosity and energizes them to explore. A non-reader may stop trying to learn, feeling it is better not to be curious than to face the struggles involved in finding out. They may be seen as the class "geek", unable to keep up with their peers. Or they may be "adopted" by classmates, who help them along in a "babying" kind of way so the non-reader has even less chance of becoming self-reliant. In Britain there is a practice in senior schools of putting all the "special needs" children in one class. The idea is that these special classes are smaller thus allowing more individual attention and the children to learn at their own pace. But many non-readers, not surprisingly, are disruptive and so a tween's struggle to learn may be exacerbated by rowdy or disturbing behaviour going on around him. Perhaps the greatest handicap for a nine year old who cannot read is that they miss out on a part of the "magic thinking" in childhood. Learning to read is often a moment when a child believes that they have shed their ignorance and are now equal to the grown-ups. It can feel a magical, powerful skill that temporarily places the child in the adults' world of "knowing everything". The child who misses out on that stage may fear that they are destined to be ignorant and hopeless for ever.

Homework

William sat brooding in my consulting room, only raising his eyes to flash me a look of utter contempt if I posed a direct question. His embarrassed parents were eager to persuade me there was "something wrong" with him, such as dyslexia. He had enjoyed his primary school years, during which he had been interested in a wide range of topics and had worked hard to achieve his good results. Both his parents were teachers and homework had been a family time, his parents helping William as necessary whilst doing their marking and lesson preparation. After a few weeks at senior school all this had changed; homework had become a battleground. His parents understood when William decided to study alone in his bedroom rather than with them, but they were frustrated when their frequent checks on him realized their worst fears, he was actually doing anything but his homework alone his bedroom! By the end of his second term, not only was his academic performance well behind, but his teachers had written to his parents about both his attitude and the fact that he was not handing in his homework.

"How can we make our twelve-year-old son study?"
William's father

We've already thought about tweens living in two worlds in two senses. They live in the world of childhood and the world of teenagers. They also live in two physical worlds; the private world of home which is (hopefully) safe, secure and free, and the private world of school which may not feel as safe, secure and free. (We must remember too, as I said earlier, they are also living in *their own world*, they are not just tweens!) Then they are given *homework* which is not about home but about school. When tweens are asked to "settle down and do your homework", unconsciously they may feel confusion over who they can be at that moment, i.e., am I now the person I am at home or am I the person I am at school?

Homework can feel invasive. It brings school into home and makes links between home and school which may be difficult for a tween to negotiate. Doing homework, i.e., school work, in a home space is using home for a different purpose and that can feel very powerful for a tween. Many youngsters nowadays do their home-work in their bedrooms, giving the bedroom a very different feel to the bedroom of a child with all its associations of sleep, tranquillity, play and bedtime stories. So it is worth wondering what the demand for homework symbolizes for a tween: what do they think the demand for homework is a demand for?

It is an endless source of fascination to me how homework monopolizes parents' time and energy much more than it does a tween's! Homework seems to be a vehicle for battles and nothing seems to cause as many frequent rows in the home. When I asked William's parents why they felt they had to police his homework, his mother replied, "*He would never finish it if we didn't ...*" That may be true, but there are times when we have to wonder about whether the end justifies the means. William's parents had stepped over the fine line between being available to support William generally as he did his homework, by answering questions or providing necessary materials such as paper and pencil, and creating anxiety and attention around doing homework. The more a tween realizes how important homework is to their parents, then the more likely they are to make an issue about doing it. If someone is looking for a fight, then it might be best not to give them a topic on a plate! I have always been of the opinion that homework is a matter between the child and their teachers. Parents can be supportive and encouraging but homework should not dominate every evening (and in some homes the whole weekend) of family life. If homework isn't done, then you might do best to inform the teacher that the homework has not been completed and arrange for them to take the appropriate action. Teachers may expect parents to ensure homework is completed and so you may have to have a delicate and tactful conversation!

Helping with homework

- Provide a supportive and facilitating environment for your tween to study. This will probably mean a quiet space, without distractions. Music in the background very quickly merges into a tween's foreground! Encourage your tween to do their homework at a regular time, probably before they do anything else once they get home from school. Give a clear message, both spoken and by the way you behave, that you expect the homework to be done as well as possible and on time.
- Remember, your relationship with your children's homework is only just beginning. Whilst it is important to take an active interest in homework, you also need to be led by them, to pick up

their hints about how *they want you* to help them. This is different from intruding or criticizing. Intruding sometimes takes the form of parents actually doing the homework for the tween or improving on the tween's efforts so that they will get a better mark. Criticizing will probably lead to rows. It may be better to let your tween know that you think the finished product is not of a good enough standard and offer ways in which they can improve it. If they don't, then again, it is something you can suggest the teacher manages. If your tween feels you are genuinely interested in their project, and you are able to help them expand their knowledge on it in lively ways, then they may not be so tempted to see homework as an opportunity to fight.

- Do not be afraid to approach your school if you think their homework load is excessive, especially with younger tweens. Homework can give the impression that school is more important than home.
- Accept that your tween is going to have strong attitudes towards homework. Be aware if they are too keen to do homework or too resistant to doing homework. Both attitudes are a communication.

Exam stress

Exams are a potent symbol for us all, mainly because they remind us about "pecking order". Tweens are becoming preoccupied with how they fit in with their peers; exams they often fear tell them exactly where they fit in! Exams are also an emotional experience because when we sit an exam, "*We invite someone to sit in judgement of us*" (Coren). An adopted tween walked out of his first set of exams panic stricken; deep down he felt he had already failed a crucial, metaphorical test and this was why his birth mother had had him adopted. A tween may feel that by sitting an exam they are letting someone else define who they are, just at a time when they are struggling to develop their own self-image.

"How can I help our eleven year old with exam stress ... she just seems to fall apart ... we tell her to just do her best ..."
Pamela's mother

So tweens often experience exams as stressful but Pamela's parents need to think about their part in her exam stress. How much pressure are they putting on her to succeed and what does "doing your best" mean? Maybe Pamela fears that to her parents, "doing her best" means passing the exam and so pleasing them. "*A lot hangs on this exam ...*" parents often say to try and encourage a tween to take revision seriously. One ten year old vomited (through stress?) in an exam and as he was led from the room sobbed anxiously, "*... but I won't get a good job ...*" Parents have to find a balance between encouraging a youngster to want to do their best without (unintentionally) making them fear that the exam is an all or nothing experience.

Parents always feel they should know best for their children and sometimes this may make you act with more conviction than you feel. At no time are parents more driven to give children the gift of their perceptions on what makes a good life than at the onset of puberty! And this can be difficult because parents and tweens may have very different topics at the forefront of their minds. You are stressing the importance of a good education, good exam results and of being able to "get a good job". Your tween, on the other hand, may be thinking that what is most important is having fun. Exams and a good job are likely to be much lower down their list of priorities than having the latest CD or designer jeans. If you are lucky and your tween's peer group are conscientious about school work, then you may not encounter too many problems.

> "The trouble is he doesn't know when to stop ... when to draw the line ... he's got national exams round the corner ... how can I convince him that nothing should divert him at the moment ...?"

Eva failed the entrance exam to her chosen school, causing a hiatus of distress in her family. Eva felt bad about it; she felt she had not only failed the exam, she had also failed everyone. She began to hate herself – initially for the distress she had caused to her family, and gradually "for everything about me". Eating disorders can arise out of the sense of self-loathing. Our self-esteem, how much we consider ourselves to be like-able and lovable, is inextricably bound up with how we feel other people see us. Whilst a tween doesn't have to be competitive and a perfectionist to develop an eating disorder – it helps! It is a hard task for parents to find just the right balance

> "We get lots of homework every evening ... it's really awful ... I can't hack this for the next seven years."
> *eleven-year-old Eva*

between motivating a child to succeed and accidentally conveying to the child that they are only lovable *if they succeed.* This is a particular issue in homes where education is highly valued and success and achievements are considered the norm. In Eva's mind, failing the exam was the equivalent to failing to be loved. And most worryingly, she clearly hated her mother. Self-loathing can very quickly turn into loathing other people. Eva was openly hating her mother as a way of expressing how she unconsciously hated herself. We will talk more about eating disorders in Chapter 8.

Managing exam stress

- The key to managing exam stress lies in thinking about the feelings and fantasies around examinations.
  Look deep inside yourself and ask what you really feel about your youngster failing. Whatever you say to your youngster you are also going to transmit those feelings. If necessary, you can say something like, "*Of course, we really want you to pass, but in a way that's our problem!*"
- Reassure them that this is not an exam on the whole of them or on them as a person, it's an examination of a small part of their knowledge. Passing the exam won't make them a better person, it might just enhance their life.

Poor attainments and coping with disappointments

This is really a question about helping Paolo to manage disappointment and frustration. In Chapter 4 we talked about the close link between disappointment and your tween's self-esteem. Paolo had an image of himself as among the brightest in the class. Like many tweens, when he moved to secondary school he found himself in a larger class with a higher proportion of children as able, and more able than himself. His image of himself at primary school was that he was clever and, as being clever was important, he was valued. This is a very common experience for tweens. Most feel surprised and disappointed, if not put out and angry, but Paolo was "devastated". Why should that be?

"Our twelve-year-old son has been devastated by his exam results. He has always been among the top of the class, now he feels he's dumb."

Paulo's mother

Sometimes, children like Paolo may feel defined by one aspect of their personality. Paolo was so busy thinking of himself as clever that he never gave much thought to what else he might be! By the tween years, he saw himself as *solely* clever, there was no more to his story. When his cleverness was challenged by these new exam results, he felt devastated, literally "wiped out". If he wasn't clever, what was he? Paolo needed help and encouragement to think about other aspects of his personality. At the same time as acknowledging how disappointed he was with his exam results, his parents talked to him about other qualities they admired in him. They also made a conscious effort to remind him of these qualities and how they were valued during everyday living. So, for example, at a relevant moment they might say things like, "We've always loved your sense of humour," or "We've always thought you were such a kind person."

Rudeness to teachers

Tweens share the common task of coping with their passions about their parents and also the need to separate from them. Flora's mother had left home when Flora was four years old. Her father managed to work from home as he brought her up – a task to which he had devoted himself until she went to boarding school. At the end of her first term away, Flora had been furious to discover that her father had had a series of casual dates during the term. However, after her initial surprise and protest, she had fallen back into her usual happy relationship with him – but she then developed a burning hatred for her housemistress!

School is a good place for tweens to displace difficulties in the family. Sometimes tweens will focus the intense feelings – be it rivalry, anger or desire – they feel for their parents onto other authority figures. When Flora was delivering a particular tirade of abuse about her housemistress one day, I said to her,

"My eleven year old is disruptive and difficult at school ... she's no trouble at home ... she seems to have it in for her housemistress in particular ... what's going on?"

Flora's father

"*Maybe there are some kinds of women you just don't like.*"

"*I like women,*" she replied angrily, "*I just don't like women round my dad.*"

By keeping her focus of hatred on the housemistress, Flora was protecting her father from her own rage. Sometimes, tweens who are particularly difficult at school are working out with their teachers what they feel they cannot work out with their parents. Deep inside herself, Flora did not want to risk hating her only parent.

The demand for social collaboration and a community spirit

The middle years of childhood are, give or take the odd dog and cat fight, a time of settled friendships. Groups form around a common interest or activity and "best friends" are made. Indeed, we should be concerned about a child of eight or nine who has not made a special, if not a best friend. Most children are able to mix with other children at this age, albeit with varying degrees of ease and confidence. However, it is not unusual at the onset of the tween years for a youngster to experience difficulties in their seemingly solid friendships. This may be specially true and normal with the transfer to the senior school. Many tweens feel uncertain and different as they struggle to make new friends in this different setting. In Chapter 1 we looked at how tweens use jokes and teasing as a way of relating to each other. Sadly, teasing can very quickly cross the fine line into bullying. Teasing is meant to be fun, two-way banter which is not intended to hurt.

Bullying and excessive peer pressure

"My eleven year old has had the same group of friends since eight years old. Recently, they seemed to have turned on her and she's feeling lonely and isolated. How can we help without making the problem worse?"

Jane's mother

Jane had always been teased; she had always been tall for her age and also had a distinguishing mop of bright red hair. She had managed this with good humour, mainly because she was a bright, quick witted girl, good at repartee, and also because her height made her a star in her position as "shooter" in the netball team. Lately, however, this teasing had taken a more aggressive form and her parents were appropriately calling it bullying.

Bullying has many faces but always involves the strong picking on the weak or a group picking on an individual. Jane's friends were now excluding her, not entirely but enough to make her unhappy. Giggling and whispering would stop as she approached a group. She felt she was always on the "outside of a secret". Of course, in the new school she was no longer playing in the netball team and the nicknames became more biting. She began to stoop in an attempt to disguise her height and was desperate to change her hair colour.

Understanding bullying

Bullying is very interesting. No other childhood behaviour makes adults as angry and yet many adults bully all the time. We seem to be ambivalent about bullying. We pass laws to prevent bullying in the workplace and yet people are often congratulated for bullying at work, for example, "I slapped her into place". And a lot of bullying can go on in families but it isn't called bullying, it's called discipline. So what is the difference between charming, persuading, coercing and bullying? Charming has been described as "getting someone to say yes before they've heard the question." But charm can easily cross the line into coercion, coercion can easily become bullying. Bullying goes against the basic human instinct to protect the weak and vulnerable and yet it also seems to be a fundamental human problem having its roots in childhood. So how can we understand the reasons for Jane being bullied?

First of all we need to remember that symptoms are a tool kit for helping us to deal with aspects of life which are new or we find difficult to manage. Symptoms are always likely to appear at transitions when we are being asked to adapt to something new. Parents tend to call children's symptoms "problems" so that they can help to solve them, because no one likes to see a child unhappy, e.g. Jane had the *problem* of being bullied.

Jane's friends were in a group of tween girls who were age appropriately struggling with issues of confidence and self-esteem. They all wanted to be popular, they all wanted to be "cool and in the group!" And they all had worries and anxieties about being excluded and unpopular. The heart of bullying lies in a power/domination relationship. At the deepest level, these girls dreaded feeling afraid, alone or isolated. By trying to isolate Jane, they were making her the "afraid-alone-isolated one", leaving them free to be "cool". Bullying can be a way of passing on our pain to someone else in an attempt to feel strong and powerful rather than vulnerable.

The relationship between bully and victim is a passionate one. The bully and victim are connected to each other – two sides of the same coin. We can think of bullying as friendship that can't find a way of making itself work. Initially, Jane had made an impact on her new classmates. She was a striking girl in many ways and for a while she drew people to her. Of course, she was pleased, but had not bargained on the rivalry this might cause with her original group. As they began to exclude her, the new girls found themselves not knowing how to be friends with Jane and "cool in the group". They joined in the bullying because, paradoxically, they were attracted to Jane but didn't know how to be close to her. Had they not wanted to be her friend, they may have taken a more neutral position.

Jane's original friends were coming from a different position. Jealous of the attention she was getting, they tried to bully her into being less appealing. In this sense, bullying can be thought of as an extreme form of persuasion. Adults do it all the time, raising their voice, or thumping a desk. Tweens who bully may need help in finding more appropriate ways to persuade other people to their point of view.

Understanding the victim

This may sound tough, but Jane did not have to be a victim if she didn't want to be one. What differentiates a forceful person from a bullying person is the way the victim responds. If the intended victim can stand firm against a bullying demand, rather than cower or give in, this prevents the other person from being a bully. So why are some youngsters more bullied than others? Unconsciously, some children try to be an irritant to others – "Mind you, she asks for it," is often the desperate last phrase in any adult's description of the frequently bullied tween. This boy preferred to feel disliked by other children to feeling unnoticed on the fringe of a group. But, of course, both feelings left him unhappy. In a similar way, although there was no doubt Jane was deeply unhappy at the way her friends were treating her, in a perverse sense, she was also the focus of their attention.

> "When they bully me, they know I've got a life, I'm not a no one."
>
> *eleven-year-old victim*

Youngsters who are vulnerable and in someway different … smaller, fatter, thinner than others or wearing spectacles, a tooth brace, or having a speech impediment are likely to be targeted by bullies. These youngsters may not invite bullying but are picked on for an attribute which other youngsters may see as a weakness. The most painful aspect here is that the tween is also likely to construe their "difference" as a weakness and so a vicious circle is begun. So how could Jane's parents help her?

Helping the victim

- Jane's parents' initial reaction was to talk to her teachers about Jane's difficulties at school even though they were afraid that she might then be accused of telling tales on other children.
- They encouraged Jane to talk about being bullied and not to feel ashamed of it. They had been stressing to her that it was not her fault that she was being bullied.
- Their acceptance and reassurance made a good platform for them to help Jane to think about her part in the bully/victim relationship. Without blaming her, they showed gentle and mild curiosity in her predicament asking her, "*We wonder what it is about you that makes your friends turn on you?*"

They were very surprised when Jane replied, "*Well I can be a bit bossy.*" They had never thought of her as a bossy child. She had always been in the centre of a group and was certainly a leader rather than a follower, but here was Jane herself beginning to think about possible ways in which other youngsters may construe her behaviour. They were able to help her to express her good ideas a little less forcefully within the group. They also took every opportunity to praise and encourage her on both her appearance and her achievements.

- If your tween is being bullied, or becomes a bully, use this as an opportunity to think about how you as parents are getting on together. Tweens' relationships with friends are likely to be a copy of how they see their parents' relationship. They are astute observers in this matter. Sometimes bullying can be a tween's way of showing parents what they are doing to each other.

Many youngsters like Jane will suffer bullying in silence. No one wants to feel different, odd or disliked. Tweens may put up with bullying for fear that if they admit to being bullied, they are also admitting to being all these things. Such a youngster is likely to suffer a further loss of self-esteem and confidence and even become depressed.

Helping the bully

No youngster should ever be allowed to bully another. As adults, we may not be able to prevent bullying but it is our responsibility to create an environment in which bullying is not encouraged and not tolerated. However, we should always be as worried about the bully as the victim. Winnicott talks of "the nuisance value of symptoms". The tween who is bullying is asking adults to take them seriously and is drawing attention to their unhappiness. A bully is always relieved when they are prevented from bullying.

"... and you mean we should be just as worried about her friends ...?"
Jane's father

If your tween is bullying:

- You will have to point out to them, kindly but firmly, that what they are doing will not be tolerated. It will not be tolerated because it is not fair to their victims, but also because it is not getting them what they want. Bullying simply isn't working for them.
- You can help to highlight the relationship between a bully and a victim by suggesting to your tween that they notice they have very strong feelings about their victim.
- You can help them to think about their victim – what do they like about their victim? What do they think the victim likes about them? This is different to making the bully feel guilty and bad with angry exhortations such as, "How would you like it?"

Bullying is always a sign that someone is feeling powerless, confused and bullied themselves. Maybe your bullying tween won't feel able to talk to you about what is troubling them. In this case, you can enlist the help of a relative or family friend, but if the bullying continues and your youngster seems seriously unhappy, then it is probably advisable to seek some professional help.

The demand for regular attendance

We have already thought about how feeling ambivalent can affect our thinking. Some tweens find it difficult to do anything with regularity or routine; they may tidy their room one week but seem totally incapable of doing so every week. Doing things regularly involves commitment and commitment means we have made a choice. No child chooses to go to school and when they go to school there is a sense in which they lose something of family life. In families, people tend to adapt to each other's idiosyncrasies; this is less likely in school where a child is being organized by something other than the family and is expected to conform. In this sense, school is bound to be less sensitive to a child's individuality and your youngster may begin to have a feeling that they are becoming more anonymous in the world. Tweens are in a state of "choosing", shall I be like this or shall I be like that? For some youngsters the demand to attend school regularly feels as though they are being commanded to abandon their freedom to choose. Others may simply find the demands of school too much.

Truancy

Casper's parents were right to be concerned. Truanting from school is worrying because youngsters are at risk if they are wandering the streets. But Casper had been returning home for the day which may make us think about what he was trying to communicate by truanting. "*Sometimes it all feels too much and I just can't hack it,*" he said dropping his head into his hands. The depth of his feelings was apparent, but he was unable to describe the "it" that was "too much". An isolated patch of truanting is no more a sign that a tween is delinquent than is, say, a tween missing one or two meals a sign that they are anorexic. Sometimes tweens feel overwhelmed by the myriad of emotions they are experiencing and decide that "he who fights and runs away lives to fight another day". They are literally fleeing the fear.

> "Our twelve year old has become delinquent. We have discovered that he was truanting from school for the whole of last week. He was pretending to go to school but returning home for the day. How can we stop this?"
>
> *Casper's parents*

Managing truancy

Casper's parents were at risk of construing his behaviour as teenage behaviour. For teenagers outright rebellion can be a way of life. Tweens may drive you to distraction as they push and pull their way to independence but they are unlikely to live in a permanent state of defiance. They may argue about how, when and where they will go to school, what they will wear and how they will behave at school but on the whole their rebellions are more talked about than acted upon. Had Casper's truancy been combined with other persistent worrying behaviours, such as running away from home or staying out all night, then it could be important for his parents to seek professional help. As it was, Casper was much more in need of his parents' compassion and understanding than he was anything else. By truanting, he was trying to tell his parents there was something he couldn't face, something that was overwhelming him. It could have been bullying, or academic pressure, or a myriad of things, but in his case it was simply the process of puberty that felt so unmanageable. In order to help him, Casper's parents had to first of all contain their shock and anger.

They also had to suspend their criticism of Casper. They were quick to accept that they felt criticized as parents by his truanting! Surely, if they were good enough parents, then their son wouldn't truant? So the feeling that there was "something unmanageable" was being compounded in the family. Once they were able to think about ways of helping Casper talk about his troubles, an atmosphere of "this is difficult but it can be managed" began to develop in the home. Casper's father helped a great deal by spending time with Casper and talking to him about the difficulties he had experienced during his early teenage years.

Tweens and school rules

Tweens are able to think about the nature of a rule and school rules and these are an interesting illustration of how they live in two worlds. In Chapter 5 we thought about the importance of rules for nine and ten year olds. As your youngster reaches the later tween years you may begin to loosen the rules and boundaries, e.g., instead of driving them to school, you may let them go alone on public transport. By doing so, you are giving them the message "you are growing up". Then they will arrive in the world of school governed by rules and boundaries. School may give youngsters a mixed message; on one hand the institution is insisting that they grow up and carry responsibility, on the other, a myriad of rules may imply that they are not capable of doing either. The tween may be left with a confusion around the issue of rules and boundaries.

Elizabeth was indeed the bane of her teachers' lives! "She thinks she's different, she thinks rules are for other people not for her," complained one and it certainly did seem as though Elizabeth felt rules were made to be broken. Sometimes tweens find out about rules and boundaries by breaking them. Both Elizabeth's parents had had very strict upbringings. From an early age they experienced the word "no" as aggressive, as withholding something from someone. They were determined that Elizabeth would have more freedom and choice as a child than they had had. They admitted to a *laissez-faire* attitude to parenting. Elizabeth had been brought up with few rules and boundaries and her parents were proud that if Elizabeth could argue coherently against a rule or boundary she would be likely to have her way. This may have worked well for Elizabeth at home but it was not working well for her at school. Rules and boundaries in school are not there to be discussed or negotiated and Elizabeth had had little practice at rule breaking. How do you learn *not* to break the rules when there are no rules? Elizabeth's problem at school was not so much that she was rebellious and difficult but more that she really didn't understand a rule was a rule until she had broken it. We can think of her as a girl unsure of her own perimeters. In breaking rules, "doing as she likes", as the school described it, she was trying to discover how far she could go in her treatment of the world and, paradoxically, the limits that defined her as a person. Breaking rules at school was actually working well for Elizabeth in the sense that she was slowly developing a sense of the meaning of boundaries but, of course, in other ways it was causing her huge problems.

> "Our eleven-year-old daughter, Elizabeth, constantly breaks school rules ... punishment seems to make no difference ... what can we do?"

Twelve-year-old Ben was in a not dissimilar position. His parents considered themselves to be trendy and easy going, well in tune with their tween children. By allowing under age drinking, late hours and over age movies they felt they were keeping the channels of communication open between them and their youngsters. But Ben saw it differently. He was currently in trouble at school for disruptive behaviour and arguing with the

> "We don't understand it, they say he argues and defies his teachers but we find him very compliant, he rarely pushes the boundaries at home."
>
> *Ben's parents*

teachers. However, his parents described him as a model child, the easiest of their three children. Ben's parents were also slightly hurt and puzzled as Ben had not confided his difficulties and unhappiness at school in them and they first knew of it when they were called to a meeting with the year tutor and the school counsellor. We came to understand that the struggles and fights Ben was having at school with his teachers were replacing those that he should have been having with his parents in order to try and establish his independence and identity. As he said, "*There's no point in arguing with them* [his parents] … *they just agree with me or say you can do it.*"

One can only sympathize with Sasha's mother. At twelve years old Sasha had decided to practise developing her emerging identity by going "Goth". This involved her and her friends not only wearing solely black, but dyeing their hair black and, whenever possible, wearing heavy black and white make-up – in complete flagrance of their school rules. Her mother explained her main worry was that if Sasha was expelled from school, which was increasingly likely then, "*She would be throwing away her future,*" as there was no school of a similar high academic standard in the area. Sasha's response was that, "*Everyone's doing it the same and they can't expel us all.*" Sasha's mother could only make Sasha well aware of her views on her wearing make-up to school. She shared her anxieties with the teachers and assured them that she would support them in whatever decision they decided to take over Sasha's behaviour. It was interesting that once Sasha's mother left the arguments to her teachers, Sasha quickly reduced the amount of make-up she was wearing to school!

> "My twelve-year-old daughter is deliberately infringing school rules by wearing make-up to school … how can I stop her?"
> *Sasha's mother*

What kind of parent is the school?

Rock may be sharing Flora's issue of transferring feelings about his parents onto his teachers. Tweens may confuse pleasing parents with pleasing all authority figures. In a sense, school as an institution becomes a parent in the tween's mind. Rock's parents had very high expectations of him from the time he was born. He was an only child who spent a good deal of time mixing with adults, and his parents demanded a high standard of behaviour and manners.

Their well meaning attempts to "bring him up properly" made him feel they were strict, critical and demanding. He took this image of adults into school with him. In primary school he had been compliant and tried hard to please his teachers. He worked hard and was successful. On moving to secondary school two changes occurred. Firstly, he found the work much more difficult and was less successful. His parents knew he was anxious about coping academically. Also, as a tween, he was beginning to feel constrained and irritated by his parents' rules. Whilst it may have been appropriate for them to correct his behaviour in public when he was very small, as a tween this had become humiliating.

> "We have always taught our eleven-year-old son to be respectful towards adults. Since he went to secondary school he has become derisory about his teachers, referring to them as 'gay', 'wack', 'stupid' and 'incompetent at their work'. Why does he do this and how can we stop him?"
>
> *Rock's father*

We can think of Rock as experiencing adults as powerful, even dangerously powerful. He was making a mockery of his teachers so that he wasn't humiliated, i.e., if adults were incompetent they were not so dangerously powerful. Also, in a way, Rock was living a reversal in the sense that he felt mocked and humiliated and he tried to avoid those feelings by becoming the one who was doing the mocking. Rock and his parents needed help to work out what it was that Rock felt he could be humiliated for, and his parents began to realize that they were urging Rock to be successful as a way of living their unlived lives. They had been disappointed and frustrated by both their lack of opportunity and their lack of success. They had been trying to do their very best for Rock and it was sad that it had resulted in their being perceived by him as critical and demanding parents whom he couldn't please.

At any stage in your child's development, it is worth asking yourself what kind of "parent" is your child's school for them. How they feel about their school, how they talk about their teachers may reflect the contrast they experience between adults who are parenting and adults who are teaching. Equally, it may reflect how they experience aspects of your parenting. For example, a youngster saying, "My teachers are too strict," may be highlighting the difference between home, where there is a flexibility in rules and boundaries, and school which demands a uniform response. Or they may be saying that their teachers are too strict in the same way as they are finding their parents rigid and inflexible. When your children are talking about school you may find it helpful to think what it is they may be saying about you and what they may be wanting from you.

Just looking? ...
just longing? ...
Starting sexual relationships

seven

"... Sigh'd and look'd, and sigh'd again."
(John Dryden from Alexander's Feast)

There are no experts on sex. This is disappointing for parents as "getting it right on sex" is often top of their worry list with this age group. Maybe this is because, as you watch your youngster take their first steps into the heady experience of boy/girl relationships, you cannot but remember how it was for you. Inevitably, your own experience is going to colour both your attitude and your desire to influence and mould your youngster's experience; and this is why, as in all areas of parenting, your best resource is the experience of other parents. Indeed, you are likely to get more "expert" opinions by sharing anxieties with other parents and discovering what they have found did or did not help than by reading this or any other book on parenting!

"His hormones have kicked in like a tidal wave ... I need some expert advice here ..."
mother of eleven-year-old boy

The reality is that no two children will develop sexually at the same rate or in the same way, any more than any two children may learn to speak at the same rate or in the same way. Our sexuality and the relationships in which we choose to express our sexuality are intensely private and personal – and idiosyncratic. So, in this sense, it is misleading to think of a norm around sexual development – it is as individual and special as a fingerprint. This is why I say there are no

"My twelve year old is showing no physical signs of puberty ... is this normal?"

149

experts on sex. In Chapter 2 we thought about common central issues but each youngster will have their own individual responses and preoccupations and their own special and unique thoughts and things to say. By twelve, many youngsters are adolescent, others may not develop physical signs until fourteen.

How much they want to say, how private your youngster wants to be about sex will depend very much on personality. Some will be open, frank, chatting about everything and sometimes trying to give you more information than you may want to hear! Others will be intensely private about themselves and their bodies. How easily you and your tween negotiate this stage will also depend very much on your personality. A very private parent may feel inhibited and awkward in the presence of a chattering tween. The parent who longs to share, discuss and guide may feel rejected and frustrated by a very private offspring. However, whether you or your tween are gabblers or reticent, we need to bear in mind that everyone has a resistance to talking about sex. It is interesting that in a society where we seem to talk *around* nothing but sex, it is still actually very difficult to talk *about sex*. Our interest and conversation centres *around* the topic, e.g., who is an item with whom? Who is being unfaithful? etc. If we add to this the fact that sex is one of the ways children separate from their parents, then the whole issue of parents and children talking about sex becomes a contradiction in terms. As one mother said, "*Maybe we need to ask ourselves what we want to pass on about sex and why do we want to talk about it?*"

"Feeling left out" seems to be par for the course in parenting tweens! Most parents hope that their children "can talk to me about anything" and sexual development is an important area you will want to share. When your children were small, you may have found it relatively easy to talk about sex, mainly because you knew that although you were giving your children the facts they were incapable of acting on their knowledge. Two six year olds may play at "being mummies and daddies" but nobody is going to get pregnant! Now you realize that your tween is on the verge of being capable of full sexual activity.

"My ten year old shies off if I try to talk about sex ... her sister was very open at this age ... am I doing something wrong?"

"... but I feel so left out ... it's so exciting, he's just joining that romantic stage, I want to watch it ... I want some of the pleasure ..."
mother of eleven-year-old boy

This may be inhibiting for you at two levels. At a thought-about level you may worry what they might do, and at an unconscious level you may feel you are intruding on a very private aspect of your tween's life. However, tweens may be more ready to share than teenagers who will regard their sex lives equally private as you may regard yours. In inviting your tween to discuss sexual matters with you, remember that it is not compulsory to accept invitations: one has the right to decline.

In a parent support group, a single father described how important he felt it was to talk openly to his daughters about petting and intercourse ... "*They've got to know what to expect and what to do ...*" Other parents challenged the explicitness of his conversations on the basis that he was risking exciting the girls to practise what they were learning. The father was quick to point out, "*There is no way they're doing anything ... they're just interested ...*" A heated discussion arose with some parents feeling that it was inappropriate for tween children to want or need such information.

"My husband and I disagree about how much detailed information my nine- and eleven-year-old daughters should be given about sex ... are there any guidelines?"

It is parents' responsibility to inform and educate children about sex. At a conscious or thought-about level we could understand this father as being straightforward and practical in giving advice but he needed to think about what he was doing at an unconscious level. By discussing sex in detail he was inviting his children to think about him having sex. There is always the risk of parents usurping their children's curiosity about sex, i.e., if parents are too explicit then they run the risk of their explanations becoming prescriptions! For example, when this father tried to explain oral sex his daughter looked slightly horrified and said, "*Do I have to do that to him?*" The father went on to say he had replied by saying, "*Yes, you jolly well do,*" because "*I need them to know what it's all about.*" It is important to go at your youngster's pace and not overwhelm them with information which, at best, may be confusing and, at worst, worrying or frightening. It can be a good idea to open conversations around a specific booklet on sexuality or health in the hope that this will invite them to ask for more information as they need it.

In Chapter 1 we thought about how tween boy/girl relationships are based on curiosity and exploration. Thinking about girls is exactly what twelve-year-old boys do! Consider this incident at a school camp. A group of twelve-year-old boys decided to invade the girls' tent after lights out. The girls responded with a typical (and seemingly essential) amount of screaming which woke the adults. The next day the boys received a public telling off and were given a letter for their parents outlining the incident and asking the parents to punish them.

"My twelve year old thinks about nothing but girls, what can I do about this?"

Some parents were outraged by the adults' behaviour. They felt the boys had been "stripped of their privacy" by being told off so publicly. "*After all,*" said one father, "*it was done as a dare, it was not sex-driven and the boys are mortified.*" The boys were bewildered, "*It was just a dare,*" said one, "*I didn't do it to get a hard on.*" These boys were enticed by the fact that they were forbidden to go into the girls' tents. They were curious, and out to excite the girls – by making them scream!

Girls are equally preoccupied with thinking about boys. Twelve-year-old Fiona was practising all week what she might wear to a party on Saturday. Each evening she came downstairs in an increasingly sexually provocative outfit for her parents to approve (or disapprove?). Her mother was becoming increasingly worried. On the day of the party, Fiona appeared in her jeans and a relatively modest sparkly top. Her mother described how, if she hadn't seen what Fiona had actually chosen to wear, she would have been extremely worried all evening. Parents' worries are likely to be far more extreme than the tween's behaviour! These stories raise interesting questions; from where will your tween learn most about sex, from romance or from pornography? And what has pornography got to do with sexuality?

"I realized that she loves experimenting with the idea, but she's not ready for anything, she doesn't want anything to happen."

Your main worry is likely to be how your tween is going to cope with sexual advances from other people. However, tweens are likely to be much more worried about coping with their own desires, i.e., how are they going to behave when they fancy someone else? Being desired is easier to manage; it may be flattering, embarrassing, welcome or unwelcome but it is a passive process. It carries an innocent "Who me?" or "I've done nothing to encourage" lack of responsibility that is clearly absent in the active process of desiring. Feeling innocent of being desired can be a cover

"How can I help my tween with fancying someone?"

story for tweens. In desire there is no innocent position but there may be a wish to be in an innocent position. You will have to help your tween to work out who and what they want and how they are going to deal with their desires, i.e., how they are going to behave when they fancy someone. They also need help to take responsibility for the effect that they have on other people. This is difficult because we can never really know how we affect other people. A twelve-year-old girl was explaining how she had gained a reputation as the "class bike" by snogging a different boy every time there was a party. "*Well*," she said, "*they were all so nice and I really didn't like to hurt their feelings by turning them down. I don't really like snogging but I did like them and I didn't want to upset anybody.*" She needed help to understand the impact other people made on her and to think about when a relationship should include sexual intimacy. (Adults do not always understand the difference between "snogging" or "necking" and prolonged kissing sessions. We tend to think they are the same thing. Not so for the tween. Kissing involves some affection and a relationship. "Necking/snogging" can happen with anyone for the sheer fun of it or for simply having the experience. Kissing is usually done in private, snogging, etc., is nearly always done illicitly and often publicly!)

This same girl's story also highlights the differing attitudes to boys' and girls' sexual behaviour. Even today parents tend to be more protective of their daughters' bodies than their sons'. We can argue a girl has potentially much more to lose from an unwanted pregnancy than a boy. But it is worth asking yourself which worries you most: the idea of someone "hitting on" your daughter or your daughter "hitting on" someone else? In one sense, girls seem more private about sex than boys who may be overtly concerned about the size of their bodies, particularly their penises. On the other hand, girls may dress and behave in a much more overtly sexually provocative way. Of course there are girls who will want to brag about their sexual exploits and there are boys who want to be very private, and it is interesting that parents of daughters often see their tweens "at the prey of boys". However, parents of sons are now worrying about the predatory nature of tween girls who seem to mature physically earlier than the boys.

In our society there is a hidden difficulty for both boys and girls about fancying someone. We live in a culture of "sugar and spice girls" whose role in life is to act as an anti-depressant for the male world. Boys are promoted as vigorous and aggressive. Tweens need to learn about all aspects of sexual relations, the tender, the loving, the aggressive, the passionate. But tweens' unconscious worries and fears give a picture of aggressive sex. How does a girl combine being "sugar and spice" with being aggressive, especially sexually aggressive? And how do boys cope with the sexually passive aspects of their nature in a culture which promotes the "thrusting male"? We cannot underestimate the influence of soaps, books, magazines and comics on this struggle. Their approach can so often leave tweens wondering, 'What *should* I be thinking or doing?" Of course, it isn't a matter of *should* and tweens are trying to discover the kind of sexual life *they* want to have without ruining the pleasure of sex. We can say that the secret of happy sexual relations lies in a person's ability to find out what really excites them and then to have the courage to find it.

"What is the difference between fancying someone and desiring someone?"

What your tween is feeling is real and serious so don't dismiss it as a crush or a passing phase. They need to know that you have some inkling of how they feel. So, talk about your first crush or your first love, how you felt, how you coped, how your parents handled it, what was helpful, what wasn't. Having laid these foundations, it may then be useful to:

"It's not just help with when she fancies someone I need ... how do I help when she's rejected?"

- Find out what your tween wants to do (it may well be nothing!).
- Follow a story line with them, "What do you think would happen if you did ..." It may be that all your tween wants to do is dream and romanticize about these feelings.
- Make your position on under age sex clear.
- Keep your tween busy. Unlike teenagers, a healthy range of interesting activities can keep a tween's mind off sex, even if only temporarily!

Tomb raiders, *Star Wars* and *Buffy the Vampire Slayer*

Sex is an intriguing topic for tweens and it can also be worrying. Their conscious picture of sex is sentimental and romantic. Girls in particular may dream of being a fairy tale bride and then of being a mother with a smiling baby in a pristine pram. They give little thought or have little knowledge of the "muck and bullets" which link these two events! This romantic view conflicts with the tween's unconscious fear about sex.

Boys' unconscious anxieties about sex

Boys' unconscious anxieties about intercourse may surface in fears around being stuck or trapped in a bad place. Sometimes they have anxieties about losing their mind or their penis, and for tween boys, minds and penises may be linked or confused. We can understand this boy, in a moment of horror (and confusion) fearing that he had cut his penis rather than his finger. Similarly, a twelve year old became highly anxious he was "going mad". He felt he was going mad, "*because I'm always worried all the time*". Eventually he sobbed he thought he was gay because when he thought about sex, which he said he did a lot, "*I get a hard on*". He was afraid that his heavy masturbating could make him lose his penis and he converted this worry to the worry that he might lose his mind.

"How can I stop my eleven year old from overreacting and dramatizing? Last night he cut his finger opening a tin ... and fainted at the sight of the blood!"

Girls' unconscious anxieties about sex

Girls have different worries. An eleven-year-old menstruating girl developed a severe tummy bug. On being told it was "a bug" causing the vomiting, she cried, "*It's killing my insides*". Distraught, she clutched her stomach sobbing and was unable to be comforted until, in desperation, her mother shouted, "*Your insides are not being damaged, the bug is coming out with the pooh.*" This girl was illustrating a common unconscious fear for tween girls. They may worry about something bad invading them and in particular, preventing them from having babies. In this instance, it was interesting the way the girl used the word "insides", a common phrase for our internal organs, rather than simply "inside".

These worries are unconscious and made sense of by the tween in their fascination with such films as *Tomb Raider* – going into a dark bad place, getting trapped but eventually discovering treasure.

Getting together their male and female sides

Popular and clever Charlotte had always been something of a star in her family. Her mother told me that the trouble began when they went to buy new school blouses. No size fitted Charlotte properly, *"Oh dear,"* said her mother casually, *"you're neither a small nor a medium, you're somewhere in between."* Charlotte had angrily protested she was not and grabbed the larger blouse saying it was fine. From then on she seemed to change culminating in her swapping her best friend. Her mother was bewildered as Charlotte tended to sneer at similar girls as, *"All they think about is clothes and make-up."* The crisis came at the year end when Charlotte gained an A* for her English exam. Her parents were knee deep in a puddle of pride but Charlotte seemed burdened by her success. She saw herself as friendless, complaining the other girls were jealous of her "brain power". However, her teachers reported it was Charlotte who was aggressive especially towards girls whom she perceived as less academic.

"My twelve year old has recently abandoned her sensible best friend in favour of a more flighty, precocious girl. We don't understand why and are worried about this change … is she going flighty?"

Charlotte's mother

One of the tasks of being a tween is to begin to work out the relationships between their male and female sides. As Charlotte approached adolescence, unconsciously she began to ask herself, "What have I got that boys might want?" She was confused. She had always been praised and admired for her brain. Her mother had given her a clear message that the best way to be a woman was to have a successful career. She wanted more for Charlotte than that she should, as Congreve said, *"dwindle into a wife"*. Her father had been slightly astonished that he had produced this "brainy" girl. At times he seemed slightly in awe of her (when she was in full verbal attack, I have to confess to being in awe of her!) and, of course, as she reached puberty, it may have suited him in some ways to keep her as a "brainy girl" rather than a "sexy girl". When Charlotte's mother made her innocent comment about Charlotte being neither "*small or medium but somewhere in between*", she spoke to a deep rooted anxiety in Charlotte. She felt between two worlds, not only the two worlds of child and woman, but also the world of brainy women and the world of sexy women. She feared if she remained a brainy girl her feminine virtues would get lost, i.e., an A* in English meant she had succeeded intellectually but failed cosmetically.

Charlotte wanted to be a bimbo and she was afraid of being a bimbo. Bimbos are not taken seriously. She wanted to be taken seriously as an intellectual and was afraid of being taken seriously sexually. She was struggling with the idea that she could be admired for something other than her brain. She was no longer satisfied with being intelligent; she realized there was more to her story.

We thought about the notion of an "intelligent bimbo", i.e., she could be both brainy and sexy. Somewhat reluctantly, her mother took her on what she called "feminine shop fuddles" looking at clothes, cosmetics, etc. Charlotte was clearly enjoying herself, and her pleasure helped her and her mother to grow closer. As a full-blown teenager, it is unlikely that Charlotte would want her mother to be so involved, but tweens will often take a real pleasure in "same sex secrets" not involving the other parent.

How to be a gentle man?

But the struggle to be a "beauty queen with a briefcase" is not only confined to girls. In Chapter 1 we talked briefly about the different ways boys and girls of this age express affection. Girls hug and share secrets. Boy friendships are no less passionate and intense but their intimacy tends to come out in rough and tumble play, described by one mother as "like large bounding puppies". Tween boys may be quickly aroused physically and such play tends to erupt into aggression.

This mother was right when she added that boys' play often "ends in tears". It would seem that boys need a climax to their play such as a punishment or violence between themselves. It all does "end in tears" because in boys' play the intention is that there will be an ending. This is different from teenage boys' behaviour, when they seem to have developed more internal control and, of course, their desire for "a climax" is much more focussed on sex.

"I simply can't stand it ... my three boys, aged ten to fifteen are so rough and aggressive with each other, I just want to yell at them to pack it in ... are they normal?"

Also in Chapter 1 we thought about how establishing yourself as a man may mean being the exact opposite of your mother and for this reason unconsciously boys may try to "get rid of" parts of themselves that they feel are like their mothers. However, I have already talked about how early intense feelings of love for the parent of the opposite sex are reawakened at this age. This boy's angry rubbishing of his mother was, at an unconscious level, also his way of preventing himself from desiring her sexually. The task for this family was to help the boy realize he could be a man and also be like his mother in some ways. And cultural trends are making it easier for boys to identify with their mothers. Many tween boys are as preoccupied with their appearance as tween girls. Whilst many small boys seem to continue to live up to the "slugs and snails and puppy dog's tails" image, there is certainly a great deal of "sugar and spice" about the tween boy. They may be less slovenly than full-blown teenagers and clothes and fashion can be very important as they have yet to adopt the teenage cult of "black only".

"My eleven year old is so rude to his mother ... we are at a loss as to how to manage it."

Talking to tweens about sex

Tweens learn their behaviour and attitude towards dress, relationships, respect for their bodies and those of others initially in the family. You will have taught these values in words and actions based on your own moral or religious code and your own experience. Now these views are going to be challenged by other influences on your tween such as their friends' and parents' views, teachers' views, views promoted by the media. Your tween may be feeling that they have to choose between your views and an outside view before they can make up their own mind. For this reason, asking questions may be the least useful way of having such conversations. You may have to depend more on what is dropped into conversations by your tween or by yourself. One mother described how she had had a long conversation with her twelve-year-old daughter about a story-line in one of the "soaps" where a thirteen-year-old girl had become pregnant. "*I know she was talking about the soap character, but I know she was also testing me out as to what we would do if she was in that situation and she was also curious about how this could happen to someone so near her own age."* Such oblique conversations can be very useful and also freeing for a tween. So you could ask, "*What do your friends think about ...* (e.g., dating, under-age pregnancy, whatever)?" It may also be useful to make statements which your youngster can follow up or not, for example, "*I hear some eleven year olds are ...* (e.g., going steady) *nowadays."*

It can be difficult for parents to start conversations about sexuality. Talking about sex will stir up your own frustrations, longing and confusion about sex. Many parents are "willing to listen" but feel bewildered and confused about listening. If you are feeling uncomfortable or embarrassed then don't try to pretend you are not! It may help to say something like "*I want you to feel that you can talk to me about anything, and I want to be able to share with you, but I do find this a little bit difficult ... so you might have to help me out!"* It will also help for you to tell your tween the story of how you ended up feeling embarrassed about sex. Explain to them how the topic was managed by your parents and your school. Don't wait for youngsters to ask you about sex, they may never do so! Hopefully, they will get better information from you than from their classmates.

"She just changes the subject or walks out of the room. What can I do?"

Think about what you are trying to do in this conversation.

- Give facts and information?
- Give rules and boundaries?
- Find out what your tween knows?
- Find out what your tween is doing?
- Share and explore issues?

As with any tween topic, it is best to ask your tween what they think about the issue first. Try to listen without overreacting or butting in and then there is some hope that they will listen when it is your turn to talk! You do not need to rush to state your own opinions, there is plenty of time to do this calmly at the right moment.

You may have to cope with the fact that you are unlikely to know exactly what your tween is thinking, or knowing or doing sexually. This is part of respecting their privacy. You can, however, make sure they have access to appropriate information and important related matters such as contraception and AIDS. It is very important to remain ready and willing to listen without too much judging, if they do want to talk. Of course, everyone feels judgemental about sexuality but now is the time for you to try and suspend your judgements.

Masturbation

It is likely that your tween's first sexual experience will be through masturbation. If there is a taboo left around sex, it must be masturbation. Sex is, for most people, a very private matter but it is not unknown to share confidences about petting and intercourse. Certainly, teenagers can be very ready to share secrets about "how far they went". Both sexes may boast about conquests and performance without any of the silences, anxiety and embarrassment that exists around the topic of masturbation.

What is it about masturbation that is so unsettling for people?

Whilst no one now believes masturbation causes blindness or any other Victorian fantasy, the jokes that surround it suggest the practice still causes people at least a mild sense of guilt. Why else would we need to raise the topic almost solely in jokes? Maybe we don't talk about it because it *is* a private matter. That said, masturbation seems to expose people's shame about sexuality, and what is it that we are ashamed of about sex?

Let's think about the link between masturbation (sex with oneself) and sex with other people. For the tween, masturbation may be a pleasurable relief from frustration and tension. Small children masturbate both for pleasure and for relief from anxiety. The difference for the tween is that masturbation is also an introduction to sexual relationships. Exploring their own bodies for pleasure is a prelude to sharing their body and exploring another person's body for pleasure. Why does anybody give up masturbation for sex with another person? In other words, how do people move from "inside to outside" in relationships?

"I know that my ten year old is regularly masturbating ... should we be worried about this?"

Masturbation only becomes a cause for concern if later on a teenager seems intent to masturbate rather than to seek out a sexual partner. Or, of course, if masturbation has become obsessive. A tween who obsessively masturbates is likely to be trying to deal with a lot of anxiety. Feeling "I am enough for myself" may be an older teenager's way of avoiding the complexities of sexual relationships. Their lives then may become isolated and lonely. If your tween raises anxieties about masturbation with you, well and good, but otherwise, you should accept masturbation as an ordinary aspect of growing up.

Homosexuality – whom should I love?

For most people, loving someone of the same sex is ordinary and normal. We all have a parent of each sex and most people will have grown up loving both parents. Children love both parents because they are different sexes. In a way it is puzzling that as adults we have to decide which sex we will love. The Darwinian answer, that the race would die out if we didn't, raises yet another question – is the point of life to reproduce? The tween years are the point at which the question of sexual orientation becomes an issue.

It is unclear how we determine our sexual orientation. At one time considered to be solely dependent upon nurture, i.e., how we were brought up and the relationships we develop with the adults looking after us, nowadays we believe sexuality may be biologically determined, i.e., depends on our genes. It is interesting how this controversy rages on. We can speculate that this is to do with a human need to make sense of more in our lives than sex. The advantage of the nurture theory is that we can somehow engineer children's sexual orientation. The risk is that someone or some people have to take responsibility or can be blamed for a person's sexual orientation. The nature lobby avoid this risk by placing themselves in the hands of fate, the idea being that our sexual orientation is pre-ordained and we can't do anything to change or develop it.

Today we live in a climate of freedom of sexual expression, gay marriages and same sex parenting. Our culture is much more tolerant to homosexuality than it has been, though we still assume it is *normal* to be heterosexual. But in tween culture, it seems, it may be cool to be black, it may be cool to be disabled, but to be thought "gay" is derogatory. Indeed, the word "gay" in tween culture is a general term of abuse. So why this hatred and mistrust? Could it be linked to the fact that homosexuality is an integral part of a tweens' development?

Girl crushes

Maisie's parents were concerned about how she spent her time. *"It's the Britney Spears thing ... it's such a waste of time ..."* Apparently, Maisie's bedroom was plastered with posters of Britney Spears and she and her friends talked incessantly about Britney Spears. Of course, Maisie was behaving age appropriately. For girls, homosexuality takes the form of "crushes" on older girls or young women. The chosen idols tend to be attractive and competent, feminine and confident, in both their status and opinions.

"My nine year old and her friends are obsessed with Britney Spears ... they seem to think of nothing else. Britney Spears is all they want to see and hear ... is this normal?"

Maisie's father

These "crushes" are one of the ways girls begin to separate from their mothers. The mother/daughter relationship is a passionate one. It involves love, admiration, rivalry, envy and rage. Both mother and daughter have to withstand these passions during early childhood until, as a tween, the daughter begins to transfer these intense feelings to her girlfriends as a kind of safe, "half-way house" towards becoming both independent of her mother and experiencing such passions in a sexual relationship.

As a mother, this can be painful and difficult; you may feel both rejected and despised by your daughter. You may be helped to remember your own experience of separating from your mother. One mother, bemoaning the fact that her mother was always saying to her, *"You are making hard work of letting go of me, you need to be more independent,"* pointed out that this same mother insisted her adult children return to the family home every Sunday. She recalled her teenage years with horror – *"I remember just trying to get away from my mum, she felt such a drain on me ... but then I felt I had never been her little girl, the others had but I hadn't."*

"I can't believe how horrid I was to my mother. I didn't see her as a person, just as this monster who was always against me."

thirteen-year-old Debbie

A tween girl who feels she has missed out on aspects of mothering faces a dilemma. She wants to be independent but how do you become independent of someone you feel you never really had? My client's longing to be grown up was mixed with an equally strong longing to be small and dependent. All tween girls will become ambivalent about becoming independent but this mother was never sure whether she wanted to be close or distant from her own mother. Such a tween girl may then seem unpredictable, moving dramatically between being content to be dependent and making sudden angry bids to be more separate and independent.

Boys' fear of crushes – on being a No. 1 fit lad

Boys have a similar but different experience. Whilst girls may be beginning to attract attention to their appearance and seeking our praise for their beauty, tween boys are beginning to emphasize what they *can do*. They display their "beauty" through such things as sport and risk taking.

Idolizing strong, successful male characters can be the boy's way of saying, "*I am a man, not mummy's little boy*". In this sense, tweens' denigration of homosexuality may have less to do with homophobia than it is about separating from the parents; it may have less to do with sexual orientation than with developing a strong identity as themselves as a male or a female, as a precursor to deciding whom they may desire.

"What should I be telling my tween about homosexuality?"

Knowing who we are may lead to all kinds of sexual relationships – heterosexual, homosexual or bisexual, exclusively or in combination. How a person works all this out will depend very much on the complexity of the personality.

Are you really letting them make up their own mind?

Francis had never made friends easily, in fact he had never had a best friend. He had recently been "hanging about" with a boy a year older than himself. The two lads got on well. For different reasons, they both saw themselves as "*outsiders*". Francis' parents' concern was that the older boy was very feminine in his ways and considered by his peers to be gay. They felt anxious on two counts. Firstly, they felt Francis was putting himself *further outside* by being friendly with this boy who was the butt of others' jokes. Secondly, they were open in their fear that if this boy were gay, he would "influence Francis that way". An interesting exchange took place in a family session.

"*Well,*"argued Francis, "*what if he is gay? What's wrong with that?*"

"*Well,*" replied his father, "*you must make up your own mind about that. I know that times are different now, you must make up your own mind what you think about that.*"

"*Yes*", said Francis, "*I don't think that there's anything wrong with being gay and as you say, I can make my own mind up.*"

"*Of course you can,*" said his father, and then there was a long pause before he added agitatedly, "*but you think that that's normal, do you, men going to bed together like men and women, you think that's normal ...?*"

"*Well, no, I'm not saying that ...*" trailed off Francis.

Francis' father was clearly not allowing Francis to make up his own mind. Of course you want to give your child clear guidelines about right and wrong, about good and not so good ways of living their lives; and parents give messages in subtle ways, not just in what you say. There is a difference between a dogmatic approach – this is the way and no other – and providing your child with a structure in which to think about how they behave and the consequences of their behaviour, both for them and for other people. A risk of taking a dogmatic approach is that your tween may be left feeling guilty and anxious just at a time when they may need support with their sexuality. Of one thing you can be sure, any sexual position which you mock and disparage will become glamorous and desireable to your tween. What is important is that your tween goes on to be able to develop their own sexual relationships autonomously.

Protection, permissiveness and under age sex

Ideally, children will begin to be sexually active when *they* feel they are ready. One of the tasks of parenting is to protect one's children's sexual life. Children need time, space and what Winniccott called, "a facilitating environment" to develop their sexual relations in their own time and at their own pace.

Curious as tweens are about which other adults may be having intercourse, they are likely to be horrified at the idea of their parents engaging in sexual activity. Two twelve year olds in the same class were embarrassed and enraged when their single parents came together as a couple. "*I just can't believe it*," said one, "*my mum is nearly forty, it's disgusting.*"

This single mother was unsure whether or not to protect her eleven-year-old daughter from her own sexual activity. Should she insist any boyfriend left the house before her daughter was up in the morning? Or should her daughter just have to accept there may be an extra one for breakfast who had shared a bed with mummy? "*I don't want her to grow up thinking I'm a nun, an asexual person, but on the other hand, she's not old enough to understand about having more than one sexual partner ... and also, it's her home, can I just dictate who she will meet at breakfast now she's growing up? ... it's difficult ... I just want to get the balance right ...*"

"Should my tween know my boyfriend sleeps over?"

In reality, parents are unlikely to "get the balance right" because of the idiosyncratic nature of sexual development. This daughter may have felt her space was being invaded. She may also have felt her mind was being invaded in the sense that she was being forced into thinking about something before she was ready. We can equally assume she would take the whole matter in her tween stride, accepting her mother's behaviour as what grown-ups do. She could also be learning that sexual relations take place in many different kinds of relationships.

The risks of being over-permissive

If parents are too permissive around sexual matters, tweens may be over-aroused and exposed to situations that emotionally they are unable to manage. All parents differ on how permissive they want to be with their tweens. You don't want to convey that sex is a dirty secret, nor do you want to flaunt your own sexuality. So how do parents decide how to convey to children that they are sexual creatures? It may be no more clear-cut when it comes to encouraging or discouraging their own sexual activity.

The parents of a twelve-year-old boy were shocked to discover his girlfriend's mother had allowed them to share a room one night after a party. She took the line, "*kids will have sex if they want to and won't if they don't want. It's got nothing to do with whether or not they are in the same room ...*" The boy's parents disagreed. They felt the youngsters were being encouraged into sexual activity before they were emotionally ready. Who was right?

The risks of over-protection

Over-protecting children from sexual activity, both their parents and their own, is likely to make them even more curious about sexual activity. They may also feel guilty. They may feel there is something they want to know about that they shouldn't know about and this can affect their academic learning as well.

Children of all ages are naturally curious about what goes on between their parents. You know this from the demanding toddler who tries to get between you in bed to the giggling six year old triumphantly announcing, "*I saw you snogging!*" Every family will have their own unique code of privacy ranging from complete openness about sex and nudity to families where almost any bodily activity seems covered by the Official Secrets Act. So are there risks in being too secretive about sex? Well, we know for children the more something is forbidden, the more curious they become about it.

Ten-year-old Leo was causing both giggling and embarrassment among his classmates. His teachers described how he was taking any opportunity to mention body parts or to describe someone or something as "sexy". He seemed excessively, and worryingly, preoccupied with sex to the point of asking the girls questions like, "Do you like my bum?" Interestingly, his parents saw none of this behaviour at home. They were highly embarrassed and disgusted by what they were told and arrived in my consulting room worried "is he a pervert?"

"My ten year old is obsessed with sex ... he describes everything as 'sexy' ... he doesn't seem able to think about anything else."

Leo was not a pervert, but he was highly excited by his curiosity. Both parents volunteered they were too inhibited to talk to Leo "on these matters". They had never allowed him into their bed, not even as a small child. They said they found it difficult to show affection to each other in front of Leo apart from a rather formal hello and goodbye peck on the cheek. Leo knew instinctively there was more to sex than his parents were showing him. His explicit behaviour was his way of asking questions. He was showing the adults, and his classmates, that he knew more than he was being told but that he was curious and confused about the facts and needed someone to explain things to him.

Laws about under age sex are based on development theories and are there to protect the vulnerable. Some under sixteens may be mature enough for a relationship involving sexual intimacy, many others will not. So much depends on the individual young-ster, their family and life experience. It is interesting that in a culture where sex is everywhere, where there is no innocence anywhere, our understanding of sexuality in the tween years is to some extent uncharted waters. In this sense, this book may be disappointing, for it can only provide you with a guide not a map.

Keeping safe: helping tweens manage unwanted sexual advances from adults

It is sad that one of the consequences of our important awareness of the sexual abuse of children is that there is now a culture of fear on both sides. In one sense, we can be suspicious of anyone who works with children and so parents may find themselves having to hand their children over to the group they can least trust! It is true that paedophiles often work with children. It is not true that anyone who works with children is a potential paedophile! Remember, statistically a tween is much more likely to be sexually assaulted in their own home and by a family member or friend than by a stranger in a dark street at night. So how do you, as parents, help children to strike a balance between being aware of potential dangers and not viewing any stranger as a potential sexual predator?

How you manage this topic will depend on how you have managed body and sexual matters with your youngster in the past. Tweens who have grown up with a sense of privacy and bound-aries around their bodies will find this a matter of continuing in the same vein. However, for all parents of tweens this is a time to remind your youngster that no one, adults, other tweens or teenagers, should touch another person's body, anywhere, without their permission and/or if they feel uncomfortable or embarrassed by the touching. Encourage them to tell you at once if this happens so you can help them to manage it. Remind them that no adult should ever ask them to keep hugs and kisses "a secret" and that such secrets are dangerous, especially if they are accompanied by dire threats about what will happen if the tween "tells". Reassure your tween these threats are rarely carried out and that "telling" is vitally important.

You can also remind your youngster that an adult who asks a tween to touch *their* body is behaving dangerously. This is a rare time when it is okay to be as rude as you like in order to warn the offender off!

It can be helpful to talk through potential situations in advance. For example, what would your tween do if they were asked to touch an adult or if they just gradually found themselves feeling uncomfortable in the presence of a familiar adult. Such conversations would not only help your tween to be aware of the dangers and the feelings invoked but would also give them a vocabulary and actions to manage them. Sadly, however, even when you have prepared your tween to manage unwelcome sexual advances from adults, you both need to be aware that if faced with this situation your tween is likely to be so frightened they freeze, emotionally and physically and can do nothing to prevent the event happening. Tweens need to know this is a normal reaction, like rabbits in the headlights of an oncoming car, and, however they may feel, this does not mean they "allowed" the assault to take place. Knowing in advance that this is how victims of assault may feel afterwards, may help a tween in the recovery process.

Sex, drugs and rock 'n' roll on a diet
Going off the rails

"Why would anyone want to stay on the rails? Aren't rails simply upturned ruts?"

(Stephen Fry, quoted in The Times, *March 2001)*

The romance of risk is an essential ingredient in child development. There comes an age when you have to let them cross the road alone, go to school alone, ride out on their bikes alone. Each of these steps to independence is risky – for both you and your child and to reduce the risk you try to balance the need to encourage independence with your child's particular emotional and physical stage. A three year old left alone in the bath to wash and then to climb out and dry herself is probably being pushed into a physical independence beyond her emotional needs. On the other hand, the eleven year old whose mother still supervises his bath is not having his current physical and emotional needs recognized. Growing up involves taking risks and practising going to extremes; if you are lucky, this risk taking will be both minor, and to some extent, amusing …

> *"At fourteen the adult rules take over … until then he's under my control and influence … but I'm failing … he's going off the rails."*
> *mother of a twelve year old*

… The eleven-year-old boy who had his hair cut in a "punk" style and then dyed in orange and black stripes …

… The ten-year-old girl who got a nose stud …

… The eleven-year-old girl who presented herself ready for school wearing a silver crop top under her coat which her mother didn't notice until they were almost at the school gate …

You may find such incidents embarrassing and they may test your patience to the limit, but they are neither beyond your parenting skills nor life threatening. They are also a safer alternative to drink, drugs and under age sex! We can argue that risk taking is an essential part of our daily life, and not necessarily a "bad thing". Some of life's most successful human beings have been people who have been prepared and able to take risks in adulthood. Politics, medicine, science and literature all owe their development to people who needed to push boundaries and go to extremes in a creative way. The worry for parents is that there seems nothing creative at all in some tweens' risk taking! As one parent said, "*We seem to live with two new family members, the Military gentlemen – General Chaos and Major Crisis!*"

"My ten year old wants a navel ring. Surely she shouldn't be thinking about things like that at ten?"

You may have very clear views on what tweens *should* or *shouldn't* be allowed to do, coloured by media hype about, and the reality of, the availability of drink and drugs to tweens. It is as natural to make judgements as it is to feel "all at sea" on these issues. Indeed, it is very difficult not to be moralistic. The hard part is to stand back and let your tween discover their own morality by making their own mistakes.

Parents may be more tolerant of boys' seemingly delinquent behaviour than girls. Twelve-year-old Mary's parents were humiliated to be called to the school to discuss her behaviour. The head teacher told them she had been given three detentions in one week, adding, "We've never had this before ... only a certain kind of boy ever gets that number of detentions ..." This attitude presupposes that tween boys and girls have different appetites. Yet we know that youngsters of both sexes are affected in different ways by puberty. Some seem to ride the storm fairly consistently with only isolated extremes of behaviour and feelings; others are flooded with anger, aggression, longing, sadness, restlessness and timidity. Indeed, it is interesting that when parents are asked to define the difference between a full-blown teenager and a tween, a common reply is, "*Oh, they* [tweens] *are much more emotional ... especially angry.*"

Tweens can be rather like exuberant puppies who may move quickly from leaping playfully around the room to digging up and destroying the plants. So, however your tween is behaving, it is likely that your main anxiety is having to live with the worry of what they "*might* do". Some youngsters may behave impulsively, taking action on the spur of the moment without hesitating or thinking, often out of outrage or concern. Tweens, like teenagers, tend to be very rule-bound. They have very definite views on what is right and what is wrong, what is fair and what is "so not fair". However, tweens and teenagers express their "rule-boundedness" in very different ways.

"My husband says I'm more worried about what she might do than what she does do. I think it's true. Is it normal?"

mother of an eleven-year-old girl

Teenagers have an acute sense of rules because one of the tasks of being a teenager is to identify and not identify with adults, so they tend to be either very defiant or very compliant. Tweens are more "goody goody", more dutiful because they are still more identified with adults. For a tween, keeping rules is one of the first ways they venture out of the home. They may want to distribute leaflets, have jumble sales, etc., in aid of good causes. Teenagers, on the other hand, find that breaking rules helps to take them out of the home.

Why do they need to take risks?

One of the tasks of a tween is to explore a whole range of attitudes and behaviours in order to discover how they will be received by family and friends. The teenage world may seem glamorous, attractive, exciting and even funny. Taking risks, especially with drugs and alcohol, may seem like a magical entrance to this world. It may also be a fantasy way of trying to get you to treat them as though they *are* a teenager. They may be trying to miss out a difficult transitional stage of development – if you like, avoiding the waiting room and trying to go straight to the main event. They are not necessarily being delinquent, they may be rehearsing a future life.

"I don't want to spoil her fun ... I don't want to dampen her vitality ... but she's laying down foundations now ... I don't want her to go off the rails."

mother of a twelve year old

Why don't they realize the risks of taking risks?

Forbidden fruits are not only sweet, they also arouse our interest. Two nine year olds found sharing a secret cigarette protested, "We just wanted to see what it was like ..." This sums up the tweens' attitude to risk – curiosity *about* smoking was what these boys were exploring, not an interest in becoming smokers themselves. This may be very different from the four year old rolling up paper and "pretending to smoke like daddy" and quite unlike the teenager who may have decided to take up smoking as a way of enhancing their image or, as one sixteen year old put it, "*It's something to do with my hands when I'm nervous about meeting people.*"

"She wants to go trick and treating with her friends without us. We're quite happy to stay in the car at a discrete distance ... but she won't have it! Doesn't she realize she could get hurt?"

Tweens don't recognize the consequences of risk taking because they live in the midst of the whirl of their immediate desires and needs. A worried father collecting his twelve-year-old daughter from a youth club disco, was shocked to see her leaving the building in a tight embrace with a boy with whom she then shared a prolonged goodnight kiss. When he tried to discuss the matter with her she said, "*Oh, dad, come on, we were just having a snog, you've got to have your fun.*" Nine and ten year olds may not experience the same sense of immediacy and urgency as older tweens do. This girl is another example of a tween "playing at being a teenager". For a teenager such an experience would be accompanied by the thrill of the risk of "what might happen". This tween seemed oblivious to, or even innocent of, "what might happen".

It is a real parenting skill to keep demands short term and relevant to a tween. So much will depend on the kind of conversation you have with your youngster. Lecturing will get you nowhere! For a tween taking risks feels good, exciting and a taste of the teenage world. Teenagers nearly always underestimate their own vulnerability – others get caught, they won't, others get hurt, they won't – and this blinds them to the long term consequences of their risk taking. Teenagers really don't want to think about their vulnerability but, paradoxically, it *may* be the only

"Everybody's doing it and I did it before and I was okay"

thing they think about and they have to find a way of coping with feeling vulnerable. So they rely on their parents to look after their vulnerability for them, saying, "*Oh, I know it's perfectly safe for me, I won't get hurt like so and so did …*" is a way of asking you to protect them by not letting them go. Tweens are similar and yet different. It is not so much that tweens don't consider the consequences of risk but that they have a different take on the consequences to the adults, e.g., your tween has not considered the long term risks of smoking but is likely to be acutely aware of the risk of you catching them smoking. They rely on parents to imagine the immediate future for them, they are not yet able to do this for themselves; their excitement lies in the risk of being caught in the here and now.

The risks for parents

You are bound to have views on your tween's behaviour and they will certainly have views on your views! The main risk for parents is that just when you need to be *thinking* about your youngster's behaviour, you will simply *react* to it by "going over the top" ("*He'll end up in jail*"); by under-reacting ("*All kids steal cars*"); … or by blaming yourself ("*Where did we go wrong?*") or blaming your tween ("*He's always been so difficult*"). In calmer moments it is as likely you and your tween will have a more *reflective* conversation sharing views and feelings. These two kinds of conversations are not mutually exclusive and at this stage of parenting, oscillation may be more important than consistency.

"Where did we go wrong?"

Delinquent behaviour is a problem for parents; for tweens it may be a solution to the difficulties they are experiencing.

Stealing

When a tween steals, they are not telling you what they need, they are telling you how they feel about themselves. Dr John Bowlby, writing in the 1970s, argued that much delinquent behaviour can be understood as "people trying to get close to each other". Jessie's parents were shocked when they discovered her stealing – "*If she'll steal from us, who's*

"I'm horrified to realize that my ten year old has been taking money from my purse. Does this mean she's going to be delinquent?"

Jessie's mother

next … shops … school …?" They had taken a strong punitive line with their daughter threatening to report her to the police. They felt their punishment had fitted her crime and the matter was over. But she did steal again, and again from her mother's purse. *"She has generous pocket money* [true], *she can ask for what she wants, she doesn't need to steal."*

"I needed something, so I stole it," said Jessie.

This was not quite the delinquent statement it sounded. Eight months earlier her mother had taken a full-time job involving her being away from home several nights a week. Jessie missed her mother whom she felt *"only cares about her job now"*. She was taking money from her mother, but money was a symbol of the time, love and affection she felt she had lost – she was trying to steal back "closeness" with her mother.

Aileen had been caught stealing cosmetics from a local store. What puzzled her mother was that Aileen had made little attempt to hide the goods she had stolen – *"It's as if she wanted to get caught,"* she said.

"My twelve year old has been caught shoplifting. What can I do?"
Aileen's mother

Aileen was the eldest of three children and the oldest by four years. When her parents separated, her maternal grandmother moved in to the family home to help her mother. Aileen's mother was distraught when the grandmother died two years later. Aileen seemed to cope well supporting her mother by looking after the younger children until she came home from work in the evening and often putting them to bed and giving them breakfast in the morning. She became something of a mother to her own mother, comforting her when she was distressed and making few demands on her for herself.

What is stealing a solution to?

Tweens steal because they feel they need something emotional which they haven't got or because they feel they had something important emotionally and have lost it and are trying to get it back. Tweens may find it very difficult to articulate what they need except in physical terms. Aileen's mother was shocked to discover how upset Aileen had been by both her father's departure and her grandmother's death …

"But you seemed to be the least affected …!"

"*Well,*" said Aileen, "*you were always crying and I couldn't bear it and I just wanted you to be happy …*"

Aileen had hidden her own sadness and distress in an attempt to protect her mother. She agreed that she had wanted to be caught stealing in the hope that her mother would realize she was also finding it difficult to cope with life. She had kept up her role of a tower of strength towards her mother at the expense of being allowed to be comforted for her own distress.

Stealing is always a communication from a tween that they are in distress and what they steal may be very significant. Aileen was stealing make-up just at an age when she was beginning to think about becoming a woman and a mother. In many ways, she had been the mother in the family for a long time. Stealing make-up was also a way of her expressing her age-appropriate rivalry with her mother over who was the woman of the house.

Managing stealing

- Is the stealing "a blip" or "a trend"? Tweens do act impulsively, or on a dare, or even "just for the thrill of it" to see if they can get away with it; such a tween's stealing can be a way of asking "Am I free?" If they do get away with it, they have a sense of being an independent person beyond the adults' control. For such youngsters, often the shame of being caught is enough to prevent them trying it again.
- If stealing is a trend, then find a quiet time to sit down with your youngster and open the conversation with something like, "*Your behaviour tells us that you are unhappy or worried about something. We don't understand, but we'd like to understand …*"
- If your tween's stealing is severe, regular and prolonged, then seek professional help.
- Paradoxical as it may seem, as we can see from Aileen's story, the tween who steals is much more likely to need spoiling than punishment.

Stealing may be regarded as an ordinary developmental stage of the tween years until it becomes compulsive. When a youngster feels unable not to steal, when they are locked into this way of behaving, then stealing has become an extraordinary problem, requiring professional help. The communication has changed. The tween is living as though they can only get what they want by stealing. They have lost the sense of listening to responsive adults who can meet their needs.

Finally, Donald Winnicott argues that stealing can be "a sign of hope". The tween who steals is likely to have hope that they deserve love, affection, time, admiration. Such a tween is fighting for their place in the world. A similar child in Aileen's position who doesn't steal, may be understood to be feeling worthless and having no right to a relationship with other people.

Smoking, drinking and drugs

This mother isn't really worrying about her boys "trying one cigarette", she is worrying that they might be developing the habit of smoking. A seventeen year old found smoking may well be at risk of becoming a regular smoker. Some ten year olds do smoke and beg, borrow or steal money and cigarettes. But it is less likely, though not impossible, that a ten year old found smoking is seriously thinking of doing so regularly. This ten year old may very well have been copying his brother or enjoying the thrill of feeling as grown-up as his brother. He would certainly have enjoyed being his partner in crime.

"I recently caught my ten year old and my twelve year old smoking. I told them off soundly but my twelve year old argues that trying a cigarette at his age is not really harmful. Could he be right?"

But what of the twelve year old involved? Was he simply aping the adults? Was he practising being a regular smoker? Or was he trying to find out for himself what all the fuss was about? This mother was intensely anti-smoking on health grounds. Sometimes tweens flaunt rules en route to accepting them. It is possible that this twelve year old was checking out for himself if cigarettes would really taste, smell and affect him in the ways his parents described. Often when tweens argue against your values they are actually arguing with themselves. The argument is not so much between you and them as between the risk taking, almost delinquent side of themselves, and a more grown-up, sensible and balanced aspect of their personality that really knows the score.

Heavy drinking is a well recognized phenomenon amongst teenagers. In Britain, heavy drinking is a particularly well recognized phenomenon amongst teenage girls. It seems to be less of an issue in mainland European countries where, of course, children are provided with diluted alcohol from a very early stage as an ordinary part of family life. Nor does it seem to be such an issue in America where there is a total intolerance to under age drinking. The legal drinking age is twenty-one and anyone giving alcohol to tweens, or indeed teens, is liable to criminal prosecution. In my clinical experience, it is not quite such an issue amongst tweens. They tend to have sudden, unexpected and spectacular outbreaks, such as the two twelve-year-old boys left alone for an evening. Their parents found them blind drunk on a mixture of white wine and brandy, "*We thought it would make Babycham*," they later explained with an air of naivety and disbelief at their fate! (Babycham is a very low alcohol drink usually considered innocuous enough to be offered to teenagers in Britain).

"My twelve year old is having a Valentine's party and wants me to provide low alcohol drinks. Most of her friends are thirteen plus years old. Should I allow it?"

How you manage alcohol and your tween is going to depend very much on your family culture and the laws of the land in which you live. In Britain, some parents allow older tweens low alcohol drinks with meals to distinguish them from younger children in the home. Of course, in England, in licensed premises, as in America, it is against the law to serve alcohol to under sixteens. And this makes it complicated if your tween wants you to provide alcohol at parties or sleepovers. Whilst as a parent you have every right to decide how, when and where your child will be introduced to alcohol, you will also respect the fact that other parents may have a different view on their tweens being allowed or encouraged to break the law. At such a time, other parents must be your greatest resource. In America, parents can be confident other parents are not allowing even low alcohol to be served at their tween parties, while in Britain the situation is more complex. If you are happy to provide alcohol at a tween party, and willing to supervise its use, then perhaps your best course of action is to contact the parents of the youngsters attending and canvass their views. Many tweens want to drink or smoke in an attempt to gain popularity with their peers to appear "cool". It may well be that your twelve year old's friend's parents would not allow alcohol at this age and your tween might be relieved if you also refused to allow it.

What are smoking, drinking and drugs a solution to?

The pain of puberty

The tween years, particularly the later years, can be a daunting time. Many tweens begin to have a sense that "*this is all too much, I can't cope with it.*" Drinking can be a way of coping. It is not so much that the tween has turned to drink as they have turned away from being a tween. Teenagers may drink to be one of the gang, to help them "loosen up", to socialize and to "kill the pain". Tween drinking has a sorrowful quality to it. In Josie's words:

"*If I'd known what puberty was like, I'd never have started it!*"
twelve-year-old Josie

"*I don't like cider … but when I'm drunk I don't have to worry about not being me … when I'm drunk that's what I am, when I'm not drunk, I don't know who I am.*"

A bid for independence

Drinking and drug abuse can be a tween's bid for independence. They are deciding what will and won't go into their body which is a way of saying "*my body belongs to me*" and challenging the notion "parents know best" or "parents know what's good for children". Many adults do things that spoil or ruin their own lives even though we are supposed to know what is good for us. We can argue that adults are making a more informed choice than tweens, but is that necessarily so? Many adults who behave in a self-destructive way do so for exactly the same reasons as tweens may. They want to feel free and they want to feel powerful in their own lives and they want to kill the pain when this seems difficult.

Modern day life is very difficult for the majority of people. We seem to need addictions in order to cope with the pressures of daily living. These may range from the relatively harmless, sport, choco-late, shopping, to the more destructive, compulsive gambling, drink and alcohol abuse. So in a sense our desire to protect our children from drink and drug abuse is an absurd hypocrisy. But we know that alcohol and drugs (and also chocolate!) are physically addictive and what parents are trying to do is to alert their tween to the consequences of too much alcohol or drugs.

Talking to a tween about smoking, drugs and alcohol abuse

- First and foremost your tween needs to know that you have discovered the joys of delinquency!
  Tell them that you understand how alcohol makes them feel grown-up, one of the gang, no longer under peer pressure. You also know that alcohol stops you thinking, makes you feel happy, less anxious, less inhibited. If your timing is right, you can add that you understand that part of the attraction of alcohol is that it's illegal, disapproved of by adults, risky and pleasurable.
- You can then move on to emphasize the risks of drink, drugs and tobacco.
  The disadvantages will obviously outweigh the advantages, but only if you emphasize the risks that are immediately important to a tween. They may need to know about long-term effects such as heart, lung, kidney and liver disease, but these are unlikely to act as a deterrent. They are more likely to respond to the fact that smoking makes your breath, clothes and hair smell like an old ashtray, your teeth and fingers can turn yellow, and that there is nothing cool about throwing up violently in public. Drinking and drugs can make you do stupid things which, if you are lucky, other people may think are very funny but it is more likely that your friends will then think you are acting like a dork.
- Try not to be judgemental – not easy as we all feel judgemental about these issues.
- You can give a clear, simple straight message on your views on the matter and what you will and will not allow in the home. You need to combine this with talking openly and calmly so as to encourage your youngster to feel they can talk to you without "getting a lecture".
- Remember, it is more important that you and your tween can talk openly and know how each other feels about substance abuse than that your tween agrees with you.

The obsession with computers

Computers are both fascinating and frustrating. They provide access to realms of information on a world of subjects, instant communications in the forms of e-mails and video links … and

"My twelve year old is obsessed with the computer. It's a constant battle to keep family life going ... it would be so much easier to just let him stay in his room doing whatever he does on his computer ... what can I do?"

"If there's a problem with the computer, or the mobile phone for that matter, it's him who sorts it out. We don't feel so irritated by his obsession with the computer then!"

mother of eleven year old

"I like chat rooms ... you can say what you like ... you can pretend to be anyone you like because no one knows you really ..."

eleven-year-old Rea

they often seem to have a mind of their own and give us nothing! In Chapter 3 we thought about mobile phones as a transitional object for tweens, and computers can serve a similar purpose by allowing them access to the outside world from the safety of their own four walls and also to source knowledge independently.

Asking other people for information, learning from other people is an interesting process. We have to begin by acknowledging we don't know and we are dependent on the other person to help us; some adults find it difficult to believe that there is nothing wrong with "not knowing". Tweens may feel embarrassed by their lack of knowledge compared with adults. They may not have yet reached the stage on the car sticker "If you want to know, ask a teenager, they know everything!" But nor do they have the small child's easy security in feeling their parents know and understand everything. Computers allow tweens to find out for themselves, with the advantage that feeling dependent on a computer doesn't have the emotional complications of feeling dependent on another person!

Accessing the net can be the tween's way of trying to feel less stupid generally. This is interesting because technology is advancing at a rapid rate and many tweens have knowledge and skills in advance of their parents and it is interesting to reflect on the impact of this on youngsters. At the very least, it is a huge life change from the stage where mum and dad solved all problems.

However, we are all too aware that not all tweens are using the computer solely to enhance their homework.

Chat rooms can have an uncanny appeal for tweens. For parents, they can be a constant source of worry and anxiety. There is no way of knowing who your youngster is talking to, what topics may be being discussed or information exchanged. Tweens are both young and impressionable, they can be groomed not only for sex by "friends" in the chat room but also into drug taking. They may believe they are talking to another twelve year old who is telling them what fun it is to be "high" when they are actually talking to a drug pusher.

"Being on the computer" is also a solitary activity and there is a real risk of youngsters like Rea relying on "cyber friends" in chat rooms or feeling the computer, with its enormous resources, is a reliable friend in itself. Many chat room friendships are healthy and rewarding, many are harmless fun, but there is always the concern that a vulnerable youngster who finds the cut and thrust of daily relationships difficult, may seek refuge in fantasy friendships in the chat room at the expense of practising making friends with their peer group. The risk then is that the youngster becomes more and more isolated. Chat rooms, of course, can also have the reverse effect. A successful internet friendship may help to boost a youngster's confidence and act as a diving board for taking further risks in making daily friendships.

"My eleven year old has begun to use chat rooms ... how do I know who she's talking to ...? I'm worried she's having chat room friends instead of real friends."

Rea's mother

All this is true, and is an appropriate worry for parents. However, it is also an inappropriate worry. The reality of the risks of the internet is that they throw into glorious technicolour the fact that your tween is beginning to have an independent, private life in which you may no longer play a central part.

Managing the computer

Parents have two tasks around the computer:

- To help your child to be aware of the risks of the internet and to use the computer appropriately.
- To recognize the general sense of unease you are feeling about your child having a private independent life.

Controlling your tween's use of the computer is a difficult task.

- Make sure the computer is in a central room used by the family, not hidden away in your tween's bedroom. If you are naturally in and out of the room whilst the computer is in use, you can both create the ambience that you are "aware" and also check what is being accessed.

- Give simple, clear guidelines about what is acceptable use of the computer, what topics can and cannot be pursued on the net. Spell out exactly when they should and shouldn't open e-mails. You may want to insist that you view chat rooms before your tween uses them regularly.

- Ask your tween to never give their address or telephone number to people in chat rooms. If you find they have done so, you can talk to your youngster about contacting the person to check them out.

- Tell your tween never to arrange to meet anyone from a chat room unless you know and are possibly going to be present at the first meeting.

- Ask your tween to tell you at once if they receive e-mails, etc., of an explicit sexual nature or which are promoting drugs or alcohol.

- Limit the amount of time that the computer can be used. A tween may be more likely to focus their computer time on e-mailing friends if they know that the time is limited.

- Excessive use of the computer seems to say something about a tween's ability to socialize. Encourage your tween to make "going on the computer" a less solitary activity by doing it with friends.

- Install a specialist programme that will both screen your tween's access to the internet and also cut the internet off at a specific time. A list of specialist websites on internet safety is available in the resource section.

Eating disorders

"My nine year old is becoming increasingly 'picky' about what she will and will not eat … I'm so worried she's becoming anorexic."

Parenting, food and feeding are inextricably bound together. If your child refuses food you are likely to feel worried and also rejected. You know this and your tween knows this and so food fads can become a useful medium for them to assert their increasing desire for autonomy. They may not be able to control how late you will let them stay out at night, but they can control what they do and do not eat.

What is an eating disorder?

Put simply, an eating disorder is when someone doesn't want to eat, even though there may be no physical cause, such as illness, why they can't eat. The "not wanting to eat" (anorexia) may be mixed with an urge to binge eat followed by self-induced vomiting (bulimia). Eating disorders tend to be associated with girls, but this is becoming an increasing problem in young adolescent boys.

"My twelve year old has put herself on a strict 'no fat' diet … she's becoming increasingly rigid about it … is this an eating disorder?"

Symptoms of eating disorders

- Sudden and inexplicable loss of weight
- Refusal to eat or disappearing at meal times
- Greed and overeating
- Consistent food faddishness, i.e., refusing fats, sugar, carbohydrates consistently rather than perhaps refusing one food for a few days and then suddenly changing to another
- Excessive preoccupation or discussion about body weight

Many tweens develop "food fads". Their heads are buzzing with puzzles about all sorts of topics, world and environmental issues, health issues and political issues, and they may express their anxieties by developing food fads. They may urge you to boycott products of a particular country or a particular food in the latest food scare. At the same time, they may demand to be provided with certain foods exclusively, like the twelve year old who wanted a packet of jelly every day because she had been told that gelatine would make her nails grow!

"How do I know the difference between a food fad and an eating disorder?"

Food faddishness may be the tween's way of trying to establish that they are individual, distinct and different from the rest of the family. Favourite foods may suddenly be refused …

"*But you've always loved banana and custard,*"

"*Yuck … it's kids' stuff.*"

… because they are associated with childhood, they are not grown-up foods.

It is not uncommon for tweens, like toddlers, to try to live on a restricted diet of favourite foods. It may not be a healthy diet, but how are you going to make them eat anything else? When a tween says, "I only eat sandwiches ..." they are also issuing the unspoken challenge, "Try and make me eat something else." Food during the tween years is about much more than eating and nourishment – mainly it is to do with the tween's urge to experiment. Tweens know you will worry about what they eat, so food can become a useful medium for them to assert their increasing desire for autonomy. Meal times may become a battle-ground for such life and death power struggles as whether or not a tween has to eat cauliflower. It is impossible to make a reluctant tween eat something they don't want, *"Chicken? Is it free-range or factory-farmed? Do you know how they keep factory-farmed chickens? ... [excessive distasteful facts] ... right, you know how they kill them ... [further excessive unpleasant facts] ... oh, look, look, there's its vein ..."*

> "My tween insists on eating only sandwiches – chicken or tuna ... surely this isn't a healthy diet?"

By the time the tween has finished, the entire family has turned vegetarian!

> "My ten year old has decided to be a vegetarian. She point-blank refuses to eat any meat. Is this a healthy diet for a ten year old?"

Vegetarianism is common amongst tweens, particularly girls. It is a healthy diet provided it is taken seriously as a balanced diet and not confined to just "not eating meat". Many tweens feel power-less in the face of more and more publicized envi-ronmental issues such as global warming and the destruction of the rainforests. Sometimes becom-ing vegetarian can make them feel that they are "doing something", that they do have some power to change the world.

> "Her pickiness at meal times infuriates me ... what can I do?"

Try not to take it personally! Food fads have nothing to do with the quality of your cooking or the food provided. Try to avoid power struggles over what they have to eat. They will always know best! Sometimes you can take the wind out of their sails with a response such as: *"Okay, I think you should eat it, but if I try to make you eat it, there'll be a fight. And then we'll all end up unhappy. So I'm going to let you not eat it."*

Allow your tween as much choice as is reasonable at meal times. Acknowledge that some youngsters may want to eat different foods from the rest of the family and try to tolerate the fluctuations in their whims. If they do turn vegetarian, respect their decision, take it seriously and support them with the information about a balanced diet. Be equally respectful if they suddenly decide they are no longer vegetarian!

Given that we live in a society where appearance is all, it is not surprising that tweens have an increasing preoccupation with image and appearance. In Chapter 7 we were thinking about how it is also appropriate and natural for them to be thinking about how attractive or not attractive they are to other people, how "fanciable" they are and also who they fancy. What we are thinking about in this section is an *excessive* or *all-exclusive* worry about appearance and in particular body weight. Whilst food faddishness is a normal stage of development, it can also be a precursor to an eating disorder.

> "My eleven year old is refusing to eat anything but salad as she thinks she is fat. She isn't, how can we help?"

Eating disorders as a solution

The need to feel in control

Eating disorders are an individual and complex solution and each youngster will be communicating their own peculiar needs. Polly illustrates a youngster trying to restore her self-confidence and feel that she has enough autonomy. She was showing the world she would decide what did and what did not go into her body. Polly's mother's authoritarian style of parenting left very little room for flexibility, and Polly had little sense of a private life. So, eating disorders may also be a means of communicating anger. You are likely to feel enraged sitting at the table with a tween who refuses to eat. Partly you feel powerless – you really *can't* make them eat – but also your tween is making you feel what they feel, i.e., angry and resentful.

> "My mother can't make me eat ... that's what I like, she can't make me eat."
>
> *twelve-year-old*
> *Polly*

A request for control

Sometimes an eating disorder can be a cry for help. Unlike Polly, Kris may be saying, "*Please put some boundaries around me and make me feel safe.*" At times, tweens are likely to feel on the brink of being out of control, if not actually out of control. Kris was enjoying a heady dose of delinquency by "hanging about" in the town centre with a couple of friends, who eventually shoplifted snacks for the three of them to eat. Kris was scared, "*I might have to do it …*" By developing an eating disorder, Kris was asking his parents to control him. He needed to feel that they were in control of him, just at a time when he was beginning to feel out of control of himself. Of course he didn't want to shoplift, but then a small part of him was secretly excited and thrilled at the prospect of doing so and getting away with it!

> "Our twelve-year-old son is refusing meals … we insist he sits at the table but he doesn't eat … yet, we think he *wants* us to make him eat …"
>
> *Kris's mother*

Anxieties about being desireable

The glamour of sexual attractiveness is much hyped in the media. Little is said about the anxieties of being sexually attractive. Children learn very early that sexual intimacy is a part of relationships. Most manage to hold a balance between their excitement and their anxiety about sex. For others, coping with their own sexual feelings and the thought of sexual demands from others is terrifying. At eleven, Max was considered "well fit" by the girls in his class. Fifteen months later, he had developed an eating disorder which arrested his physical development. Asked one day what would be different if he still had his "No. 1 fit boy" looks, he replied: "*Girls might want to snog me … I might want to snog everyone.*" Max was so anxious about his ability to control his sexual desires, he was managing to avoid adolescence by physically remaining a child.

> "Does puberty hurt?"
>
> *nine-year-old girl*

> "How long is adolescence? I can't hack too much of it …"
>
> *twelve-year-old boy*

Just at an age when he should have been revelling in his good looks and attractiveness he had become fearful and anxious about them. This affected not only his ability to socialize with other youngsters, but also his general performance in school. He moved from being something of a star on the sports field to being listless and apathetic. His school work began to suffer because most of his mental energy was being used to suppress the thoughts that he was afraid to have; he had, if you like, put a brake on his naturally enquiring mind.

The risks of promoting healthy foods

If there is a theme to this book, it must be that parents cannot get it right. Overly promoting healthy foods can make children rebellious about what they eat; it may be better to encourage an overall healthy diet, with hopefully only small amounts of junk food included. Perhaps this girl is reacting to her mother's promotion of healthy eating by beginning to feel she is only attractive and loved if she remains thin, and in her mind, therefore, healthy.

Managing eating disorders

Most children have conflicts over eating at some point in their development. So try not to panic. Tweens with eating disorders are often baffled by their own problems and make them worse trying to make them better.

"I have always encouraged my children to eat healthily, they know the difference between good and bad foods. I taught them to check fat contents and to avoid unhealthy snacks like potato crisps and sweets. But now I am finding chocolate and crisp packaging in my twelve-year-old daughter's room. What should I do?"

- Explain to your youngster that what they are doing simply isn't working; neither you nor anyone else can understand their worry and so cannot help them to understand it either.
- Reappraise the ways in which you boost your tween's confidence and self-esteem. Draw attention to their qualities and character traits rather than their looks. It is all too easy to unwittingly enhance society's quest for physical perfection. A twelve year old who had consistently refused to wear her spectacles, volunteered one day that when the spectacles were first prescribed for her, aged five, she had overheard her mother on the phone saying, "Oh, it's such a shame, we've just found out today that she needs glasses …"
- Remind your tween that most people feel dissatisfied with some aspect of the way they look.
- A family meal may give you the opportunity to both monitor what your tween is eating and also to model a healthy eating pattern. Socially, meal times can be an excellent opportunity for families to talk and share news, views and information. In a household of tweens and teenagers, this may happen only rarely!

- Think about whether you are giving your youngster enough freedom and choice. Sharing with your youngster how you felt on the verge of adolescence and the difficulties you had in making contact with the opposite sex may help your youngster's confidence by making them feel normal.
- If you really feel that an eating problem is making you or your child too unhappy then you should seek professional help.

Under age sex and promiscuity

We tend to associate promiscuity or under age sex with older teenagers but it is becoming an increasingly worrying issue for tweens; the prevalence of HIV, AIDS and sexually transmitted diseases are increasing parents' anxieties. Experimenting sexually is one way teenagers find out who they are and what they want. Tweens are less likely to experiment to any serious level but some do; what matters is how much they feel intimate in the sexual relationship. If they don't, and if they seem to be moving from partner to partner in a rather cold manner, then we must presume that their behaviour is a way of their asking for help about how they feel about themselves.

What is promiscuity a solution to?

- Promiscuity is a way of dealing with feelings.

A tween may become sexually active when they can't find a quick enough way of feeling confident with their body and emerging sexual urges. Paradoxically, adults may regard promiscuous tweens as overconfident in their bodies, but promiscuous tweens may have serious worries about their attractiveness and their ability to be loved. They may try to meet their longing for love and acceptance through sex and so confuse sex with affection and someone loving them. Promiscuity and casual sex may be fine if you're looking for orgasms, but what these tweens are seeking is intimacy and acceptance.

- Tweens are flooded with all kinds of feelings other than sexual which they may find difficult to manage. Many are terrified of feeling lonely as they take the gradual step from home into the outside world.

A twelve-year-old girl began a sexual relationship with her boyfriend within weeks of her father leaving home. Her mother feared she was "bad" or "delinquent", but the girl explained that she couldn't end this relationship because, "... *there's no one else on the scene and I'll just be by myself.*" She was trying to replace the intimacy she had had with her father by a different kind of intimate relationship with a boy.

It is not uncommon for tweens, especially tween girls, to think that they can solve their painful feelings of being unloved by finding someone to love. The notion is that loving someone will make them themselves feel loved. Teenage girls may feel that they can solve the problem by having a baby – "*Someone who's mine and I can really love and who loves me back.*" As we have seen throughout this book, the roots of disturbing teenage behaviour are sown in the tween years.

Managing under age sex and promiscuity

Whilst we have to acknowledge that every tween is unique and different from other tweens, it is a good generalization that tweens are psychologically and emotionally not ready for sexual relations. A tween having under age sex needs to be told that they have to stop doing so! Sometimes parents feel the best course of action is to ensure that such a tween is using as safe as possible contraception. On one hand this is eminently sensible but bear in mind that if you offer your tween contraception you are implicitly giving them permission to have sex. How you stop them having sex is a huge problem but nonetheless telling them to stop should be your main aim!

It is realistic to acknowledge that youngsters today face serious temptations and they face these temptations at a much younger age than previous generations. However, this realistic position is different from feeling that the world is a hostile place and your youngster will have no autonomy but to succumb to temptations. Your anxiety about your child taking risks is going to be exacerbated if you view, however faintly, all strangers as potential paedophiles and all other youngsters as potential seducers. For the time being you will have to learn to tolerate not knowing what your tween might be doing all the time outside the home and also learn to trust that you have given your youngster a good enough foundation in life for them to make wise choices – give or take the odd dramatic mistake which we are all allowed to make in life.

Lone parents and tweens

"Holding the fort alone ... but crisply"

One of the risks of writing such a book as this is that it can be read as though I am presuming all children are brought up by two parents who love both the children and each other and who are living together. This is not my intention and, indeed, such a presumption would be missing the mark. There are now so many ways of being a family: lone parent families, adoptive families, same sex parents, older parents, grandparents parenting, mixed race families; and I hope as I write this book, that I have found a philosophy appropriate to some extent for everyone. It is potentially comforting that there are so many people trying to make it work in so many different forms, races and cultures. The relative success of so many of these families gives us hope for future child care practice. That said, it is a fact that all children originate in a couple (sperm bought on the internet still involves a couple!) It is also a fact that children are influenced for the rest of their lives by both people in that couple, whether they know them, let alone live with them, or not.

The influence of an absent parent

"He's never even met his father ... surely you can't say his father is influencing him ...?"
mother of eleven-year-old boy

For a child, the influence of an absent parent is that, although the parent is absent *physically*, they are *emotionally* present in ways in which the child may not necessarily be aware, i.e., consciously or unconsciously the child has to imagine living, laughing, fighting and loving this parent. In this sense, there is no such thing as an absent parent as parents cannot be *emotionally* absent.

Children find different ways of dealing with having an absent parent. Some deny their feelings. A ten-year-old boy was anxious to reassure me that he was *"glad that my dad has gone"*. Asked how he knew, he replied he remembered overhearing his mother saying, *"Oh, I'm glad he's gone ... I'm glad to be rid of him ..."* He had adopted his mother's view as an instant and acceptable explanation of what he might be feeling. Feeling glad is always preferable, we can argue, to feeling sad and angry! Maybe he felt closer to his mother by instantly identifying with her at a time when, of course, he may have been very anxious that she too might disappear.

Other children may idealize the absent parent. A sad and bewildered eleven-year-old girl who had not heard from her father for over a year, sobbed her way through a distressing list of events such as him not acknowledging her birthday, ending, *"My dad is the best dad in all the world."*

In this chapter, we are going to think about issues specific to lone parenting tweens. Nowadays many parents are not necessarily living together but may both be active in the upbringing of their child, both physically and emotionally. Other lone parents may be alone and unsupported. However, children draw even the isolated single parent into a couple by their relationships with teachers, friends, childminders. So to some extent, all that is written about the relationship between tweens and parents is relative to a lone parent. The friend, relative or childminder who may share the care of your tween and who may be seen to be openly supportive of you, may very well come into the kind of conflicts with your youngster that I have written about as often occurring between parents. I am also aware that much of what is said in this chapter is true of lone parenting children of any age. I am also only too aware of how difficult it is to offer separated parents help in managing their tween without making them feel that it was not in their childrens' best interests that they separated in the first place.

The issues faced by a lone parent will be coloured by the circumstances in which you have become a lone parent family. You may be parenting alone because of a death, or a divorce which you may or may not have wanted. You may always have been a lone parent. Your tween may have frequent

"So many of her friends are in lone parent families ... surely it's perfectly normal now ...?"

mother of nine-year-old girl

or infrequent contact with their other parent and the quality of this contact will vary.

Most children in lone parent families have friends in the same position. However, how you came to be a lone parent family may colour your child's notion of a family; a nine-year-old boy whose parents had divorced when he was a baby used to moan, "*I just want to be in a real family, an ordinary family.*" He saw what he had as a family as not as good as family life with both parents. Such lack of self-esteem can be crucial for tweens. Media preoccupation with single parent families may exacerbate the situation. An eleven-year-old girl had swapped an affluent lifestyle for a more meagre one following her parents' divorce. Watching the news on television one day she suddenly asked, "*Mum, do we get benefits?*" She was having to deal not only with her own individual feelings, but also how a lone parent may be construed in society.

What is a family?

Historically, we have thought of a family as two parents of opposite sexes loving each other and creating (typically) 2.5 children! However, our idea of a "family" is now evolving to include, as I said earlier, a much wider range of possibilities. Marriage does not necessarily equate with family and home. These are three separate ideas which may overlap and interlink but which may be able to exist independently as well. Single parent families have their struggles, which make them real families. They are *ordinary* families and some may even be "extraordinary" families.

How lone parent families differ

A lone parent family is more than just a two parent family with one parent living away from the childrens' home. Lone parent families have their own unique structure and dynamics which may work for and against the childrens' best interests. Family life is stressful and there are no absolute truths, but there is the risk that the tween in a lone parent family, particularly if the parent is unsupported or openly unhappy, may feel the need to look after or befriend their parent. They may feel less free to focus on their own development than the child who has parents who are openly supportive of each other.

Eleven-year-old Louise was such a child. Within ten months of her parents' hostile divorce, her father died suddenly and unexpectedly. Her traumatized mother had suffered ever since from severe migranes. Louise was referred to me by her teachers who described her as unsettled and unhappy, frequently saying that she felt unwell with a headache and wanted to go home. I suggested to Louise that she was worried about her mother whilst she was in school. "*Yes,*" she replied, "*I worry about her, because I'm the only one that can make mum happy.*"

> "Since her parents divorced, Louise has been unable to settle in school, frequently crying and saying she feels unwell."
> *Louise's teacher*

"*And isn't it interesting that mum gets migranes and you're getting headaches?*" I commented.

"*Yes,*" she said, "*because we're alike, that's how I know how to look after her.*"

Louise was setting herself an impossible task. No child should have to be a parent to their parents but many sometimes will. When that happens, it can be that someone loses something and someone is placed under strain, and it is usually the child. Louise needed permission not to take on that responsibility and to be reassured that there were adults around who would look after her mother. The same situation can, of course, arise where parents are living together in a warring relationship and where one parent may recruit the child as an ally against the other.

The dynamic of availability

In a two-parent family, there is a chance that one parent will always be available to the children (and, of course, fathers are available to children in different ways to mothers). In a lone parent family, where a parent may be working full-time and doing chores in the evening, with younger children to look after, you may be less available. For this parent it was a choice between the match or the ballet. On the other hand, in some families, particularly if the parent is not working outside the home, the lone parent may be totally available to the tween.

> "I can't say [to partner] ... You watch him playing in the match and I'll go and watch her doing her ballet."
> *lone mother*

Being part of their lives by proxy

Zac's father had died when he was seven years old. As he grew up, Zac became more and more enthusiastic about sport. His friends' fathers both helped him to train and took him to matches. His mother was beginning to realize there were fewer and fewer family activities they could share. She felt that had his father lived, "*I would have been there when they came back from matches and heard all about it, probably more from his father than from him, but I would still have been part of that part of his life ... even if only by proxy.*" As it was, she was feeling a double loss. She was feeling excluded from a whole area of Zac's life, as well as the absence of his father to share the loss and also to "fill in the gaps". She took comfort in the fact that sometimes Zac would come home bubbling over with excitement and share every detail of his trip. However, she also had to respect that at other times, he would want to share very little.

"How can I stay close to my eleven-year-old son now he's into boys' things?"
Zac's mother

We talked of the importance of her knowing Zac's world ... if only by proxy. She made sure that she flipped through his sport magazines, kept abreast of his favourite footballers, tried to learn the offside rule and to be aware of "who was hot and who was not!" Zac's response fluctuated between being acutely embarrassed by his mother's attempts to appear "cool", and feeling connected to her by her interest.

No one to moan to ...

Something that everybody knows but which is very little talked about is that, at times, all parents hate their children. For some people, this is never more true than at the onset of the tween years! Just as tweens need to moan about their parents, so parents need to moan about their tweens. When parents complain to each other about their offspring, the criticisms are voiced under the umbrella of their inclusive acceptance and love of their children. A dynamic of a lone parent family is that lone parents feel supported by complaining to friends or relatives about their tween's latest outrage but are then left feeling guilty. As Zac's mother said, "*I always end up saying rather lamely, 'but he's a*

"... but I feel so guilty if I moan about him ..."
Zac's mother

good lad really'." No one else was thinking that Zac wasn't a good lad! His mother felt she was being disloyal to Zac and so found it difficult to easily get the support she needed.

The need to moan may be particularly poignant for lone parents. As children approach the tween years, parents have to begin to consider what their lives will be like when the children have gone; for some lone parents this may seem an exciting chance to, as one mother said, "get my life back!" For others, it will raise anxieties about a lonely future.

Lone families may be coping with trauma

All families have their upsets and difficulties, if not their share of trauma. Tweens in lone parent families may well have had to cope with two of the biggest stresses of life – death or divorce. How your tween experiences being in a lone parent family will be coloured by both their age and stage of development at the time of the trauma, and also how the events were managed by the adults around them. Death and divorce can be potentially catastrophic for both the adults and children involved. Both may feel bewildered and disorientated and that terra firma has been replaced by shifting sands. Something that everybody, but particularly the children, took for granted and permanent has turned out not to be so.

> "I'll always be a little less than myself now."
>
> *twelve-year-old girl on the death of her mother*

"Dad left a jumper and it smells of his aftershave, and I smell it when I'm sad," said a ten-year-old boy describing his feelings of loss after his father left home.

Believing you can come through it must be half of the battle, for such parents convey to the child, consciously and unconsciously, "This is difficult but it can be okay" – a very different message from, "This is terrible and it's all our fault you are miserable." Whilst no tween should ever feel responsible for their parents, tweens can be helped in time of crisis to feel that they can contribute something reparative to the situation. A tween may feel less out of control and bewildered by a crisis if there is a sense of the family sharing the project of how to deal with this new situation.

> "How can we help our tweens to make the best of it, to keep alive the fact we are divorcing and yet not let it spoil everything?"

Tweens' reactions to trauma

Of course, there are as many reactions to trauma as there are children and it is unwise to generalize. However, children of different ages have different developmental and emotional needs. Young children need first and foremost to feel close to someone, to feel attached securely to an adult who will anchor them in the face of trauma. Teenagers are more able to verbalize their feelings such as grief and anger. They are also more likely to have developed a life outside the home to which they can turn for both solace and distraction.

Younger tweens may experience their share of guilt and sadness in the face of death or divorce, but it is likely that they will be dominated by a sense of rage and injustice. They need time, space and permission to be angry but they also need help in keeping their anger focussed. Mabel found it easier to contain her anger when her mother adopted a reflective, rather than a confrontational approach – no easy task! For example, when Mabel flew into a rage over a particular skirt not being ironed, her mother would calmly and firmly say, "You're angry that dad and I don't live together, it's not about your skirt not being ready." Such reflection seemed to help her understand that however much she protested, she could not influence the situation. In common with many children of divorced parents, she was harbouring a persistent hope that her parents would get back together.

> "I can't do anything right for my nine year old ... I don't know what she wants. She's been so rude and angry with me since her father left home ..."
>
> *Mabel's mother*

Herbie's father described a typical example of Herbie's greed. Herbie returned from a trip to a local store with a school friend, laden with gifts bought by the friend's father. He came home hugging a CD, a computer game and a pair of jeans, more in a sense of greed and possessiveness than in glee and satisfaction.

> "I'm shocked that since my ten year old's mother died several months ago, he's become more and more greedy and demanding ..."
>
> *Herbie's father*

"*Gosh,*" said his father, "*not many ten year olds would get so much from a Saturday shop.*"

"*No,*" responded Herbie, "*and their mums aren't dead either.*"

Children of this age may be preoccupied with comparisons, who has what, and where they fit into the pecking order; and their pecking order may change radically on becoming a lone parent family.

We can think of Herbie's behaviour as his way of telling his father that he felt deprived ... he was deprived of the mother he had so adored. It was unjust and unfair that his mother had died and this was leading him to believe that he was entitled to more material goods than other tweens and also that possessions could in some way compensate for his loss.

Older tweens are more capable of verbalizing their feelings of loss than younger ones. They will be more likely to talk about missing not only the absent parent but also how they feel about any other losses and changes occurring through their becoming part of a lone parent family. However, this may not stop them from falling back on behaviour as a communication.

Simon's mother left home a week after his eleventh birthday. It emerged that he didn't want a party because, "*My mum always did it [the celebration] and now she's not here.*" This sensitive father was quick to suggest a few days away for his birthday, placing it in a different context from those previously. He made no attempt to "cheer Simon up", but accepted how painful and difficult it was for him this year and helped him to find another way of having a birthday.

"My twelve-year-old son is refusing to celebrate his coming birthday. He just keeps saying, 'I'm not bothered.' I think he does want a party ... but something is stopping him."
Simon's father

How do parents know which child to worry about?

In my clinical experience, whilst there are common themes for all tweens, stresses, crises and traumas are also a unique experience. Some tweens seem to take matters in their stride, others may be inconsolable. What are the signs that a child is suffering? Sadness, anger, quiet and withdrawn behaviour, regressed behaviour are all indications; and so too can be pseudo-maturity, hyperactivity, "coping too well", and quickly becoming attached to other adults.

It is interesting how, in the face of trauma, adults tend to speak of how "the children" are reacting, implying that there is a generic reaction, regardless of the child's individuality, age and stage of development. Thinking of "the children" in a blanket way can be the adults' way of coping. Childrens' pain and distress is very difficult for adults to witness when their own resources may be low. Sometimes one child in the family can carry all the distress, grief and anxiety for everyone. By becoming "the unhappy one" in the family, that child allows other people to get on with their lives. It is important to keep an eye on the balance of distress in the family. Everyone should be a bit upset and everyone should be a bit coping.

Helping tweens to cope with trauma

- Whatever the crisis, tweens need a clear, direct message, "It's not your fault, this has nothing to do with the way you have behaved or the way you are." In terms of divorce and separation, it can be useful to highlight that "this is adult business". They may feel powerless and angry at such a message, but they will also feel relieved of an unnecessary burden. However, you also need to bear in mind how, sometimes, apparently very clear messages just don't get heard and you will have to be prepared to keep on repeating them.
- In order to make sense of emotional experiences, tweens need to be told the facts. That said, we need to keep in mind that facts are always coloured by feelings and so it is not always clear exactly what are the facts. Indeed, it may well be that there is no such thing as an unambiguous fact from anyone's point of view.
- Your tween is likely to be shocked and bewildered. They are likely to express this with two questions: "What has happened?" and "What will happen to me now?"
- Remember, at any age, goodbye makes us sad and angry.

Death and divorce: different kinds of bereavement

Tweens recovering from a death or divorce have not only emotional feelings but also emotional tasks. For both adults and children, the experience of divorce may be very similar to that of a bereavement – but the two are alike and unalike. They have in common the fact that the tween has to realize that life has changed irrevocably and nothing will ever be the same again. Not only has their security been shattered but for many tweens their worst fears will have come true. In coming to terms with this fact, the feelings may be the same in both death and divorce but the life tasks involved are different.

When a parent dies a tween has to come to terms with the fact that they will never see the parent again. Even in religious households where belief in an afterlife may be prevalent, it would be unusual to lead the child to believe that after death the relationship will be exactly the same as it was in life. Rituals such as the funeral help the tween to say goodbye and to accept the finality of death. In the following months, the tween may be encouraged to "let go" of the dead parent mentally and rebuild their own life in which the deceased has an integral, but historical part.

In divorce, the tween has to negotiate a different kind of being together with the departed parent. The sense of loss may feel as acute as if the parent had died; it is important for parents to keep on making it clear that the parent has *not* died. You should not encourage your tween to let go of the absent parent; rather, they need to be encouraged to establish a new *way* of having a relationship. Your tween may feel as though they are having to establish "a new relationship". It is important to remind them that the fundamental relationship is the same; it is the *way* of having that relationship that is different.

Boundaries and discipline in a lone parent family

When a couple are parenting together, the tween's rage will fluctuate from one parent to another, according to the tween's mood. Lone parents are likely to endure a constant wave of passion because, as Guy's mother said, "*He has no one else to be angry with ...*" There was no other adult to step in and protect her from Guy's rage: firstly, by confronting Guy, "*Don't speak to your mother like that*," and secondly, by being there for her to "sound off to" in private.

"How do you cope with a ten-year-old boy who is permanently angry and abusive and you are a lone parent?"

Guy's mother

She was bewildered by Guy's increasing anger "*I know he was angry about the divorce, but we've been through all that and he's had a very settled twelve months until his hormones kicked in ...*"

Guy, like all tweens, was moving towards becoming more self-contained. Let us think about this developmentally; children's feelings can be very strong. A child of four needs an adult to contain (i.e., think about and withstand) their rage so as to ensure they do not feel engulfed by it. Teenagers need help to manage their own rage and help to bear their rage without being self-destructive. A tween needs both! By this I mean, Guy needed his mother to be able to not only withstand his rage by not yelling back, but also to help him to understand and think about it. This is always a difficult task, but can be a particularly difficult task when a lone parent is raising a child of the opposite sex. Another mother of a twelve-year-old boy described how he would push past her in a room or hallway, shoving her just a bit harder than was necessary. She was aware that as he grew older and stronger, she was not going to be able to cope with him arguing with her physically.

Guy's mother was also finding it difficult to know which battles to fight with Guy. As everything was a fight, she found herself getting increasingly entrenched as the days wore on and insisting, or trying to insist, on things being done in a rather rigid way. This, of course, simply caused the battles to escalate. When parenting together sometimes one parent can help the other to realize when a particular battle isn't worth fighting. In the long run, many single parents will get this sense of perspective from other people in their support system but this is not the same as having another adult there at the time to help to diffuse the situation, often with humour. Guy's father, had he been around, may have taken on his truculence in a good humoured, rough and tumble manner not available to his mother. It is also true that a tween boy may be less inclined to take his mother on if there is a male figure around to support her. As a small boy of four or five, Guy may have lived in a magical world of differences. He may have had ideas about getting rid of his father and having his mother all to himself. By eleven, he would be beginning to learn how to do this and also to understand the significance of having his mother to himself. When his parents separated, having his mother to himself became a realistic possibility and in some senses, a worrying one.

> "There's no one to say ... 'Better let this one go' ..."
> *Guy's mother*

Managing anger and abuse

Guy's mother had several tasks to practice:

- She resolved not to yell back at Guy (as much as she could!) She knew this only exacerbated the situation and also did not provide him with a good model of how to handle anger (see Chapter 5).
- She decided to say quietly but firmly to Guy that she was not going to discuss things with him while he was being so disrespectful. She would then leave the room.
- Of course, this sometimes meant that Guy got away with not finishing chores he was being asked to do. When this happened, she tried to weigh up how important it was to insist that the chore was completed and what consequence she was going to put in place if Guy refused to complete the chore.

"But Dad lets me ..." – divorce and separation

Children are always prone to playing parents off against one another. It can be hard enough for parents living together to find ways of supporting each other in the face of constant assaults on them as a couple, but for separated parents it can be a nightmare. At the same time, it may be even more in the child's best interests to do so, even if only through gritted teeth! If parents could easily support each other then they wouldn't be separated. It is a very difficult task for separated parents to remain together as a parental couple, but it is possible as a task and it is necessary as an aim. Parents need to be together in their concern for the wellbeing of the child but this doesn't mean that they have to agree about everything.

Sexual relationships run their course and a couple may decide for a myriad of reasons, they no longer want to be a sexual couple. The resonance of such a decision through the family is very powerful and difficult to capture in words. Sex is usually a strong bond between couples so when a sexual couple separate from each other, but hope to remain together as a parental couple, relationships become very complex. Are the children a compensation for sex as may be the case with couples who "stay together for the children"? We can argue that it may be a greater burden for a child to be brought up in the atmosphere of a home where their parents have no sexual passion for each other than to be brought up by separated parents who have acknowledged openly that they no longer excite each other. In the latter case, a child may feel sad and miss the constant presence of both parents. They may be puzzled about why their parents no longer love each other but the agenda is on the table to be discussed. This is very different from the former situation, put into words so exquisitely by a six year old, "*Why is mummy nice to daddy when she doesn't like him?*"

The grown-ups have to be very grown-up indeed to succeed as a parental couple who are no longer a sexual couple. At no stage is this more important than at the tween stage as tweens are always eager to exploit any situation to their advantage.

This tween has found an interesting way of showing his mother who is "the man of the house" and who is in charge. Again, let us think about this developmentally. As a five year old, Charlie could play at being a caricature of the "man of the house". We can imagine him "being a big man" by imitating his father. As a teenager, he would be likely to take on his father as "man of the house" in a more extreme and strident manner, but it would be a realistic version of a man. Tweens are both extreme and realistic.

> "At twelve, my son is making access visits directly with his father rather than through me. However he's now refusing to share their plans with me. What can I do?"
>
> *Charlie's mother*

Charlie's parents had decided jointly that it was appropriate for his father to make access visits directly with Charlie rather than through his mother. They did so because they felt that as the tween in the family he was being most affected by arrangements for access visits. His teenager brother already made his own arrangements to see his father. His parents made arrangements for his five-year-old sister without needing to involve her more than necessary. Charlie, however, because of his developing social life and because he was not yet fully independent, felt right in the middle of planning access visits about which he was always irritable. It seemed the process of making arrangements to see his father stirred up his feelings of being "a turkey wishbone", emotionally torn between his parents. However, Charlie's refusal to share these plans left his mother not knowing whether plans had been made or not and, if they had been made, what was her part in them, e.g., driving to an agreed meeting point.

Tweens need concrete evidence that they are facing a solid parental couple. Charlie's father had to tackle Charlie about his behaviour and they decided to revert to arrangements being made with his mother until he was "grown-up enough to handle it". This was not presented as a punishment; Charlie's parents simply pointed out to him that his difficulty in being adult about the arrangements told them that emotionally he wasn't yet ready to take responsibility for arranging visits to his father.

In a similar situation, a twelve-year-old girl was repeatedly placed on report at school for failure to do her homework. Her mother was eventually called to the school to meet the teachers. Although her father lived some distance away, both parents thought it was important that they went to the meeting together, giving the girl a clear message that they were both concerned about her behaviour and that neither of them were going to tolerate it.

Sonya's father was understandably anxious that visits to him should go as smoothly and happily as possible. He only saw Sonya once a month. She wanted to stay up late with him and he allowed her to do so for two reasons. The first was that he wanted to please her, and the second was that he didn't want to risk "having a row and spoiling the weekend". He then added that he felt his ex-wife was far too strict in insisting on set bed times even at weekends – "That's so she can have an evening … she likes evening time to herself, it's not because she thinks it's good for her."

This father was confusing good parenting with a desire to get back at his ex-wife. Obviously it is in a tween's best interest if parents can agree on a general set of rules, which will apply in both homes. There are all sorts of reasons why this may not be possible and so the way you explain differences to your tween is crucial; "I don't care if your dad lets you, you're not doing it here," is not helpful.

> "My ten-year-old daughter is allowed to stay up late every night on her weekend visits to her father. She returns home tired and irritable and finds it difficult to cope with school on the Monday. How can I tackle my ex-husband about this?"
>
> *Sonya's mother*

Indeed, it can make the tween feel they have to choose between their parents' views. When a tween does this, they are less likely to see it as favouring one parent and more likely to feel that they have rejected the other parent. Saying something like, "*Dad and I see this differently. It doesn't mean one's a good person and the other's a bad person. It doesn't mean one is right and the other is wrong. It just means we see it differently. When you are at Dad's you can do it his way; here I'm afraid, you have to do it mine.*" It may not stop the protests or the resentment, but it will help the tween to have a sense of their parents' being together in issues of parenting and not at war over them. They will feel more secure in the knowledge that they cannot cause or exploit further hostilities between their parents. Some lone parents will be unsupported or have no contact with their ex-partner. Whenever possible, it is useful to enlist the support of a friend or some family member who can offer some consistency in managing your tween. However, it is a wise parent figure (or step-parent) who knows when to back off and not cross the boundary of being the child's blood parent.

Advantages of single parent families

"Life as a single parent can be crisper ... I don't have to discuss everything with someone else, I can just issue a decree. I don't have to cope with them saying 'Dad says ...'"

single mother

"It's a parent thing ... if your parents go out ... you get more fun ... my mum doesn't go out ... she just watches TV."

eleven-year-old boy

There are benefits in being brought up in a lone parent family. It is interesting to reflect on the advantages you think you might have had if you had been brought up by only one of your parents. If you are reading this as a lone parent, you may like to think about what your child would lose if they were brought up by a couple. This mother felt her children didn't have to cope with two adults trying to have a relationship as they parented; she felt her energy was less dissipated by arguments with another adult. There is nothing like a tween "in a strop" for causing a row between parents!

This boy felt his social life was limited by his mother's lack of social life. (His comment raises an interesting question as to who is responsible for pleasure in the family.) He was aware he was missing out on pleasures shared by his friends in a social circle. We can think of a correlation between a good social life and the capacity for pleasure. It is true that some lone parents are isolated and lonely, but it is not an exclusive experience. Many tweens would feel just as socially isolated living with two parents who had long ceased to enjoy each other's company with the result that they seldom entertained friends, or indeed were entertained. Such parents are together, but not together, in that they can no longer have fun as a couple.

Many of the social aspects of family life are casual and spontaneous – friends call in, spontaneous invitations are made at the
school gate, impulse decisions made on the weather ... Many lone
parents may have to work hard to arrange a social life and role
models for their tweens. Family life necessarily has to be much more
planned and thought about. The advantage for the tween is that they
may be exposed to a much wider circle of people than otherwise.

Other tweens in lone parent families may have the advantage of
learning that there are very many different ways of having successful sexual relationships. Hopefully, they will have observed their
lone parent in all kinds of social, emotional and sexual relationships. On one hand, they will have to tolerate sharing their parent
with other adults, but in doing so, the tween may be prevented
from feeling that they are responsible for their parent. Such tweens
may also have the advantage of a more rich and more broad
contact with life outside the home.

Step-parenting and reconstituted families

There are, of course, as many tween reactions to becoming part of
a reconstituted family as there are tweens. Indeed, if separated
parents can manage to keep the tween in a "secure base", i.e., not
tear them apart emotionally, many children seem to negotiate this
process relatively smoothly. Much will depend on the individual
tween's personality, needs and how disruptive the change is for the
tween. Have they had to move house, school, even the area in
which they live? Is the reconstituted family going to
live in a totally new house for everyone, or is one set
of children going to have to join another set in their
family home?

Rana's parents had been separated for four years
but, like many children of divorced parents, she
had always hoped that one day her parents would
be reunited. For some children, such a hope can
almost become a purpose for living. It wasn't that
Rana didn't like her future step-father, it was that
the remarriage was forcing her to realize the finality
of her parents' separation. At this moment, some
children may face for the first time the irrevocable

"I'm shocked by
my eleven year
old's reaction to
the news that I'm
going to marry my
long-term
boyfriend. She is
distraught ... she
feels, 'It's the
absolute pits ...
that's the end'."

Rana's mother

truth that the adults have known for many years and presumed that the tween has also known. Remarriage is "adult business" in that it is a choice that the adults make and which may be foisted onto the children. I was slightly amused once by a couple who sought my advice on how they should tell the husband's children.

"*We've thought of asking them if it was alright if we got married.*"

"*And what will you do if they say no?*"

By virtue of their existence, reconstituted families are often more complicated than biological families. Both adults and children will be dealing with a variety of relationships, old and new, and the adults will have to negotiate, not only the practicalities of bringing together two families and two family cultures, but also doing this in conjunction with their ex-partners. Everyone will need to be aware that this may not work out in the way that everyone would wish.

How reconstituted families differ

The fundamental difference between a biological and a reconstituted family is that not all the members are blood relations. Instinctively family members will feel differently towards those who are blood relations and those who are not. Most step-parents start out with the best of intentions or at least want to have the best of intentions, but of course it is difficult because a step-parent may never feel for a stepchild as a parent does, and nor indeed should this be their aim. Many are surprised, if not overwhelmed, at how angry, jealous and resentful they may feel towards a stepchild who has a special relationship with their partner, may upset their own children in the family and, of course, who is a constant reminder of a previous relationship. These strong feelings make parenting complex. One of the most shocking things for a step-parent in a reconstituted family to discover, is that they maybe do not love or want to include the stepchild. So even with the very best of intentions, parents parenting in reconstituted families may come from very different, rather than common, positions. A natural parent is likely to feel defensive of their own child. A step-parent may very well feel that if the stepchild wasn't living with them, then

"After all, she [step-daughter] is nothing to me ..."

step-father of twelve-year-old girl

these disruptions wouldn't happen or that the stepchild "needs more discipline". Every family has to find its own particular way of drawing these disparate relationships together in order to make a group which can live together in *relative* harmony. A good step-parent, of course, can transform a family who has previously endured trauma and misery, but in a reconstituted family, running into problems along the way is natural and almost unavoidable.

Reconstituted families are likely to have some unrealistic expectations and it takes time for these expectations to become more realistic. Parents may be full of optimism and have a joyful sense of new beginnings. They may presume that the children will be sharing these feelings, even when there have been previous difficulties between the children and the new partner. There can still be a sense that "it'll all be alright when we are living together". Parents may also have to cope with jealousy or hostility from the previous partner who may try to sabotage the new family through the children, by arguments over access and money.

When words fail ...

Tweens in a reconstituted family are often dealing with painful and conflicting feelings that they may not know how to put into words. This is because some things are impossible to put into words; people only speak when they are ready. They may feel intrinsically loyal to their own parents and it is common for step-children to feel they are in some way betraying their natural parent if they become fond of the step-parent. One eleven year old described how she hid presents from her step-mother in the garden, "*Because I don't think mum would like it ...*" So tweens need time and space to develop relationships within the reconstituted family. They also need permission to feel indifferent to their step-siblings. Remember, you chose this partner with their children; it is unlikely that your children chose their step-siblings who then provided a partner for you!

Signs a tween may be struggling ...

Aggression and competition

Jack and Gemma share a common problem: a sense of loss of identity. For both parents and tweens, loss and change are a key issue at

"My ten-year-old daughter has become increasingly difficult since I told her about my new boyfriend six months ago. She refuses to share, and always has to win."

Gemma's mother

"My husband's son is rude and aggressive towards me. He refuses point-blank to do anything I ask him and if I try to insist, he shouts, 'You're not my mum, you can't tell me anything'..."

Jack's step-mother

"Since I remarried last year, my nine-year-old daughter has become quiet and anxious. She has gradually dropped all her out-of-school activities."

Karen's mother

this time. Tweens may have lost daily contact, sometimes all contact, with one parent. Like Jack and Gemma, they may also have lost their position in the family. "*I used to be the oldest son, now I'm just number three boy ...*" said an angry and confused Jack. Gemma felt she had lost a share in her previously single mother. "*I used to have one third of mum, now I only have one fifth ...*" she said after her step-father and step-sister moved in with her and her brother. Both Jack and Gemma felt threatened and displaced by the change and showed it in different behaviour. Gemma had become competitive, exploding, "It's not fair ... you always choose her ... I never get a go ..." if she wasn't chosen for an activity. She always wanted to win or come top and would become very distressed when she didn't. We can understand her as both fighting to regain what she felt she had lost and also fighting to ensure that she didn't lose anything else!

Jack's aggressive behaviour was communicating his fear that his step-mother was going to replace his mother whom he saw rarely. However, he was less angry with her than he was with his step-siblings, whom he felt had demoted him to "number three boy" in the family. He was most angry with his father for causing this mess – "They're not going to leave, are they ... my dad really likes them ..."

Insecure and anxious behaviour

Adults find it difficult to tolerate the ambiguity and uncertainty involved in change and loss. It's not surprising, therefore, that children can find it traumatic. It sounds as though Karen may be acting out exactly what she is feeling, i.e., unsure. Anxious and insecure behaviour is a way of regressing to an earlier stage of development. It is almost like Karen at the beach at a much younger age, rushing into the sea until a huge wave knocks her over. She may then retreat to the shoreline to paddle safely for a little while.

Older tween girls may have particular issues when their mother begins a new relationship. Maybe Oriel feels that if anyone in the family is going to have a boyfriend it should be her! Such jealousy is very common and it is also quite usual for a tween like Oriel to flirt outrageously with her mother's man.

"Having been a single parent for five years I have recently made a new relationship. My twelve year old is trying to wreck it by her angry and awkward behaviour. What can I do?"

Oriel's mother

Managing worrying behaviour in a reconstituted family

Jack, Gemma, Karen and Oriel are showing very different behaviours but they have very similar needs.

- They need permission to feel what they are feeling. They may also need to be helped to name what they are feeling, e.g., Jack needed to understand that he was confusing "being angry with his step-mother" with a "fear of losing his natural mother".
- They need help to link their feelings with their actions, e.g., Gemma needed to be told, "It's okay to feel angry and resentful, it's not okay to be horrid to your step-brother." She also needed permission to know that it was okay not to like him.
- They need to have their feelings normalized. Saying something like, "Lots of twelve year olds have secret feelings about their step-siblings. Some feel very jealous ..." may help them to feel there is "nothing wrong" with them and also offer them an invitation to talk about how they feel.
- Remember, some things are just confusing! What you are trying to help your child to develop is the capacity to bear compromise (we could also wonder why we think compromise is a good idea.) Once Oriel understood her jealousy of her mother's new boyfriend, she and her mother could move into a closer relationship sharing more grown-up "girlie" things.
- They need reassurance that, however they feel, they still have their own special place in the family. Special one-on-one time with the natural parent may encourage tweens like Karen to understand that, although the environment has changed, her relationship with her parents is still the same.

When a new baby arrives

Why would any child want a sibling? By the tween years most children will feel there are no more babies to come. So Eddy may be surprised at your news. He may also be shocked by the fact that you are having sex! He may experience all the usual anxieties about being usurped or having to share, but the most important part to bear in mind is that your new baby will be a constant reminder to him of what he doesn't have. If he doesn't live with you, he will be reminded of this fact when he sees the baby; if he lives with you, he will be reminded that *his mother doesn't live with him*. This is extremely difficult for the tween because for them it is irreversible. It is a safe bet that any difficulties you have with your tween over the new baby are likely to be rooted in this fact and that is what you should address. Of course it is necessary to reassure them that they have not lost their special place with you but most of all, you need to let them know that you understand how they feel about not having one parent living with them.

> "How can I prepare my twelve-year-old son for the fact that my partner and I are having a new baby?"
> *Eddy's father*

Reconstituted families are not the same as nuclear families

There are going to be constant interruptions to family life. Parents have to work with children together to create new family rules, rituals and boundaries. These changes can be painful and difficult for you all. It is especially difficult for parents to witness their childrens' unhappiness. However, the easiest way for children to learn how to be flexible, how to compromise and how to understand their own and other people's points of view, is to have flexibility, compromise and understanding modelled by all the adults who surround them. Of course, this is not always possible, nor indeed do you have to model these qualities full-time; what matters is that your children see them within their parents' repertoire of relating to each other.

Further reading

Books for Parents

Ayolan, O. & Flasher, A., *Chain Reaction – Children and Divorce* (London: Jessica Kingsley, 1993).

Bradley, J., *Understanding Your 10 Year Old* (Great Britain: Rosendale Press Limited, 1993).

Brumberg, J. J., *The Body Project: An Intimate History of American Girls* (New York: Random House, 1997).

Clifford-Poston, A., *The Secrets of Successful Parenting* (Oxford: How-to-Books, 2000).

Hartley-Brewer, E., *Talking to Tweenies* (Great Britain: Hodder & Stoughton, 2004).

Jackson, D., *Letting Go as Children Grow* (London: Bloomsbury, 2003).

Knox, D. & Leggett, K., *Divorce Dads Survival Guide: How to Stay Connected with Your Kids* (Massachusetts: Perseus Books, 2000).

Leach, P., "Getting Positive About Discipline: A Guide for Today's Parents," London: Barnardos Booklet (1997).

Lush, D., *Understanding Your 9 Year Old* (Great Britain: Rosendale Press Limited, 1993).

Maughan, S., "*Be Twixt and Be Tween,*" *Publishers Weekly* (US, 11 November 2002).

National Family & Parenting Institute, *Over the Top Behaviour in the Under 10s*, London: NFPI Booklet (2002).

Orford, E., *Understanding Your 11 Year Old* (Great Britain: Rosendale Press Limited, 1993).

Panzarine, S., *A Parent's Guide to the Teen Years: Raising Your 11–14-Year-Old in the Age of Chatrooms and Naval Rings* (New York: Checkmark Books, 2000).

Rosenberg, E., *Growing Up Feeling Good*, (New York: Puffin Books, 1995).

Strauch, B., *Why Are They So Weird? What's Really Going on in a Teenager's Brain?* (London: Bloomsbury, 2003).

Wiseman, R., *Queen Bees and Wannabees*, (London: Piatkus, 2002).

"*Substance Abuse: Student Workbook and Parent/Student Workbook*," Middle School Health: Partners in Health, St Louis: Parkway Health Education Program, Parkway School District (1996).

Fiction

Bloom, J., *It's Not the End of the World* (London: Macmillan Children's Books, 1998).

Bowler, T., *River Boy* (Oxford: OUP, 1997).

Crompton, R., *The Family Roundabout* (London: Persephone Books, 2001).

Elliot, M., *The Willow Street Kids: Be Smart, Stay Safe* (London: Macmillan, 1997).

Hill, S., *I'm the King of the Castle* (England: Penguin Books, 1981).

Shearer, A., *The Great Blue Yonder* (London: Macmillan Children's Books, 2001).

Streatfield, N., *Saplings* (England: Persephone Books Limited, 2001).

Wilson, J., *Bad Girls* (London: Corgi Yearling, 1996).

Wilson, J., *Sleepovers* (London: Young Corgi, 2001).

Wilson, J., *The Worry Website* (London: Corgi Yearling, 2002).

Non-Fiction

Frank, A., *The Diary of Anne Frank* (London: Penguin Books, 1997).

Books on Theory

Blos, P., *On Adolescence* (New York: The Free Press, 1966).

Coren, A., *A Psychodynamic Approach to Education* (England: Sheldon Press, 1997).

Erikson, E. H., *Childhood and Society* (England: Vintage, 1995).

Winnicott, D., *The Child, the Family and the Outside World* (England: Penguin Group, 1964).

——, *The Family and Individual Development* (England: Tavistock Publications, and New York: Methuen Inc, 1965).

Website Addresses

jillcurtis@family2000onwards.com

BBC Parenting Website: www.BBC.co.uk\Parenting, Hasbury Team Section

Parenting Education & Support Forum: www.parenting-forum.org.uk

Young Minds: www.youngminds.org

www.raisingkids.com has a pre-teen section

www.parentlineplus.org.uk

The Body: http://www.thebody.com

PREVLINE: www.health.org (information and publications for parents and youngsters on alcohol and drugs)

NationalParentInformationNetwork: www.npin.org

www.amasassociation.org.adult.hmt (information for parents on a variety of topics related to Tweens)

www.kidsource.com

Specialist Websites on Internet Safety

www.bbc.co.uk/webwise/basics

www.getnctwise.org

www.nspcc.org.uk/kidszone

Useful organizations

UK

National Family & Parenting Institute, Unit 4301 Highgate Studios, 53–79 Highgate Road, London NW5 1TL, telephone: 0044 (0) 20 7424 3460

Kidscape, 152 Buckingham Palace Road, London SW1W 9TR

Anti-Bullying Alliance, telephone: 0044 (0) 20 7843 6000

Advisory Centre for Education (ACE): www.ace-ed.org.uk

National Association for Gifted Children, telephone: 0044 (0) 8707 703217

Eating Disorders Association (EDA): www.edauk.com, helpline: 0044 (0) 1603 621414

One Parent Families, 225 Kentish Town Road, London NW5 2LX, telephone: 0044 (0) 20 7428 5400

Child Bereavement Network, telephone: 0044 (0) 1159 118070, e-mail: chn@nch.org.uk

USA

Boys Town National Hotline, 1–800–448–3000 (provide short term crisis counselling to youngsters and parents, open 24 hours, 7 days a week)

National Mental Health Association Information Center, 1021 Prince Street, Alexandria, VA, 22314–2971

Sexuality Information & Education Counsel of the United States (SIECUS), 1–212–819–9770, 130 West Forty-Second Street, Suite 2500, New York, New York 10036

National Parent Information Network, 1–800–583–4135 (9am–6pm EST Mon–Fri)

References

Angelou, M., *BBC Radio Broadcast*, 2003

Balint, M., *Basic Fault* (London: Tavistock, 1974).

Birtin, E., quoted in programme notes for *The Book of the Banshee*, by Anne Fine (Guildford: Yvonne Arnaut Theatre, 2003).

Bowlby, J., *Attachment and Loss*, Vol. 2: Separation: Anxiety and Anger (London: Hogarth Press, 1973).

Coren, A., *A Dynamic Approach to Education* (London: Methuen Press, 1997).

Driscoll, M., 'Stealthily Stealing Their Innocence', in *The Sunday Times*, 19 January 2003.

Erikson, E.H., *Childhood and Society* (Great Britain: Vintage, 1965).

Freud, S., *Jokes and Their Relation to the Unconscious* (London: Penguin Books, 1976).

Hill, A.J. & Franklin, J.A., 'Mothers, Daughters and Dieting: Investigating the Transmission of Weight Control,' *British Journal of Clinical Psychology* (1998) 37, 3–13.

Hill, A.J. 'Developmental Issues in Attitudes to Food and Diet,' in *Proceedings of the Nutrition Society* (2002) 61, 259–266.

Hill, A.J. and Pallin, V., 'Dieting Awareness and Low Self-Worth: Related Issues in 8 Year Old Girls,' Division of *Psychiatry and Behavioural Sciences*, School of Medicine, University of Leeds, UK, May 1997.

Hobson, R., 'Loneliness,' *Journal of Analytical Pyschology*, Vol. 19 no. 1, 1974.

Ingram, M., 'Age of Discontent,' in *The Times* (London) 16 February 2004.

Jackson, D., 'What's Got into the Tweenies?' in *The Times* (London) 28 July 2003.

Luxmoore, N., *Listening to Young People in School, Youth Work and Counselling* (Great Britain: Jessica Kingsley, 2000).

Maher, M., 'Bullying – The Lover, The Pimp and The Coward,' in *Educational Therapy and Therapeutic Teaching*, issue no. 3, March 1994.

Phillips, A., Personal communication.

——, *On Kissing, Tickling and Being Bored* (Cambridge, MA: Harvard University Press, 1993 and London: Faber & Faber Limited, 1993).

Sinason, V., 'Face Values', in *Free Associations* (1985) 2, 75–93.

Strauch, B., 'The Weird World of a Teenager's Brain,' in *The Times*, 17 February 2003.

Trenenan, A., 'Sugar, Spice and All Things Nasty,' *The Times*, 6 August 2002.

Weldon, F., *Independent on Sunday*, 5 May 1991.

Winnicott, D.W., *The Child, the Family and the Outside World* (Penguin, 1964).

——, *Playing and Reality* (Tavistock Publications, 1971).

'Little Girl Chic,' *Sunday Times*, 6 April 2003.

Index